Dub Techno
The Orphic Experience of Sound

Bahadırhan Koçer

Contents

I am indebted to my friend, who argued that seeking a philosophical aspect in dub techno is fruitless. His perspective served as inspiration for this study, as I held a contrary belief.

Foreword

In the midst of a rainy autumn night in mid-October of the year 2019, I found myself sitting with three of my acquaintances in a dimly lit, low-ceilinged lounge situated on one of the streets in Beyoğlu. It was not customary for me to be in such a place, but there we were, engaging in a series of dialogues that, by their very nature, were not likely to reach any sort of conclusion. Topics ranged from Kant's noumenon to Baudrillard's thoughts on stereophonic music to Bentham's panopticon and its influence on Foucault's conception of power. Outside, the rain fell heavily, and its gloom seemed to have permeated everything, rendering the dialogue meaningless in the face of the profound agony of existence. Suddenly, I became aware of the beguiling strangeness of the music that had been playing in the background for some time. The music drew me in, lifting me out of the space and demonstrating the relativity of time. Descending the stairs, I approached a turntable that sat alone in front of a window overlooking the rainy street. The shadows of the raindrops cast upon the window seemed to dance in time with the music. To the right of the turntable sat a stack of records that had already been played, while to the left sat a stack of records waiting to be played. As I bent down to read the label on the spinning record, a man appeared. He revealed to me that the current record spinning on the turntable was *Fetch* by the Moritz von Oswald Trio, while the previous selection was *An Evolutionary Music* by Ariel Kalma. While returning, I found myself engrossed in discographies during a boat trip. For weeks, I listened to countless albums. After some time had passed, I had the opportunity to meet Ariel in person and engage in profound conversations, which led to me drawing numerous sources of inspiration from him. Moritz, on the other hand, was a coincidence that introduced me to dub techno, a style of music that I would later attempt to explore deeply through an album project. Ever since that day, dub techno has remained an enigma that is worthy of deeper contemplation and more profound comprehension on my part. It is akin to a mystery that begs to be decrypted and fully apprehended.

Although coincidences can be unpredictable at times, they are longstanding companions that simply need permission to exist. In fact, the deep fascination I have with the subject matter of this book is a consequence of granting permission to these interwoven coincidences, which have enshrouded my life like a mist.

At the outset, I owe an immeasurable debt of gratitude to three altruistic souls who made this research endeavor possible. My mother, who had always listened to me with unwavering interest, my father, who embodied the quintessence of selflessness and sacrifice, and my sister, Lect. Zeynep Afra Soyuer, who provided me with the sanctity of seclusion, which was vital for all my scholarly pursuits. Also, for our long, eye-opening, and unhurried walks on the seaside, I owe my gratitude to Prof. Dr. Rahim Horuz. I extend my thanks to my advisor, Assoc. Prof. Dr. Ozan Baysal, for his valuable collaboration, close follow-up of the process, critical contributions, and tolerance. I express my gratitude to Ronny Pries, who unconditionally spreads the courage to create, and to Dub Monitor for his close interest in this book and for opening the way with his pioneering studies. Lastly, I thank Zahid "Hard Reset" Sarıhan for his support and courtesy during the interview process.

Bahadırhan Koçer
İstanbul, 2023

Introduction

From a developmental standpoint, techno music serves as an all-encompassing umbrella that subsumes all of its sub-genres. Though techno music emerged initially as a genre that resisted mainstream popularity, it has since evolved into one of the most widely consumed music genres worldwide. Attempting to explain the widespread popularity of techno music through a single cause or theoretical lens would be oversimplifying the complex nature of this phenomenon and lack objectivity. Nonetheless, it would not be erroneous to suggest that over the span of more than forty years since its diffusion from Berlin and London, techno music has undergone a transformation in stylistic, practical, social, political, and cultural aspects. It is equally true that new stylistic elements, sub-genres, and methodologies continue to emerge and perpetuate in a dynamic manner within this field. Dub techno, as a sub-genre under the techno umbrella, serves as an exemplary manifestation of various characteristics of the transformative process. Dub techno is notable for its relative abstraction from the various functions typically exhibited by sub-genres such as Detroit, acid, hardcore, or minimal techno on the dance floor. In this regard, dub techno has boldly liberated itself from the paradigms and stylistic hegemony of these functions over time. Furthermore, it represents a multifaceted transformation that extends beyond a mere musical shift, as it sets itself apart from the context in which techno music is consumed and utilized more broadly. It is conceivable to argue that the nature of this transformation lies fundamentally in a shift from communal to individual listening. Of course, this change has spatial dimensions. Nevertheless, a spatial change, or rather a change in the context of music consumption, does not merely entail a shift in the physical space where music is consumed. The transformation also leads to an evolution from an external to an internal music listening experience and a corresponding alteration in the affective relationship established with the music.

The issue of the individualization of the act of listening to sound, which includes the act of listening to music, can be discussed from an eccentric perspective in the light of the orphic media concept created by Mack Hagood, a media researcher who recently took inspiration from the *Argonautica* epic and drew inspiration from the myth. Through various individual technological devices and media contexts, such as noise-canceling headphones, individuals can isolate themselves from the sonic environment that surrounds and relentlessly coerces them, thus achieving 'sonic self-control' freedom by creating a 'filtered bubble' of sound-in a crowded subway train with the help of headphones, for instance. This is seen as a new media consumption form that has been opened up for discussion within the framework created by Hagood. Deliberating on the concept of orphic media at its core necessitates considering the politics of the individual's spatial connection to sound. In this regard, the concept invokes the ideas of Gilles Deleuze, Felix Guattari, and Henri Lefebvre in connection with concepts such as *milieu* and abstract space. Moreover, grounded on the neoliberal self, a concept that has been widely debated for a considerable period, the orphic media concept serves to address both the individual's place in society and the most individualistic form of consumption that society has engendered. The individual's consumption of media is unquestionably restructuring the nature, form, and essence of media. In the framework drawn by Hagood and expanded by a handful of researchers, experiencing media in an orphic way causes an 'orphic remediation' which occurs as a result of a hierarchical relationship between the spatial sound experienced by the individual, for example through headphones, and other sounds. Remediation can occur through two modes: intramodal remediation involves the suppression or filtration of spatial sound by another sound, such as white noise, while crossmodal remediation involves overlaying spatial sound with another sound that alters affect and transforms the individual's perception and relationship with the world. In both cases, the individuals take control of their sonic self, freeing themselves from the hegemony of spatial sound and placing their desired sound in a higher position in the hierarchy. In this respect, orphic remediation is reconstructive. Especially when remediation is crossmodally realized through a musical piece, both spatial sound and the musical piece undergo numerous transformations. This reconstructive experience of music listening is precisely what is termed the 'orphic experience' in this study. Ultimately, the individual consumption of music, which is offered in various formats as a fundamental mediatic element, can also be examined in light of the orphic media concept. Dub techno, with its various qualities gained from the development journey of techno music, can be used as a musical example in the context of orphic media. Examining dub techno from this perspective has created 'the right room issue' in this research. This issue revolves around the question of whether the context of dub techno is the dancefloor or headphones. Headphones being the main medium of a sub-genre within the techno music cluster carries clues about the orphic experience that gains meaning with the individuality of listening. In summary, in this research, the key concept created by Hagood is assumed to open a new door to interpret the music-experiential aspects of techno music through dub techno, and the clues that dub techno carries about the orphic experience have been explored. While examining the orphic experience of dub techno, a context was also created to analyze the genre from a musicological perspective. This research has become versatile thanks to this context.

As mentioned above, the hypothesis that the relentless transformation of media and media tools derives strength from a transformative force that promotes the orphic experience has been a critical aspect of this research. In addition, the impact of this transformative force on dub techno, which played a significant role in establishing the concept of orphic media, has also been discussed in this study. This specific transformation, which can be discussed through the dub techno genre, created by eccentrically blending dub and techno styles, also alters the listener's music interaction experience by affecting and influencing it. Traces of the individualization of consumption, interaction, and affect can be traced in the sound, spatiality, stylistic elements, and historicity of dub techno. Dub techno has experienced a shift that is almost the exact opposite of the 'hardcore continuum' that Simon Reynolds outlined (as cited in Nye, 2013, p. 165), which is characterized by the axiom of 'harder-faster-louder'. On the other hand, researchers such as Sean Nye (2013, p. 165) have proposed to classify electronic music genres that are moving towards the opposite idea within the minimal continuum which follows the axiom of 'softer, slower, quieter'. Although there are many noteworthy points indicated by these classifications and thoughts, this research discusses how dub techno, with its minimized and relentless nature, became subject to individual listening and the associated orphic experience. It is precisely at this point that a blank page is opened, not only musically but also politically, sociologically, culturally, and philosophically.

The fundamental purpose behind the emergence of this thesis is to evaluate and discuss the transformation and evolution processes that techno has undergone since its inception, carrying the reflections of individualization through genres, and to examine it through dub techno. Through this examination, it is hoped that a fruitful way of evaluating the issue of the individualization of the experience established with music, as well as spatial, instrumental, social, and philosophical aspects, will be discovered by accepting dub techno as a reference point and an example. The idea of individualization has been approached not only through headphones. This research revolves around the question of 'how dub techno provides clues in the transformation of music into a formal and functional orphic experience'. In this regard, this research delves into the short history and foundations of dub music, which is the first pillar that dub techno focuses on, followed by an examination of the nature of techno music, the second pillar, and finally an exploration of how dub techno, which was brought into the techno music realm by blending various aspects of these two genres, prepares the ground for altering the listening experience through its musical aspect. In the research process, various methods such as compilation, musical analysis, survey, and interview have been employed to illuminate the field. These methods are elaborately explained under the heading of methodology.

This research consists of four fundamental themes: orphic experience, dub music, techno music, and dub techno music. Under the orphic experience theme, the concept of orphic media is elucidated, and the background of individual music listening experience is discussed in relation to the sonic self-control achieved by the listener, who is isolated from the communal listening act by means of headphones. In the remaining three themes, discussions are conducted to understand the linear transformation undergone by dub and various techno sub-genres in connection with dance. All of these debates have been conducted with the aim of illuminating the communal experience of the relevant music genres. Communal listening is accepted as the gathering of individuals to listen to music, dance to music, and socialize around music. Thus, it is evident that music has various functions both on the audience and the space. Dance music, which serves various functions such as fueling uninterrupted entertainment and altering the external and internal influences of the community on the dance floor, is partly utilized, and this utilization naturally determines the sharp precedents, aesthetic paradigms, or consumption culture that are valid in the music production process. The orphic experience, as explained above, is a vital perspective for thinking about the individualization of listening, in other words, a way to break free from communal listening. Therefore, both dub music and techno music, although they have existed separately in different geographies and cultures for a long time without contact, were born in environments where people came together, coded with the culture of being together, and accepted music as a catalyst that is listened to and influenced together. Dub music's default context is large, handmade sound systems. Initially, these systems were used in outdoor events and dub listeners danced to dub versions dominated by low frequencies, played by performers operating the sound systems. The collision of sub-frequencies with the individual's body on the dance floor and the internalization of this physical activity by the listener established dub music as sound system music. Although there are technically distinct qualities in sound systems, they have also been determinative in the first examples of techno music. Therefore, the idea of increasing the volume of music with amplification devices is a determinative aspect of listening to music in both genres. The performance techniques used in dub music transform sound engineers into artists who have the power to mesmerize the crowd. They are comparable to wizards who enchant their audience and hold them under their spell. Similarly, some researchers refer to DJs as modern shamans for techno music (Becker et al., 1999, p. 64), and they are on the stage to interact musically with the crowd. Indeed, techno music, according to popular belief, should be DJ friendly by default. Sound system operators, sound engineers, DJs, and deejays are figures that shape the idea of communal music listening for both dub and techno genres. For these reasons, the dancehall for dub music and the dancefloor for techno music have permeated the structure of these two music genres, shaped their aesthetics, and determined the direction in which production and consumption paradigms would evolve. However, in addition to all this, dub techno, as a mixed genre of dub and techno music, has shown a breakaway movement from this origin. This situation indicates a turning point. Dub techno is considered a genre that can test the idea of orphic experience with the help of technological devices and changing media characteristics when communal listening turns into individual listening.

In the section discussing dub music in the context of the ideas above, the historical context of the genre was explained, certain fundamental techniques were emphasized, and the relationship between the music and communal listening was examined in various ways. Immediately thereafter, a similar approach was taken in the techno section, with a focus on historical context and the development of an approach to three sub-genres of techno: Detroit techno, acid techno, and minimal techno. This approach has both an analytical and a narrative nature, allowing for the demonstration of the linear transformation that techno music undergoes in the context of dance, over short periods of time. In the section dedicated to dub techno, a definition of the genre was attempted with the help of various interviews conducted with producers, performers, and listeners. Following this, several analyses were carried out to determine the orphic experience, and ultimately, the potential of dub techno as a subject for the orphic experience was discussed based on survey data. One of the primary goals of this research was to develop an approach to the basic aesthetics, characteristics, consumption practices, and problematic issues of dub techno. Considering the scarcity of scientifically valid sources produced solely for dub techno, defining and approaching the genre with consistency in scientific terms is inherently complicated. However, the fact that the analysis or discussions of dub techno are weak in the literature of musicology and other fields makes this study important. Therefore, the originality of this study lies in examining dub techno, a subject that has not been widely explored, through the lens of orphic media, a contemporary concept that also attracts attention for its unexplored nature. As a result, this study was produced with a tendency to embrace innovation in terms of both the research subject and framework. For this reason, a consistent scope, a narrative created for readers to grasp nuances, and a scientific framework with a discursive and analytical basis were considered to be important for inspiring future research that may be conducted later.

Although this study aims to explore an untouched subject, there are several limitations that need to be considered. The first of these limitations is undoubtedly due to the scarcity of studies conducted in the relevant field. This situation, which arises from the lack of consensus and the shortage of sources in the literature, compelled this study to make objective fundamental descriptions and to comprehensively address the research subject as far as possible. Indeed, most of the topics examined have been almost entirely new in the literature of this field. Although the idea of utilizing surveys, interviews, and musical analyses in a compatible way to make various initial definitions contributing to the literature was considered, this study has been limited by the relatively low number of pieces analyzed[1], the restriction of the number of survey and interview participants to 41, the absence of a participant or observer field research on the direct effects of orphic experience on individuals, and, consequently, the relatively weak a posteriori data. Nevertheless, it is believed that the conclusion of this study has ignited the fuse of the information cascade that may emerge in the future regarding dub techno and orphic media studies. These limitations offer indications for possible future research endeavors that can be more sophisticated. So, it is hoped that this research will inspire enthusiastic scholars to remedy the aforementioned deficiencies in the literature by conducting further research.

---

[1] In order to provide exemplification of specific aesthetic situations, great care has been taken to create certain footnotes for most of the analyzed and exemplified pieces, which would at least include the names and credits of various other examples that share a similar context. This would enable the reader, while tracing the names of other examples provided in the footnotes, to discover certain aesthetic paradigms on their own.

2

Methodology

In this research, the primary focus was to provide a consistent analysis of the research problem by first defining the orphic experience, followed by revealing the historical and musical aspects of dub and techno music, and ultimately shedding light on how the orphic experience occurs through the characteristics of dub techno that emerge from the fusion of dub and techno music. In line with this priority, four fundamental data collection tools were utilized in this study, namely, compilation, interviews, surveys, and musical analysis. All of these tools were harmoniously combined and correlated to serve the purposes and priorities mentioned above.

The compilation of relevant data from various sources covering all of these areas has been essential in creating the groundwork for this study, enabling the definition of the orphic experience within the conceptual framework of orphic media, the development of approaches to the historical and aesthetic aspects of dub, techno, and dub techno genres, and most importantly, revealing the clues they carry for both communal and individual listening practices. The compilation method is appropriate for unifying old and new discussions from relevant sources, comparing debates made within the specific paradigms of various fields, revealing common and rare views, and adapting them to the central discussion of this research. Therefore, this study has gained a guiding quality for future research on dub techno and the orphic experience through the compilation method.

In this research, defining the short history, aesthetics, musical, and philosophical aspects of dub techno as a research subject has become a convoluted process in itself. This is mainly due to the scarcity of scientific literature produced on dub techno. In this context, it has become necessary, by the very nature of this research, to at least define dub techno at a basic level and make a literary contribution. To define dub techno more objectively beyond limited internet content, short interviews were conducted with 41 participants consisting of electronic music producers, performers, and listeners. Participants were asked to describe the sound of dub techno. These descriptions were used to define dub techno in the relevant section of this research, allowing for the creation of a more insider definition of dub techno through the intersection of different perspectives and insights obtained from the interviews. The interview process consisting of seven different questions has not only benefited the definition of dub techno but also facilitated the exploration of techno music's dance culture, production practices, and social and political domains on the dancefloor. The subjective verbal data collected in the interviews have been incorporated into the narrative of the research while ensuring scientific objectivity.

This study was initiated by the question of how dub techno provides clues in the transformation of music into a formal and functional orphic experience. Additionally, it explores the inherent aesthetic qualities of techno as a catalyst for dancing. With these aesthetic qualities in mind, examining dub techno as a sub-genre of techno in order to distinguish between communal and individual listening and to detect the orphic experience has created a central issue for this research. This significant dilemma has been named 'the right room issue' which is a product of the question of whether dub techno and similar sub-genres are best enjoyed through headphones or on the dancefloor. This dilemma fundamentally refers to the idea of communal listening becoming individualized. To examine this idea, a survey was conducted with 41 participants consisting of electronic music producers, performers, and listeners. 32 (%78) of the participants were male, and 9 (%22) were female; 17 (%41.5) were EDM producers, 6 were EDM performers (%14.6), and 18 were EDM listeners (%43.9). 22 (%53.7) of the participants were familiar with dub techno, while 19 (%46.3) reported being unfamiliar with it. Interviews were conducted with the 22 participants who were familiar with dub techno during the process of defining dub techno (see Chart 2.1).

Participants played eight tracks from the dub techno and ambient techno categories and were asked whether they were best suited to be listened to through headphones or on the dancefloor. Participants were also given the option to leave questions unanswered. The responses of the participants led to a predominance of either headphones or dancefloor in most of the tracks played, which allowed for a discussion of why these tracks were primarily considered suited for either headphones or dancefloor. Thus, a discussion of the characteristics of communal and individual listening actions that could be considered within the context of orphic experience was conducted through the right room issue. Therefore, the survey method played an important role in this research, as it anchored the discussion on scientific grounds, triggered the analysis process, and helped shed light on the connection between dub techno and orphic experience.

Through the application of musical analysis methods, as well as data collected through surveys and interviews, the core hypotheses outlined in the introduction have been critically evaluated. Additionally, the musicological analysis method was primarily adopted to examine the dominant aesthetic scales found in early examples of techno music within the Detroit techno, acid techno, and minimal techno genres. Each track selected for this study underwent the same analysis process. The music analysis process involved the creation of a spectrum image, the extraction of a structural diagram, the transcription of the main harmonic and melodic sequences, the identification of primary riffs, the visualization of drum patterns using both sequencer and notation images, and finally, the linear narration of the occurrences identified in the initial sequences. This analytical method was deemed fruitful for obtaining results as it facilitated multidisciplinary discussions throughout the research process and, in conjunction with the survey and interview data, contributed to the testing of the core hypotheses, leading to a broader perspective. In summary, all the methods discussed above played a vital role in creating a wide perspective to approach and resolve the problem investigated in this study, within the bounds of scientific rigor.

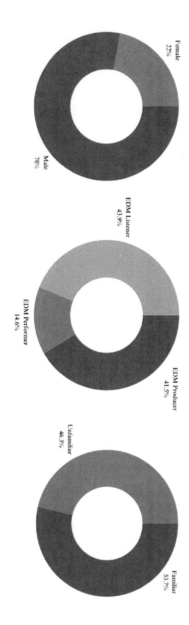

Chart 2.1 : Gender, role, and familiarity ratios of the participants

3

Literature Review

This research is based on three separate topics, namely orphic media, dub music, and techno music. Therefore, the focus has revolved around these three fundamental topics in order to associate the listening experience, spatiality, and aesthetics of dub techno with the orphic experience. In particular, data related to the relevant topics was first obtained from historical and philosophical sources produced in the media and music fields, and subsequently from technical sources related to music production in the process of compiling and defining. The fact that the topics under scrutiny in this research are intertwined with internet culture in cultural and practical terms has also made it necessary to use internet sources for most of the research.

Orphic media is a concept coined in Mack Hagood's 2011 article, *Quiet Comfort: Noise, Otherness, and the Mobile Production of Personal Space* (Hagood, 2011), and further developed in his 2019 book, *Hush: Media and Sonic Self Control* (Hagood, 2019), which explores various related ideas. As a relatively new approach, the notion of orphic media or the orphic experience of media has only been touched on in a few review articles (see Marazi, 2020). Consequently, the sources available to understand Hagood's framework and to qualify the orphic approach are quite limited. This is problematic since this concept, which could be useful in examining topics such as the individualization of media experience, the relationship between spatial sound and politics, the self recreated through technological devices, the connection between the abstract idea of isolation and sound and music, sonic self-control, and the sonic power of music, has yet to receive adequate attention in the relevant literature. A significant gap in the field exists. Therefore, this study represents an effort to apply the ideas of orphic media, orphic experience, and sonic self-control in a systematic manner to the field of sound and music, inspired by Hagood's framework, and can be perceived as an attempt to adapt these concepts to a specific methodological approach.

The assertion that dub and techno have been scrutinized from various perspectives in the literature by numerous researchers would not be unfounded. Particularly, given that dub music emerged in the 1960s, which is older than all the phenomena discussed in this study, it has become a field of research where canonical and non-canonical texts discussing political, technical, philosophical, and aesthetic debates have been published. However, this research has focused only on two aspects of dub music: the communal listening culture of dub music and how basic production techniques have permeated dub techno.

To discuss these two fundamental aspects, Lloyd Bradley's *Bass Culture* (Bradley, 2001), and Julian Henriques' study, *Sonic Dominance and the Reggae Sound System Session and The Vibrations of Affect and their Propagation on a Night Out on Kingston's Dancehall Scene* (Henriques, 2003), were illuminating at the initial stage. Additionally, Thomas Vendryes' *Versions, Dubs and Riddims: Dub and the Transient Dynamics of Jamaican Music* (Vendryes, 2015), Alexandre Fintoni's *The Reggae Sound System: Sound, Space and Politics* (Fintoni, 2014) and Anna McLauchlan's collaboration with *Assembling the Dance: Reggae Sound System Practices in the United Kingdom and France* (Fintoni & McLauchlan, 2018) have inspired the foundations of the relevant topic in this research[2]. To delve deeper into the subject, the sources utilized have been employed on the aforementioned foundation. It is noteworthy that the sources in which the analytical methodology for dub music is utilized are limited in number. For instance, there are few sources that examine the historicity of performance practices, how sound engineers can transform into creative musicians, and how dancehall and soundsystem traditions determine the aesthetics of music. Consequently, in terms of historical research on dub music, it is more substantial compared to technical research.

Techno music, like dub music, is one of the main pillars of this research. Similarly to dub music, there are quite a few sources that analyze techno music from various aspects. Journals such as *Dancecult*, which publish articles solely focused on dance music and related issues, seem to play an important role in compensating for this deficiency. Additionally, various internet magazines that are customized for the field of electronic dance music, especially in terms of production techniques, can be considered important sources given that techno

_____

[2] The sources listed here are not presented in order of importance. It is important to emphasize that these sources are of a nature that will contribute to the discussion that this research specifically focuses on. Furthermore, in this research, many other sources that have not been mentioned here have been consulted.

music is currently produced through digital audio workstations and the production and consumption processes have become almost entirely digitized.

For the section of this research that discusses the politics and aesthetics of techno music, Dan Sicko's *Techno Rebels: The Renegades of Electronic Funk* (Sicko, 1999), Graham St. John's *Rave Culture and Religion* (John, 2017), Hillegonda C. Rietveld's *Global Techno Resistance: The Underground Resistance and Detroit Techno* (Rietveld, 2018), and Ansgar Jerrentrup's *Techno Music: Its Special Characteristics and Didactic Perspectives* (Jerrentrup, 2000) have been considered as enriching sources.

Beyond all of these sources, it is evident that techno music is a subject of research that requires deeper examination not only from a musicological but also a sociological and cultural perspective. When examining the existing literature on techno music, it is apparent that there are not many studies that incorporate musical analysis, delve into the aesthetic and political dimensions through specific techno tracks, and adopt a non-solely sociological analytical approach. It is hoped that this research will act as a trigger for producing fruitful results by intertwining the analytical perspective with the purely conceptual perspective in the field of electronic dance music, even if it is a small one, and by addressing precisely this deficiency.

In this study, the reason for separately discussing dub and techno music was to comprehend the aesthetics upon which dub techno has risen above these two genres. Initially, the aesthetics of dub techno, without delving into minute details, were discussed, and in the next stage, they were brought into interaction with the orphic experience. Nevertheless, like orphic media and other related concepts, dub techno is a subject of weak research in terms of academic literature. There have been only a few sources written about dub techno. While some esteemed researchers have engaged in discussions about the political, social, and cultural dimensions of dub techno, for example, its relationship with post-Fordism, it is difficult to find such data in academic literature when it comes to sound. Moreover, it would not be wrong to say that dub techno is subject to very little discussion regarding its political, social, and cultural dimensions. There could be various reasons for this, but the primary reason is that this genre of music seems uninteresting for music research at first glance. Interviews conducted with various individuals in this study also support this idea. Therefore, a closer examination of dub techno from both conceptual and technical perspectives by researchers familiar with its nature could yield fruitful results. It can easily be said that dub techno, which is interpreted only through the orphic experience in this study, has multiple connections and aesthetic paradigms that are worth exploring. Therefore, in this study, an attempt was made to fill this significant gap in the literature, but further research, perhaps

even field research, is necessary to examine the history, aesthetic paradigm, and social and cultural dimensions of dub techno.

4

Orphic Experience
A New Way to Engage with Sound

In order to contextualize the concept of orphic experience, it is necessary to first examine the concept of 'orphic media'. This includes providing a definition of the concept, explaining the influence of related concepts, and identifying the fundamental elements that make up the framework.

Orphic Media

Mack Hagood first introduced the concept of orphic media in his work *Hush: Media and Sonic Self Control*, published in 2019, defining it as a desire for abstraction from unwanted stimuli and basing it on this particular need (2019, pp. 6-8). The trigger for the thought process that resulted in the emergence of the concept of orphic media was the sociological and psychological interpretation of the noise-canceling feature (Hagood, 2019, pp. 177-194). Inspired by the *Argonautica*, a work by Apollonius of Rhodes, Hagood imbues his concept with symbolic meaning by drawing upon the mythos (Malitoris, 2019). In the epic, Orpheus accompanies the five Argonauts on their long and arduous journey home. As they near the end of their journey, the Argonauts encounter the Sirens, whose alluring and seductive beauty lures humans to their death through the power of their mesmerizing music (Sotirios, 2021, p. 6). The Sirens attempt to ensnare the exhausted Argonauts through their music and ultimately kill them. However, Orpheus, "through his songs, manages to drown out the seductive songs of the Sirens, who were trying to entice the sailors to their love" (Sotirios, 2021, p. 6). In the end, the Argonauts are able to evade death by yielding to their passions thanks to Orpheus. In this way, Hagood highlights the influential power of sound through this symbolic context (Malitoris, 2019).

As individuals are increasingly forced to live in crowded spaces, they can utilize the technological resources available to them to alleviate their anxiety about being isolated from crowded places where their personal space is likely to be violated, by taking advantage of the power of sound to alter, transform, subdue, and affect them (Hagood, 2019, pp. 189-191). Today, individuals can use orphic media to filter and select what they want to hear and feel, just like Orpheus, altering the sonic environment. In this context, Hagood, mentioning the concept of the 'filter bubble' by Eli Pariser, emphasizes the demeanor of individuals to "hear what I want to hear" (2019, p. 222) and illustrates how the individual, subject to the power of sound, can escape being passive in the face of sonic power.

Orphic media is a concept that goes beyond visual, written, or auditory media, and in this study, all playable media material and media player devices, forms, and types that create filter bubbles as described above are also referred to as orphic media. In this sense, orphic media serves the function of sonic self-control[3] for the individual (Malitoris, 2019). Hush, which discusses the types of orphic media defined by Hagood and examines the concepts of control and power while conducting this discussion, and fuses the concept of self and affect theory to make various determinations (Marazi, 2020, p. 2), offers an alternative path for new media research by focusing on the current issues brought by digitalization.

Hagood appears to suggest that new methods and approaches may be relevant in media research when discussing the action of sonic self-control. This is because the action of sonic self-control shapes our perception of media in contemporary societies (Hagood, 2011, p. 574). Hagood identifies the 'inflammation' of social spaces over time with more auditory information and stimuli as a problem. Moreover, he states that individuals are caught in a consumer trap through the creation of these stimuli in areas such as shopping centers and airports through market capitalism. At this point, orphic media, which can be important in enabling the individual to escape from a hegemony that suppresses consumerism (Hagood, 2019, pp. 184-185), can also serve to allow the individual to temporarily feel unique by breaking away from neoliberal self-creation and confinement. All of these connections considered, tthe concept of orphic media has a wide range of applications. This is because the phenomenon of unstoppable sonic self-control can occur in any space where sound is present, and the act of experiencing and benefiting from orphic media can also occur in any space where sound is present. Therefore, rather than ignoring the aforementioned phenomenon of unstoppable sonic self-control, it is vital to examine the new relationships that media establishes with space and the new

---

[3] The phrase 'hear what you want' from a headphone company that markets its active noise-canceling feature is mentioned by Hagood (2019, pp. 198-204) as a representation of the liberation of individuals to control their own sonic experience. The widespread use of active noise-canceling headphones has contributed to the creation of disconnected masses that prefer to perceive space according to their own desires and are isolated from each other in terms of communication.

habits created by these relationships. In this research, a similar examination was carried out on dub techno.

It is undeniable that the act of masking noise enables the creation of a new and freely shaped soundscape separate from reality. In this context, canceling noise supports the visual experience with a new auditory dimension and transforms its nature. Additionally, noise canceling can be considered not only as a factor that increases the quality of audio media but also as an action that provides an alternative way of experiencing the process of separating from the mass. In sum, the act of canceling noise and masking it with sonic media or even using headphones may sometimes serve to break away from the sonic hegemony of the space by recreating the individual's soundscape. When it comes to space, it seems that the examination of the concepts of 'abstract space' and '*milieu*' is considered crucial for providing a piece of contextual information.

Abstract Space and *Milieu*

In analyzing the relationship of noise masking with space, the concept of abstract space by Henri Lefebvre is utilized. Lefebvre (1991) defines the concept in his work *The Production of Space* (pp. 49-52). Under the light of his definitions, the concept of abstract space is interpreted as, "the capitalist production of space as a process of abstraction, through which capitalist social relations and reductive technocratic representations of space are progressively concretized in lived material reality, and through which this reality is itself rendered increasingly abstract" (2013, p. 366). Abstract space is equipped with capitalist directors, tools, indicators, and functions. In connection with this definition, it has been stated that an individual who passes to the action of canceling noise, "creates a small field of Lefebvre's abstract space, in which difference is minimized so that the informatic circulation of texts and commerce can be maximized" (Hagood, 2019, p. 194). On the other hand, the individual is also able to break away from capitalist social relations and the sonic hegemony of abstract space and create a personal space isolated through headphones. For this reason alone, noise-canceling headphones have caused a significant change in the way we interpret devices that produce sound, which we have been using for a long time (Marazi, 2020, p. 6). In abstract space, our technological devices that create individual voids isolated from capitalist consumption directives have transformed the acoustic environment into a content pool that suppresses "biological, social, and material differences that make us who we are" (Hagood, 2019, p. 6). Additionally, noise-canceling headphones and other devices with similar functions further abstract the relationship between space and sound, allowing for the possibility of "navigating abstract sonic spaces" (Hagood, 2019, p. 185).

While establishing a connection between the noise-canceled environment and the individual, Hagood also utilizes the concept of *milieu* created by Gilles Deleuze and Felix Guattari (2019, p. 8). According to Deleuze and Guattari (1987, p. 311), the *milieu* is a powerful, resultless void. It has been possible to approach spatial practices that shape cities and relational conditions with a conceptual perspective, through the contribution of the concept of *milieu* and multiple thinkers referencing this concept (Çoruh, 2019, p. 1122). The concept of *milieu* creates an intermediary between space and ontology. Through this intermediary, the concept describes the atmospheric conditions such as "timeliness, value systems, codes, rules" and "ways of establishing relationships" that the urban environment carries (Çoruh, 2019, p. 1123). Hagood (2019, pp. 9-10) states that to understand the noise in a specific *milieu*, it is necessary first to understand the ambient sounds, ways of listening to and evaluating sounds, definitions and theories of noise, and practices of producing noise. According to him, only then will it be possible to contextualize the action of canceling noise.

Furthermore, concerning the concept of *milieu*, which serves as a mediation between ontology and space, the individual exists in three fundamental domains: *umwelt*, which is the environment in which objects surrounding the individual are located; *mitwelt*, which is the domain of relationships and social existence with others; and *eigenwelt*, which is a unique domain of existence specific to humans and referred to as the inner world of the individual (Miyer et al., 2021, p. 54). The idea that the concept of orphic media encompasses these three fundamental domains in establishing a sonic relationship between the individual and space has been accepted. When an individual cancels ambient noise, they displace the natural content of the existing soundscape and introduce a new one, re-coding the *umwelt*. In addition, the individual's isolation from auditory information coming from other people also changes the content of the *mitwelt*, which is formed by the individual's relationships with the external world. This situation may also be related to the inflammation of the *mitwelt* in terms of information. According to Richard Sennett (2015, p. 121), the increase in the volume of information leads to the receiver showing "less responsiveness" to it. Hagood and Sennett's approaches to information intersect at this point. In light of Sennett's thought, the canceling of ambient noise can also be considered a process in which technological equipment and software, which increase the volume of information, eliminate "all behaviors relating to mutual communication" (2015, p. 121). In this approach, it would not be incorrect to say that the mitwelt undergoes a transformation as a result of the individual canceling noise and isolating themselves from the information. In the end, all these transformations create a new *eigenwelt*, as the *eigenwelt* is integrated with the manifestation of the *umwelt* and *mitwelt* (Miyer et al., 2021, p. 54).

After establishing a connection between Lefebvre's abstract space and Deleuze and Guattari's concept of milieu, Hagood discusses the notion of 'neoliberal-self'. At this point, Hagood aligns closely with the conclusions of Pierre Bourdieu. According to Bourdieu, neoliberalism is a black utopia that 'enslaves' a small number of people who "perpetually jet around the world and earn more than they could dream of spending in four lifetimes" (Bourdieu, 1998, p. 43). According to Köse and Bingöl, "the rest are already the remnants kept at the bottom by the system's self-exploitation programs and self-responsibility incentives, plebs" (2021, p. 11). Hagood also makes observations in line with this thought, pointing out that freedom in neoliberalism is an individual matter full of contradictions, recalling Bourdieu's plebs[4] (2019, pp. 178-180). However, when individuals are forced to gather in public spaces irrespective of their individual freedom of choice, such as when "rude, smelly, greasy, chatty, and ugly" (Hagood, 2011, p. 583) passengers are seated together in airplane passenger cabins; when, in the jargon of Bourdieu, 'plebs' come together and congregate, there is a reaction that generates the desire for abstraction mentioned earlier. This is where, according to Hagood, orphic media comes in: to satisfy this desire for abstraction. When the issue is cramped airplane passenger cabins, this is an inevitable end due to the sales policies of the airlines. Since it is not possible to fly passengers other than by seating them and because airline companies "surcharge" bodies that disturb others, they offer noise-blocking options as a service to their passengers (Hagood, 2019, p. 189). In this case, an individual who is forcibly mixed with the crowd benefits from the freedom to 'shut off' the voices of other individuals and reduce external stimuli. Shutting off the individual from external stimuli is mentioned as the remediation function[5] of orphic media.

In this respect, one should take a closer look at the two types of orphic remediation: 'intramodal' and 'cross-modal' (Marazi, 2020, p. 2). In the case of the intramodal type of orphic remediation, the act of fighting against sound with sound or suppressing, masking, blocking, or redirecting auditory attention to another direction is involved. In the case of the cross-modal type of orphic remediation, the transformation of the perception of modalities, affective states, or the passage of time through the use of silence or sound is involved (Hagood, 2019, p. 25). In this context, orphic media provides individuals with the freedom to 'hear what they want' and create a 'filter bubble' for themselves as a smaller part of Lefebvre's abstract space. Orphic media highlights the "deep desire for control as freedom", and this desire "motivates the use of nearly all electronic

---

[4] Hagood refers to the people who 'jet around' described by Bourdieu (2019) as "road warriors" and connects the act of canceling noise with earphones to class politics in this context (pp. 180-182).

[5] Orphic remediation is described as one of the primary functions of orphic media (Hagood, 2019, p. 6)

media today" (Hagood, 2019, p. 4). Hagood points out that the use of orphic media in an *ad hoc* manner involves a fight against sound with sound, using the example of an airplane passenger cabin, and draws on the mythos at this point (2019, p. 189). This narrative can certainly be expanded by considering other spaces as examples rather than the airplane passenger cabin. In one way or another, the individual using orphic media transforms the soundscape. This transformation can be carried out not only with noise-canceling headphones but also with any media player that produces sound.

Orpheus and the Sirens

The person who alters the soundscape substitutes their preferred noises for the undesirable ones. This activity can be viewed as a conflict between sounds. The principles of orphic media have been connected to a particular scene in *Argonautica* by Apollonius of Rhodes when Orpheus fights sound with sound to protect the Argonauts from the Sirens' fury (Malitoris, 2019).

The concept of orphic media, in this sense, references the way Orpheus used the power of sound and music. In ancient Greek mythology, Orpheus was a musician, singer, and poet. In mythology, Orpheus' connection and ability with sound and music are divine and he is considered "the mythological expression of the delight which music gives to the primitive races" (Lang, 2016, s. 32). Orpheus, was able to soften "all animals, plants, living humans and spirits" (Dönmez and Kılınçer, 2011, p. 108) and he "could sing so sweetly that wild beasts would follow him about; trees and plants would bow down to him and the wildest of men would become gentle" (Grimal, 1986, p. 315). Orpheus' ecstatic music, according to mythology, has the characteristic of befuddling the human mind supernaturally and enabling the comprehension of unconventional and extraordinary ideas by expanding one's imagination. Lee (1960) claims that Orpheus "has access to the secret of all knowledge" (s. 8). According to Hagood, the passage from Apollonios featured in the myth of the Argonauts symbolizes the transformative, hypnotic, and subjugating power inherent in the nature of sound and music. Orphic media enable individuals to resist the dominance of ambient sound by harnessing the power of another sound[6], thereby liberating them from the role of passive consumers in a sonic-abstract space. According to Hagood (2019, pp. 217-218), noise canceling is nothing but the sonic self-control that enables the freedom to hear what one wants to hear. Orphic media[7] is there

---

[6] 'Another sound' can be a piece of music, a podcast broadcast, a movie sound, white noise, or a phone conversation that is delivered to the individual in a highly personal manner and is not present in the soundscape of the physical space.

[7] Orphic media, as defined in this study, can include any type of media content and player. Hagood (2019) explains the scope of orphic media by using the example of three

to help the individual break free from unwanted sounds they are exposed to in the physical world and, in a sense, remind them of their individuality amidst the crowd, allowing them to live without being affected by a constantly changing, anxiety and stress-inducing, and distracting environment (Hagood, 2019, p. 3). On the one hand, the freedom to hear what one wants carries the risk of "fostering intolerances both sensory and political" in a world where the flow and intensity of information reach high levels (Hagood, 2019, p. 4); on the other hand, it provides access to the protected space needed for "sensory and emotional self-care" (Hagood, 2019, p. 4). At the center of orphic media is the transformative and influential power of sound, and therefore music. In this context, orphic media have also been seen as connected to the theory of affect[8] (Hagood, 2019, pp. 49-50).

An Approach to Orphic Experience

Orphic media is a concept that refers to the use of sound and music as a means of personal and emotional self-care, as well as a way to challenge and resist the power of ambient sound in our environments. This concept is closely related to the transformative power of sound and music, as exemplified in the myth of Orpheus, a musician and poet in ancient Greek mythology who used his musical abilities to tame wild beasts and bend nature to his will. In the context of musicology, orphic media presents a new perspective on the role and function of music in individuals' lives. While traditional musicology tends to focus on the historical, cultural, and social contexts of music, orphic media highlights the individual and personal experience of listening to music and the impact it can have on our emotional and psychological states. This approach is particularly relevant in the digital age, where individuals are constantly bombarded with information and noise and where the ability to control and curate our auditory environments has become increasingly important. Orphic media plays a role in the collective and individual listening of music from a musicological perspective. It allows individuals to redefine their relationship with sound and music, enabling them to create their own sonic environment and break free from the

---

nested circles. The first and smallest circle includes devices such as white noise machines, various sound-blocking digital applications, headphones, and other devices. The second circle is composed of sound media such as music or film sound that shapes, connects, calms, dominates, or scares the area in which it is found. The third and largest circle includes all media (p. 23).

[8] Affect can be interpreted in multiple ways and is still the subject of debate (Ott, 2018, p. 2). Hagood (2019) notes that contemporary media theorists such as Mark Hansen, Bernard Stiegler, and Brian Massumi highlight the importance of affect as a power in the modern media environment, but also express doubt about its ability to produce concrete results in media and music analyses by researchers who use the theory (p. 21).

constraints of the physical space they are in. This can allow for a more personalized musical experience and can potentially allow for the emergence of new musical styles and forms. Additionally, orphic media can facilitate the creation of new musical communities, and the exchange of musical ideas and experiences between individuals. However, it is important to consider the potential risks and limitations of orphic media, such as the potential for oversaturation of information and the risk of isolating individuals from their physical surroundings. Considering this context, it is possible to define the orphic experience.

Orphic experience involves using sound and media to create a sense of personal control and autonomy in the face of overwhelming sonic stimuli in contemporary society. This can include using headphones or other devices to block out external noise and create a private, isolated space, or using music or sound to regulate one's own emotions or mental state. In this sense, orphic experience can be seen as a way of resisting the sonic hegemony of abstract space and the consumption directives of capitalist society and finding a sense of individuality or authenticity through sound. From a Baudrillardian perspective, orphic experience can be seen as a form of simulation or mimicry, in which the individual seeks to create a personalized version of reality through their choice of media and sound. By selecting and filtering the sounds they encounter, the individual can create a simulated version of the world that conforms to their desires and preferences. In this sense, orphic experience can be seen as a way of escaping from the demands of the real world and constructing a self-contained, artificial reality. According to Bourdieu and Lefebvre, orphic experience can be understood as a form of symbolic capital, in which the individual's choices and preferences in terms of media and sound serve to differentiate them from others and signify their social status or cultural capital. By carefully curating their auditory environment and creating a personalized soundtrack to their lives, the individual can signal their taste and distinction to others, and distinguish themselves from those who do not possess the same level of cultural capital.

Overall, the concept of orphic experience can be seen as a way of navigating and shaping the sonic landscape of contemporary society and creating a sense of personal control and autonomy through the use of sound and media. By carefully selecting and filtering the sounds they encounter, individuals can create a customized version of reality that conforms to their desires and preferences and differentiate themselves from others through their choices in media and sound. Here, headphones can play a significant role in facilitating orphic experience, as they allow the individual to create a personalized auditory environment that is separate from the sounds of the surrounding world. By wearing headphones, the individual can block out external noise and distractions, and focus on the sounds they have chosen to listen to. This can create a sense of isolation and detachment from the external world, and allow the individual to escape from the demands and distractions of the real world. In this sense, headphones can be seen as a key tool for facilitating an orphic experience, as they allow the individual to create a customized, self-contained sonic environment that is separate from the noise and distractions of the outside world.

5

Echoes of the Past
The History and Evolution of Dub Music

Dub is a multifaceted musical genre that emerged in Jamaica in the 1960s and 1970s as a psychedelic and prominent dimension of reggae music (Vendryes, 2015, p. 6). It was developed and refined during the 1970s, with a structure that combines various cultural practices and technical elements. In the late 1970s, it spread from Jamaica to the United Kingdom and the United States. In the 1980s, dub became well-known in the UK as a culture that embodies a particular musical form, under the guidance of skilled and knowledgeable producers such as Dennis Bovell, Adrian Sherwood, and Mad Professor (Vendryes, 2015, p. 6). The independence of cultural expression that followed Jamaica's liberation from British colonization helped to make dub-associated philosophy and music practices widespread on the globe. Mimi Haddon (2017) refers to the spread of dub culture from Jamaica to the UK and other countries as "transplantation" (p. 9). The transplantation has made dub culture visible in several locations on the globe, as depicted in Figure 5.1. According to Haddon (2017), reggae and its sub-elements interacted with other musical cultures after this process, resulting in a "punk-reggae alliance" in the UK (p. 9). It has been suggested that producers such as Brad Osborne and Lloyd 'Bullwackie' Barnes played a significant role in the establishment of dub music in the US (Vendryes, 2015, p. 6). Osbourne 'King Tubby' Ruddock, Lee 'Scratch' Perry, Keith Hudson, and Horace 'Augustus Pablo' Swaby are considered to be the four pioneers of the genre (Masterclass, 2021). Thomas Vendryes, who has published a detailed research paper on dub, notes that dub culture and musical style emerged in Jamaica through innovative and experimental music mixing techniques. Dub music inspired numerous other musical genres after its inception, but it almost disappeared[9] in its homeland,

---

[9] The demise of dub in Jamaica should be viewed in relation to its proliferation in other parts of the world. Dub has not vanished, but rather, it has survived through

Jamaica, after spreading to other parts of the world. Vendryes (2015) calls this a "paradoxical aspect" of dub music (p. 6)

Figure 5.1 : A simple chronology of dub music from 1960 to 1990

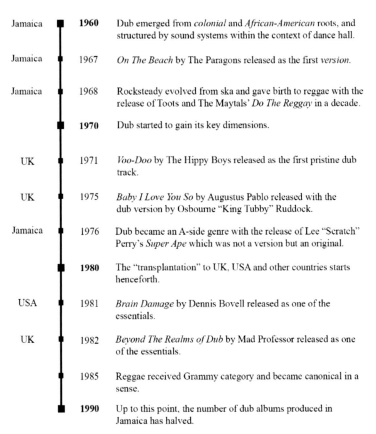

Jamaica	1960	Dub emerged from *colonial* and *African-American* roots, and structured by sound systems within the context of dance hall.
Jamaica	1967	*On The Beach* by The Paragons released as the first *version*.
Jamaica	1968	Rocksteady evolved from ska and gave birth to reggae with the release of Toots and The Maytals' *Do The Reggay* in a decade.
	1970	Dub started to gain its key dimensions.
UK	1971	*Voo-Doo* by The Hippy Boys released as the first pristine dub track.
UK	1975	*Baby I Love You So* by Augustus Pablo released with the dub version by Osbourne "King Tubby" Ruddock.
Jamaica	1976	Dub became an A-side genre with the release of Lee "Scratch" Perry's *Super Ape* which was not a version but an original.
	1980	The "transplantation" to UK, USA and other countries starts henceforth.
USA	1981	*Brain Damage* by Dennis Bovell released as one of the essentials.
UK	1982	*Beyond The Realms of Dub* by Mad Professor released as one of the essentials.
	1985	Reggae received Grammy category and became canonical in a sense.
	1990	Up to this point, the number of dub albums produced in Jamaica has halved.

According to multiple electronic and written sources, dub music is said to have originated from a mistake made by producer Byron Smith and sound system operator Rudolph "Ruddy" Redwood (Barrow and Dalton, 2004, p. 216). Internet sources suggest that Ruddy went to Treasure Island Studio to acquire songs for his next dance and that, by accident, Byron Smith gave Ruddy an instrumental version of The Paragons' 1967 release *On the Beach* (Future Music,

---

transformation and evolution. The genre has also left a lasting impact on performance and production techniques. For example, the dancehall genre owes much of its style and aesthetics to dub music (Vendryes, 2015, p. 15). Additionally, the emergence of various music genres such as dubstep, dubtronica, dub techno, psy-dub, and trip-hop can be traced back to the creative reimagining of traditional dub form (Masterclass, 2021). It could also be argued that the dub culture has helped to legitimize the process of turning sound engineers into creative artists.

2021). Ruddy played this version at his dance and it gained popularity. This instrumental version, which was essentially the result of a producer's mistake, unexpectedly won the favor of the audience, and this positive response became the spark that ignited the development of dub music (Masterclass, 2021). However, it is important to note that dub music did not emerge from a single source, and multiple catalysts were involved in its creation and evolution. The Treasure Island Studio, founded in 1951 by Jamaican businessman Stanley Motta, is also said to have played a significant role in the development of dub music. It is believed that the recording and editing processes at the studio drew from two distinct cultural sources in terms of style and form (Chen and Chang, 1998, pp. 14-19). According to Vendryes, one of these sources was the "colonial history, in the inheritance of African, Christian, and Caribbean mixed musical forms", while the other was the popular music forms of the time, such as big band jazz and R&B, created by African-American cultures (Vendryes, 2015, p. 7). From this perspective, the emergence of dub culture was influenced by both traditional forms and popular music of the period. In terms of form, it is also claimed that the first example of the genre, which had fully consolidated its distinctive features, was The Hippy Boys' *Voo-Doo* in 1971 (Barrow and Dalton, 2004, p. 216), although some sources consider *On the Beach*, as mentioned above, to be one of the first examples.

There is a tendency in both canonical and non-canonical sources to attribute the emergence of musical practices, such as dub, to a single reference or specific historical milestone. Some sources point to 1951 (Chen and Chang, 1998, pp. 14-19), some to 1967 (Barrow and Dalton, 2004, p. 216), and some to 1976 (Vendryes, 2015, p. 8) as the year of emergence, development, or distribution of dub music. While all of these sources contain important information, researching and interpreting what occurred at these key moments can lead to the "A-side and B-side" issue, as discussed in this study. The music release format available in post-1950 Jamaica is said to have changed when producer Byron Smith accidentally gave sound system operator Ruddy an instrumental version of a track. When Ruddy played this instrumental version on his sound system, he noticed that the audience appreciated it. This incident sparked a new trend: on vinyl records, which typically had completely different songs on each side, the B-sides began to be filled with instrumental and reinterpreted versions of the songs on the A-sides. According to Rick Anderson (2004), dub music emerged thanks to the B-side versions, as this method made sense for 'thrifty' producers (p. 209). Including an instrumental version on the B-side of a recording reduced production costs, and the appeal of this cost-saving approach, as well as the popularity of these versions with the audience, led to the adoption of this style by King Tubby. It is rumored that King Tubby believed that "pared-back" dub versions would have a creative impact at sound system events and impress the audience (Future Music, 2021). This situation also contributed to the increasing number of dub recordings in the market over time (Barrow and Dalton, 2004, p. 217-219). In the early days, ska, rocksteady, and reggae were the dominant genres on the A-side of vinyl records. Dub, on the other hand, created a distinct sound by removing the lead vocals from A-side songs and emphasizing the drums and bass, using a specific effect chain (Masterclass, 2021). At this point, it is possible to see the thin line separating reggae and dub. Reggae is a music genre that centers on the vocals and conveys the narrative through the lead vocals, while dub music, which emerged from the reggae style, is defined as "reggae without the original lead vocals" (Masterclass, 2021). There is also a status difference between the A-side and the B-side. At the time, a song on the A-side was considered the original, while the version on the B-side was seen as a secondary reinterpretation (Vendryes, 2015, p. 8). However, with the release of The Upsetters' *Super Ape* album, produced by Lee Perry in 1976 and released on Island Records, dub rose to A-side status as a musical genre with its own aesthetic (Sullivan, 2014, pp. 45-49). The relationship of B-side reinterpretations to financial constraints is clear. Additionally, the influence of necessity, as seen in the emergence of the sound system tradition (which will be discussed later), should not be overlooked in the B-side issue.

In Jamaica, the primary focus of dub music production was at dance hall events, which were open-air gatherings where people came together to listen to and dance to music played on large sound systems installed in dance halls. As a result, Jamaican dub was produced for a particular kind of consumption at dance hall events and was shaped by this criterion in many ways (Vendryes, 2015, p. 7). Because of its history, dub has always been closely connected to dance. According to Vendryes (2015), the "essential musical objective" of dub music production was to facilitate dancing (p. 7). Therefore, dub music should be viewed as a phenomenon closely linked to the sound system culture. The form of dub music is based on experimental practices[10] which eventually became a vital part of Jamaican popular music culture.

The Sound System Culture

Sound system events that emerged in Kingston, Jamaica in the 1950s took shape as a source of entertainment (Fintoni and McLauchlan, 2018, p. 2). Sound systems, which facilitated the development of a genuine culture that spread to

---

[10] The mixing practices that emerged as a result of an initial error were later intentionally employed due to their power to engage the listeners of the time (Anderson, 2004, p. 209). The fact that the characteristics of the dub sound are implemented in various music genres today, to some extent, suggests how these practices that originated from an error could become widespread.

many countries after the 1950s, were referred to as "mobile apparatuses" due to their portable nature (Henriques, 2003, p. 454). Examining sound system events can provide insights into staging music in dance halls, interacting with the crowd, and most importantly, designing the space. While sound systems are crucial to the historical development of dub culture, they are also essential in reflecting the aural aesthetics of dub music to the listener. In the reggae music scene, which encompasses dub culture and practices, live bands were largely absent. Music was played through reggae sound systems and interacted with the listener through customized sound systems (Fintoni and McLauchlan, 2018, p. 2). As a result of the aforementioned historical development, sound systems have become a means of listening to Jamaican music, emphasizing low frequencies and authentic dynamics in a dance hall where people gather and dance[11]. Subsequently, sound system practices began to spread to other countries, particularly the United Kingdom, due to factors such as the immigration of Jamaicans to Britain after World War II in search of new opportunities (Fintoni and McLauchlan, 2018, p. 2). The process of 'transplantation' led to some changes and developments in the sound system tradition. Each country had its own scene, and the reaction of the sound system tradition to these existing scenes resulted in the incorporation of new cultural elements or the alteration of existing ones. Henriques and Vidigal describe this process of transformation as the "outernationalization" of dub culture (as cited in Fintoni and McLauchlan, 2018, p. 4). In other words, dub has undergone a process of exchange between countries after initially emerging in Kingston, Jamaica. This has resulted in a new quality of dub that has not only affected the form of the music but also transformed the style of consumption and the dance floor where music is consumed. For example, while music consumption in Jamaica's sound system culture took place in a bright and open space, it became more introspective and took place in dark indoor spaces when dub culture spread to the United Kingdom (Fintoni and McLauchlan, 2018, pp. 12-13). Additionally, the United Kingdom's dub scene lacks a dress code, unlike the Jamaican scene which has a specific dress code and does not use deliberate darkness or lighting during concerts (Fintoni and McLauchlan, 2018, p. 13). According to research conducted by Fintoni and McLauchlan (2018), data from interviews suggests that the barrier between performer and listener has disappeared in sound system-centered dance halls in the United Kingdom, particularly due to the positioning of the stage and sound system, as well as the performer-or traditionally the operator

---

[11] On the other hand, for many researchers who have done research on the sound system phenomenon, this issue does not only center on dance and is not superficial. It is useful to examine the issue without ignoring the existence of politics, a conscious break from self and space, "libidinal and commercial economies" and many other elements on the dance floor (Henriques, 2010, p. 64).

(p. 11-13). This creates a more intimate and non-hierarchical interaction, in contrast to rave events where the atmosphere is described by Graham St. John (2017) as meditative and introspective, with the effect of darkness being decisive (p. 281). The discussions of Julian Henriques (2010), who commented on the sound system phenomenon in light of affect theory, are worth considering at this point. For Henriques, the loud sound produced by sound systems generates a physical force and creates sensuousness in the crowd on the dance floor (p. 79). From Henriques' perspective, sound systems create a new context with multiple dimensions. The flow of the performance, the sequence of the pieces played, the editing of the transitions between the pieces, the attitude adopted by the operator, the positioning of the sound systems, and many other factors produce a "vibration of affect" (Henriques, 2010, p. 79). This vibration of affect can disable the "rational subject" and unleash the "relational subject." In this case, the audience in the dance hall is able to shed what is "autonomous" and "self-consistent" thanks to sound systems (Henriques, 2010, p. 79). Accordingly, if we examine closely, it is evident that there is a deep aspect of escape and unity that takes place under the guidance of unique cultural codes in sound system events. On the other hand, according to Henriques (2010), Kwesi Johnson's bold use of the phrase 'bass culture' in the 1980 album title[12] highlights nothing but the fact that bass is the foundation of the politics of sound system culture (p. 63). The concept of bass culture also supports the legitimacy of the vibration circulating in the atmosphere during a performance and provides an opportunity to theorize about this issue in its entirety (Henriques, 2010, p. 63).

In addition, it is believed that the spoken word, when delivered live, along with a live musical performance, has a significant impact on the dynamic between the performer and the audience within the sound system culture. Fintoni and McLauchlan (2018) point to toasting as a longstanding tradition in which the spoken word is central, particularly in reggae events, and the role of the Master of Ceremony (MC) who performs it (p. 3). Savishinsky's work views toasting as a message-transfer ritual that contextualizes the music being played – "where 'dread talk' or the modification of Jamaican slang used by Rastas expresses their heightened consciousness and deep understanding of the inherent power of the spoken word" (as cited in Fintoni and McLauchlan, 2018, p. 3). This performance, which is often based on an improvised spoken word section by Jamaican deejays, adds another layer to the music (Masterclass, 2021). On the other hand, there is ongoing debate as to whether the deejay phenomenon, with its incorporation of Caribbean spoken word into the performance, inspired rap music (Future Music, 2021).

---

[12] Although not mentioned in Henriques' text, Lloyd Bradley's book published in 2001 was also titled with the same phrase.

The production quality that defined dub music was the reinterpretation of an existing piece through the use of creative techniques to serve the purpose of facilitating dance (Vendryes, 2015, p. 12). Jamaican deejays, or "macro-composers," as Vendryes referred to them (2015, p. 15), played remixed American R&B and ska records at events in Jamaica, with sound systems serving as the central hub for these events as both a sound source and a medium (Haddon, 2017, p. 8). In the 1950s, when reggae music began to emerge and radio was not yet accessible, sound systems were the only way for people to listen to recorded music (Bradley, 2001, pp. 125-136). Therefore, similar to the B-side phenomenon, the sound system tradition can be seen as being related to financial constraints. The sound system culture also placed a significant emphasis on the role of sound engineers, who were responsible for controlling the consoles and played a creative role in performing music through the use of various specific techniques (Vendryes, 2015, p. 12). The positioning of the sound system was also a key factor in this culture. For instance, Henriques (2010) cites an engineer from Stone Love, one of Jamaica's largest sound systems, who asserts that there is a soundscape in the dance hall. The engineer argues that the proper setup of speakers comprising multiple sections (as depicted in Figure 5.2) is crucial for spatially arranging the SFX used during the performance in a way that engages with the audience (p. 65). By examining Figure 5.2, which is based on Fintoni's technical research (2014) and data from various sound system blogs, it is easy to see that each stack from top to bottom covers a specific range of the audible frequency spectrum, from low to high. Thus, each stack is essential in that sense, as they collectively cover the full range of 30 Hz to 20 kHz.

Figure 5.2 : An illustration of a four-stack reggae sound system setup

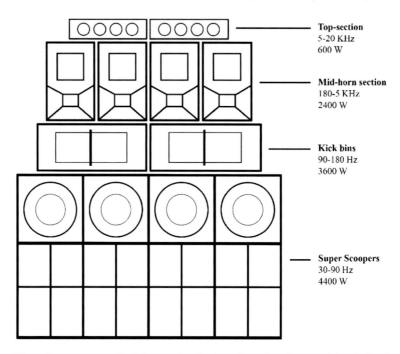

The advancement of mixing technologies also played a crucial role in the emergence of the dub style, as the dub phenomenon[13] was built uponthe capabilities of mixing equipment (Vendryes, 2015, p. 13). The dance hall, where reggae music encountered its audience, was originally an open space in Jamaica. The phrase "a dancehall night out" among communities, therefore, describes an activity that continues until dawn, with people gathered in the open air in the streets (Henriques, 2010, p. 61). In particular, outdoor sound system events in Kingston served a dual purpose, providing both entertainment and a means for producers to gauge the reaction of listeners to new recordings through the operators of the sound systems (Anderson, 2004, p. 210). This method of observation through sound system events was found to be effective in determining whether a new song was worthy of a wider release.

The sound systems used to play dub music in dance halls were not commercially manufactured, but rather 'homemade', which remains a common

_____

[13] On the side, Vendryes (2015) raises another point: Although the active involvement of sound engineers in the performance of the music took place on the Jamaica stage; from the 1960s to the 1970s, there was a period in which engineers did not only play a technical role in the general popular music field, but were also actively involved in artistic creation (p. 13).

practice (Fintoni and McLauchlan, 2018, p. 6). Each sound system has an owner, and these owners often build their own systems. During the construction process, owners incorporate various customizations to their sound systems, the main goal of which is to create systems that can effectively deliver the distinctive feel of dub music (Fintoni and McLauchlan, 2018, p. 7). Additionally, high kilowatts are neither necessary nor desirable in the sound system culture. According to Albah, commercially manufactured high-kilowatt sound systems diminish the dynamic richness of the music and degrade its aural quality. He asserts that ravers, rather than dub listeners, prefer high-kilowatt systems. However, sound systems are expertly crafted to showcase the quality of the dub music played (Fintoni and McLauchlan, 2018, p. 12). When conducting basic historical research on dub music, it is quite common to encounter phrases such as 'sound system owner' or 'sound system operator'. Upon examination, it becomes clear that these sound systems hold a certain level of identity. Albah, speaking on behalf of the Welders Hi-fi system, stated that individuals who attend dub events do so not just to dance and listen to music, but also to experience the sound of a particular sound system (as cited in Fintoni and McLauchlan, 2018, p. 6). As a result, a sound system becomes known by the name of its builder or operator, conferring an altered identity on the owners of the sound system within this realm, which Lloyd Bradley referred to as "bass culture" (2001). Therefore, each sound system has a unique name and owner.

The construction of a sound system is a highly specialized and intricate process that necessitates a nuanced comprehension of technical details, the functionality of various components, and aesthetics. According to Fintoni and McLauchlan's interviews (2018) for the above-mentioned research, mastery develops during the process and the sound system builder becomes more familiar with the technical details mentioned while building a system. In contrast to industrial systems commonly utilized for musical playback, sound systems offer a more rich and more vibrant auditory experience, according to another interviewee who provided data for the same research (p. 6). Reggae sound systems do not produce a 'crystal-clear' sound[14], and unlike most

---

[14] It could be argued that the belief that 'perfect sound is not pleasant' is not exclusive to dub culture. It is not uncommon for contemporary music producers in various genres to prefer a sound that is not entirely high-quality, noise-free, and crystal-clear. In fact, there are specialized software plug-ins that aim to replicate the sound characteristics of analog hardware using digital tools. For example, a blog post introducing and reviewing various such plug-ins, including TAIP by Baby Audio, PSP Vintage Warmer by PSP Audioware, Console & Tape Machine Emulation by Overloud Tapedesk, and J37 Tape by Waves, concludes with the statement: "Digital recording technology offers myriad benefits over an all-analog studio, but you still can't beat the sonic supremacy of recording sounds directly to tapeor can you?" (Sweetwater, 2022). This suggests that the belief that 'perfect sound is not pleasant' is also present in the production stages of other genres beyond dub.

fabricated sound systems that come off the production lines, they are not flat[15]. Sound systems toned especially for reggae music should be relatively dominant at low and high frequencies (Fintoni and McLauchlan, p. 7). A non-flat output is a very basic and understandable criterion, given the importance of low-frequency musical elements in the sound system tradition, especially in the 30-300 Hz range (Henriques, 2003, p. 452). Sub-bass and low bass should be taken as the "musical material" of the sound system culture. The low-frequency range and especially the reggae bass line, which affect the listener with a high physical force that "touches" but not hurts, in Henriques's words (2003, p. 461), are the signature of sound system events (Henriques, 2010, p. 63). In other words, the materiality of sound, through low frequencies, touches and "vibrates" the crowd in the dance hall. The sonic force, which is "embodying as well as disembodying", kneading individuals with a sense of "unity" is a unique element of the dub dance hall (Henriques, 2003, p. 461). The underlying source of this force is nothing but sound systems. As such, it is evident that sound systems play a decisive role in shaping the culture and aesthetics of dub music.

Exploring the Production Foundations

It is important to understand the unique remixing practices of dub music when studying the foundations of production, as these practices have been a defining feature of dub music and have inspired the production techniques of punk, hip-hop, and various electronic dance music genres since 1970, influencing the evolution of these genres (Howard, 2004, p. 231). The origins of dub can be traced back to a mistake made by producer Byron Smith, who created a vocal-less version of a 1967 single. Sound system operator Rudolph 'Ruddy' Redwood played this version on his system, leading to a chain of events that sparked the trend of including an instrumental version, or dub, on the B-side of a recording as an alternative to the A-side, in order to save on production costs (Barrow and Dalton, 2004, p. 216). This allowed producers to fill both sides of a record without incurring the expense of creating a new B-side and marked the birth of dub and the era of versions (Anderson, 2004, p. 209). Dub versions were created by rearranging the tracks of A-side songs in creative ways using mixing consoles, showcasing the live mixing nature of dub music. As a result, dub music came to be associated with the B-sides of new singles, resulting from the reinterpretation of Jamaican singles using a specific effect chain (Veal, 2007, pp. 68-75). This reinterpretation style became a defining characteristic of dub music and shaped

---

[15] Flat systems that the interviewee almost pejoratively talks about are gears that do not boost or cut any frequency while producing soundwhich is trendy in the music production industry. These systems, which generate 'honest' audio are important for the blind listening process during the production phase. If a mixed track is heard well in a flat system, it is said that it will sound well in an end-listener system (Sweetwater, 1997).

the basic features of the genre. By the 1970s, dub had gained recognition as a standalone genre on the A-side, with its own distinctive aesthetic (Vendryes, 2015, p. 8). The production foundations of dub music, particularly in its early stages, were based on deconstructing and reconstructing new singles using a specific effect chain. Later, dub evolved beyond being a version-based genre and established itself as a new musical field, heavily influenced by traditional dub reinterpretations.

Today, it is traditional for dub interpretation to involve the specific use of signal processors and extemporaneous dynamic amplitude controls. Echo/delay and reverb are the sound effects that have contributed the most distinctive sonic characteristics to dub music (Haddon, 2017, p. 17). Osbourne 'King Tubby', Lee 'Scratch' Perry, Augustus Pablo, and Keith Hudson were key producers who shaped the sonic characteristics of dub through the heavy use of echo, amplification of low frequencies, distinctive vocal integration, and the inclusion of high-pitch instruments to balance the frequency spectrum (Future Music, 2021). In the dub style, a track should have a sense of an 'organic' feeling after the production process. This feeling is also considered an essential criterion on several tutorial-based internet platforms that outline current production methods. For example, music producer Ronan Macdonald believes that a finished dub track should have a "laid-back vibe" (Macdonald, 2021). Macdonald emphasizes the importance of prioritizing "human timing" in consistent dub music production as it adds a sense of organic imperfection to the mix. He also suggests using the mixing console in a way that allows for "spur-of-the-moment" results, such as by keeping the delay tempo sync turned off and manually adjusting delay time and filters in real-time using faders and knobs (Macdonald, 2021). Macdonald's approach is focused on achieving a humanistic feel by avoiding machine-like precision in the timing of the music. The practice of "drastic" reinterpretation is still prevalent in dub music, as it has been since the era of B-side versions in the early 1970s (Anderson, 2004, p. 209). Music producer Daniel Boyle (2020) claims that "sending the delay back to itself" is fundamental in dub music. Like Macdonald, he also emphasizes the importance of manually adjusting a particular knob in real-time, rather than relying on computer automation, when controlling faders, muting groups, and reshaping the arrangement of a song. In particular, it is a classic technique in dub to improvise the rate and feedback ratio of the delay manually, rather than setting a synchronized rate.

> "To make a real dub, it's got to be done with your hands. Otherwise, it isn't from instinct; it's from thought, which is why dubs made with edits and automation sound cool, but they're pretty predictable because it's kind of the way you'd expect it to happen. When you're doing stuff through a console or a MIDI controller; hitting mutes and pulling faders, turning knobs, etc., you do stuff by

accident but it sounds great! That's really when dub comes into its own-when there's mistakes" (Boyle, 2020).

In this passage, Boyle speaks of "sudden muting", a technique for performing dub music. This technique exists to pull the entire multitrack into a "sparse" spot (Boyle, 2020). In an almost traditional way, especially the drum and guitar tracks are passed through a spring reverb processor. Reverb should also be used with an "intrinsic" procedure, as emphasized as a basis in the application of the delay effect (Macdonald, 2021). In addition, to create a classic dub echo effect with relatively high (and often unstable) feedback amount concerning the organic feeling, it is recommended to use tape echo hardware as in the early periods or up-to-date emulation plug-in software that serves the same purpose in the digital environment (Masterclass, 2021). The same advice applies to reverb and other effects, as the idea that analog equipment provides a 'warm' output with rich harmonic information is very common in electronic music production, as mentioned above. In today's digital environment, it is necessary to "warm up the mix" for a consistent dub sound (Boyle, 2020). Modulation effects are considered another key ingredient of dub music. For this reason, it's common to apply flanger to hi-hat or guitar tracks or to use a phaser for delay return (Macdonald, 2021). Boyle (2020) recommends creating a spring reverb aux for the drums and blending the aux channel with the main channel after it is finally cleared of the low end with the high-pass filter. According to him, this is the most common method for creating classic dub version drums. In addition to the above-mentioned details, Wayne Chen and Kevin O'Brien Chang argue in a related study that dub music has three main production elements: a determined rhythm section, emphasized low frequencies, and syncopation (1998, p. 43). Also, Future Music, a music production magazine, states that dub music has three essentials: tape echo, spring reverb, and melodica partition[16] (2021). Similarly, in the Masterclass, a platform where experts in their fields give narratives, dub music is defined with four characteristics: no lead vocals, riddim emphasis, sound effects, and space for toasters (Masterclass, 2021). The number of these sources can of course be multiplied. But from these three examples, it can be implicated that the foundations of dub music are mostly based on a specific sound design

---

[16] The three essentials are put forward with their reasons in the relevant text. According to the text, tape echo is the first essential because the sound and effect produced by the hardware used in the early periods are classical. Creating this classic effect is important because tape echo gives the output an organic, loose feel. Spring reverb is the second essential because the twingy metallic sound character produced by spring reverb in dub music is as classic as in the first essential. The third essential is the melodica score. The reason for this is explained in the text by producing high-frequency information that will balance the dominant frequencies by creating contrast. As it is said in the main text, it is difficult to comment on the ranking and selection criteria of these three essentials (Future Music, 2021).

rather than mere instrumentation. This seems quite understandable given the historical development processes. On the other hand, there is an undeniable subjectivity in these three texts, since it is not clear what criteria should be adhered to when creating basic determinations about the essence of a particular musical genre.

The riddim

Dub music has a distinctive rhythm section consisting of a characteristic drum pattern that serves as a specialized foundation for percussion. The harmony of all elements within a certain groove in dub music is referred to as a riddim, which is Jamaican patois for rhythm. As a method of arrangement, riddim shares some similarities with the concept of a backing track. Riddim can be thought of as a context in which other layers integrate and harmonize, typically including a percussion track that is spontaneously reinterpreted along with the other tracks. Also known as a reggae concept, the riddim method involves the use of instrumental tracks as the basic building blocks of dub music, with each instrument track that is harmonically consistent being individually manipulated by the operator using processors and volume controls and re-arranged through improvisation (Future Music, 2021). This allows the "selector" performing in the dance hall to create a percussive and melodic sound that enhances the atmosphere (Vendryes, 2015, p. 15). According to Macdonald (2021), in addition to the use of percussion, the ability to create and shape a consistent feel for the dub using existing tracks, or understanding riddim, is essential. Michael Veal argues that the emergence of the riddim method led to sound system operators adopting the role of "macro-composers" (2007, p. 85). From this perspective, sound system operators can be seen as composers capable of conveying an improvised interpretation to the audience in the dance hall through the deconstruction and reconstruction of the whole. As such, the riddim method creates a unique mode of conveyance in dub music – one that is worth considering in light of the fact that familiarity with riddim is treated as a prerequisite in dub music production. In the 1980s, operators or music producers who had been using the riddim method with existing tracks began to create original riddims. This expansion of creative possibilities for producers was made possible by the development of music technology, particularly drum machines (Vendryes, 2015, p. 17).

Drum kit notations provided after this point are created in accordance with the standard shown below in Figure 5.3.

Figure 5.3 : The drum kit standard

Explaining the patterns of riddim, Macdonald (2021) makes a basic classification of three basic drum styles: "one-drop, rockers, and steppers". The author's use of kick's accentuation as a criterion when introducing patterns seems worthy of attention. According to Kevin Zahner (2022), who exemplifies these three basic drum beats, one-drop is one of the most characteristic patterns of reggae, with the kick played on the third beat and upbeat hi-hat accents (Figure 5.4).

Figure 5.4 : Basic one-drop pattern

Rockers, on the other hand, is a pattern that can be encountered in several music genres with the kick played in the first and third beats, and the snare played in the second and fourth beats (Figure 5.5). Rockers pattern also indicates the above-mentioned ska and rock connections.

Figure 5.5 : Basic rockers pattern

Steppers is the four-on-the-floor pattern of reggae music with the kick played on each beat (Figure 5.6). This pattern provides a solid basis for the variation of other elements such as cymbals, toms, snares, and percussion. The four-on-the-floor structure of Steppers has enabled it to be characterized as a "modern" pattern (Olivas, 2018).

Figure 5.6 : Basic steppers pattern

Instead of thinking that all these patterns are immutable, it is important to know that they are played by alternating, embellishing, or blending with other patterns (Figure 5.7). In particular, the hi-hat is claimed to be a decisive element to support accentuation (Olivas, 2018).

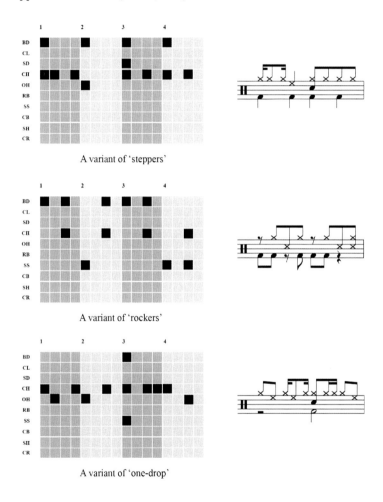

Figure 5.7 : The basic variations of the three core patterns

At this stage, it is useful to briefly discuss the fundamentals of the reggae bassline. Because the three basic patterns and variations exemplified above form the building block of the riddim concept by showing their unique intricacy with the reggae bassline. The relatively accepted method, written by Chris Matheos, was found useful at this point. Likewise, the theoretical characteristics are discussed at a basic level in light of this source. According to Matheos (1998), the reggae bassline is an element that should always be considered in patterns (p. 5). This paternal structure also gives clues about the concept of the riddim. The most commonly used pattern was identified as "root-fifth-octave" by Matheos (Figure 5.8). Another common pattern is "root-third-fifth" (Figure 5.9). The number of patterns can be multiplied and more complex examples can be given, but at a fundamental level, reggae music is based on altering basic patterns with various additions, ornaments, alternations, and so. Therefore, basic patterns also function as a template on which to be creative (Matheos, 1998, p. 5-6).

Figure 5.8 : Root-fifth-octave pattern

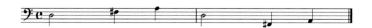

Figure 5.9 : Root-fifth-octave pattern

Matheos points out that some bassline patterns do not always start from the root note as is customary. For him, "reggae is a groove-based style" and "changing up the starting notes of a pattern can make [the] groove less repetitive sounding" (Matheos, 1998, p. 6). Similarly, down beats can be skipped when playing reggae bass. Matheos describes resting in down beats as a quality that supports the groove and refers to this technique as "breathing" (Matheos, 1998, p. 6). According to Matheos, there are several techniques that can be used to support the reggae groove. The first of these is "rhythmic displacement". Rhythmic displacement is simply shifting a bass pattern to different spots of the bar without changing the melodic information (Figure 5.10). In other words, it is the horizontal displacement of the bass pattern. Displacement often goes unnoticed by the audience if it is done without exaggeration, but it "instantly makes the groove more interesting" (Matheos, 1998, p. 7).

Figure 5.10 : Rhythmic displacement

According to Matheos, another technique used to create the reggae groove is 'crossing the barline'. This technique can be used "when working with two bar phrases" by holding a note over the barline. Matheos claims that a "tasteful" effect can be achieved by using the crossing the bar line technique properly (Matheos, 1998, p. 9-10). Also, occasionally putting rests on the same spots instead of tying notes may create an alteration (Figure 5.11).

Figure 5.11 : Crossing the bar line or using rests

'Using dead notes' is another technique that can be used to add a percussive character to the bass groove (Figure 5.12). Matheos argues that a bassline with consistent use of dead notes can act almost like percussion and alter the feel of the rhythm section (Matheos, 1998, p. 11). In summary, using dead notes can add a percussive quality to the bassline.

Figure 5.12 : Dead notes

Matheos argues that instead of fretted, fretless bass can make the slide movements on the bassline sound more "organic" (Matheos, 1998, pp. 13-14). He states that when playing fretted bass, it is reasonable to replace rests with slides so that the groove can be variegated in a unique way (Figure 5.13).

Figure 5.13 : Replacing rests with slides

Another technique that Matheos describes is moving patterns. This technique is only concerned with performing the music live on stage, rather than creating an aural aesthetic in the bassline section (Matheos, 1998, p. 17). This technique described by Matheos basically mentions a simple transposition, but the pattern structure of reggae music seems to have pushed the author to define this technique as "moving patterns" with a specific phrase (Matheos, 1998, p. 17). In this technique, there is a vertical replacement of the melodic patterns on staff.

It should be taken into account that all these techniques, articulations, and alternative bass interpretations mentioned at the basic level exist with consistent low-frequency information in the dance hall since reggae comes to the forefront with its relationship with sensation, not with its interpretation dexterity as mentioned in the relevant section. When it comes to sensation, low frequencies are claimed to be crucial in sound system culture by several researchers — which was discussed in the related chapter. Dub emphasizes low frequencies, either through arrangement style or boosting. Dub music's criterion for emphasizing low frequencies is undoubtedly closely related to sound system culture. "This is one area where size matters and bigger really is better" (FabFilter, 2022). The sizeable sound systems used in the dance hall allow the sonic details of the music to be reproduced in a wide range. The impactness of low frequencies is increased through the use of multiple large cabinets in the systems. Sound systems have transformed low frequencies into signatures for Jamaican music production (Hitchins, 2014, pp. 34-37). Low frequencies have a physical impact on the bodies of people who gather on the dance floor where the sound systems are located. This effect was named "sonic dominance" by Julian Henriques and described as "the bassline beats on our chest, vibrating the flesh, playing on the bone and resonating the genitals" (2003, p. 452). Boosted low-end was fundamental, especially in the early stages of dub music. This essence is still present. Hence, the dance hall audience dances to music dominated by low frequencies (Veal, 2007, p. 57). In events where music has "mass," thanks to sound systems, especially low frequencies make a touch that connects individuals in the dance hall with a physical force (Henriques, 2003, p. 452). The situation where low frequencies vibrate all surfaces of the skin rather than just being heard with the ears is considered a specialized issue for dub music (Henriques, 2003, p. 453). In other words, the emphasis on low frequencies should be taken as one of the unique qualities of dub music.

Syncopation is one of the characteristics of dub music. According to Vendryes, syncopation in dub music has its origins in the ska, with its accentuation structure emphasizing after-beats (2015, p. 13). Syncopation has become one of the hallmarks of Jamaican music and has evolved on an identical basis, especially with dub music (Barrow and Dalton, 2004, p. 3-4). Guitar chops played in off-beats are one of the standard articulations of dub music. This main element is also called *skank* in jargon. Skank fills in between two main beats with "scratchy" chords (Mcdonald, 2021). Syncopation, or the disruption of a regular rhythmic pattern, is an important element in EDM and has been widely studied in the field of musicology. Syncopation has been found to elicit pleasure in listeners and encourage spontaneous rhythmic movements, which is why it is often used in dance music (Sioros, 2015, p. 120). Syncopation can add complexity and interest to a musical piece and can also help to create a sense of tension and release, which are important for creating a compelling and engaging musical experience. Syncopation is often achieved through the use of off-beat accents, or by placing accents on weak beats rather than strong beats.

Dub music is a genre of electronic dance music that originated in Jamaica in the 1970s. It is characterized by the use of extensive sound processing techniques, such as reverb, echo, and delay, to create a spacious, immersive soundscape. It spread around the world, affecting the global music production field formally, interpretively, transferably, and philosophically. Dub's influence on modern music seems undeniable as "there are genres which borrow explicitly from the bass-heavy, sound system-driven approach, such as dubstep, trip-hop, and dub techno" (Future Music, 2021). Dub music often features stripped-down, repetitive rhythms and a heavy emphasis on bass and drums, as well as the use of samples from other sources. It is closely associated with the development of reggae music and has had a significant influence on a range of other genres, including hip-hop and electronic dance music and specifically, dub techno. In terms of its cultural significance, dub music is often seen as a reflection of the social and political conditions of Jamaica in the 1970s and 1980s, and has been described as a form of 'sound system culture' that embodies the values of community, collaboration, and resistance.

Fundamental deconstruction of the dub echo

In this section, a simplified deconstruction of the genre-specific echo practice, deemed to hold paramount importance among the characteristic sound-processing methodologies of dub music, is undertaken. In this regard, rather than compiling ideas that have been discussed in other sources[17] regarding the sound of dub music and the production paradigm in which echo

---

[17] For further research on related topics, see Sullivan, P. (2014). *Remixology: Tracing the Dub Diaspora.* Reaktion Books., D'Aquino, B. (2008). Rewinding the Tape of History: King Tubby and the Audiopolitics of Echo. *Riffs Journal, 2*(2), 66-72., Henriques, J. (2011). *Sonic Bodies: Reggae Sound Systems, Performance Techniques, and Ways of Knowing.* Bloomsbury Academic., Roholt, T. C. (2014). *Groove: A Phenomenology of Rhythmic Nuance.* Bloomsbury Academic. On the other hand, the cultural, political, and sociological aspects of dub music and its place within the Jamaican diaspora, as well as the authentic aspects of commercial record publishing practices, have been studied in multiple sources, in contrast to the scarcity of technically oriented research. These issues have also been attempted to be discussed in the previous headings.

occupies, it is intended to carry out a direct, fundamental level analysis and develop an approach to how echo effect holds a place in the musical structure as only one form of implementation. Through this analysis process, a visual and auditory representation of the authentic dub echo style, which has been known to inspire other genres such as dub techno (Vendryes, 2015, p. 6), is brought to light. The practices of manipulating various parameters through knobs and faders on equipment used for production and performance in the early examples are often considered to embody the human aspect of dub music. As previously discussed, the idea that the echo parameters must also be improvised in a "spur of the moment" (see Macdonald, 2021) manner, akin to manipulating other signal processors or controllers, is crucial in dub music. In this section some parameters are automated to mimic the human influence, experimenting with the idea of randomness and improvisation in the use of echo effects in dub music, incrementally within a software environment[18], utilizing only an echo processor. As Sullivan puts it, echo should be regarded as a crucial effect in the production of dub music, in which "the engineer can also be an artist in his own right" (2014, p. 47). By examining the thought path created by Sullivan, the idea of how engineers can intervene in the musical structure with their 'instruments' will also be discussed under a separate heading, taking into account the use of the echo effect in an articulative form, specifically in terms of the 'feedback amount' value, using examples as a basis.

Additionally, how the basic parameters are transformed into the final sound is exemplified within the context of dub music. The results of the experimentation, in the form of experiential data garnered throughout the process from start to finish, are listed as the fundamental principles of dub echo and are appended at the end of this section. To provide a more cohesive narrative, the discussions within this section have been divided into two categories: technical and musical. It must be considered a major limitation that the following conclusions are based on an expandable and evolving experience and are designed to be definitive only for the subject of dub techno within this research.

The technical aspect

In this section, a sine wave sample will be the reference point. So, a dominant pure sine wave is generated at C4, 261.626 Hz, using Live's wavetable plug-in, adhering to the A440 pitch standard. The selection of a sine wave is motivated by the desire for the subsequent series of processes to be discernible in the

---

[18] The process was carried out utilizing *Ableton Live 11*. To execute the process at a fundamental level, recourse was made exclusively to Live's stock plug-ins, namely the *echo* and *LFO*. Spectral representations were obtained via *iZotope RX9 Audio Editor* software.

spectrum during the initial phase. The experimentation carried out using the sine waveshape will provide fundamental examples as the entire process is ultimately applied to a musical context, with the effect being subsequently discussed in relation to this outcome. The majority of the ADSR values of the generated signal, as well as all other parameters of the wavetable plug-in, were left in their default positions at the start, and the output, as shown in Image 5.1, is exemplified[19] in its unprocessed state.

Pure Sine Wave Sample

Image 5.1 : Spectrum image of the pure sine wave sample

In the initial phase, a series of processes was carried out on the waveshape in question utilizing the echo. The first process, conducted with no alteration of any parameter, has resulted in an echo applied in the default setting. As shown in Image 5.2, the echo plug-in, by default, has linked the echo modes of the right and left channels, synchronized with a dotted accent to an ⅛ beat, chosen a delay offset value of 0% for the right and left channels, set the feedback value to 50%, the dry/wet[20] balance to 70%, disabled the panning modulation, and processed the output signal with a band-pass filter with a soft slope ranging between 50.0

---

[19] In the following phase of the procedures undertaken in this section, the waveshape was transformed into a pure sawtooth. Additionally, it has been deemed beneficial to remind that some values in the basic processing experiments were exaggerated to represent them in a visually and auditorily salient manner.

[20] The dry/wet balance ensures the blending of the signal before and after the FX. This sort of blending can be achieved through various methods in digital or analog echo processing.

Hz and 5 kHz without any set Q value. These parameters, without any change, will provide a sensory outcome of the FX-processed sound as rather mechanical, steady-paced, and straight. The circular illustration placed in the center of the plug-in interface indicates the spatial representation, and also provides a hint of the 'non-organic' perfection of the yet insufficiently modulated values.

Image 5.2 : The parameters of the echo effect applied in the initial phase

The sound sample obtained from the echo effect applied with the values shown in Image 5.2 is described as 'non-organic' above. In this context, the spectral image in Image 5.3 shows that the right and left channels are perfectly identical copies of each other in a rhythmic context, and both channels are perfectly superimposed in terms of amplitude and frequency values. The sound signal that is heard after the echo effect almost fades away, with the amplitude dropping below -85 dB after the fourth second. The symmetry that is shown in multiple values in the spectral image is a good representation of the constant sensation that emerges from the applied values.

Non-Organic Echo Feel

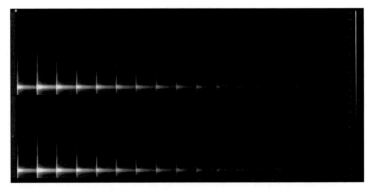

Image 5.3 : Spectrum image of the echo effect applied in the initial phase

It has been deemed significant to take into account that one of the fundamental characteristics of dub echo is that the continuously varying feedback amount often creates overlaps in the result that is heard after the echo effect. In Image 5.4, the feedback amount[21] has been set to 100%. The spectral representation of how the high feedback amount affects the signal is shown in Image 5.5. In authentic examples of dub music, it is deemed important to consider that, both in production and performance, the level of feedback is subjected to sharp fluctuations through improvisation. The feedback knob is a significant factor that impacts the 'density' and 'dynamism' of the outcome heard after the echo FX.

Image 5.4 : A graphic representation of 100% feedback amount

In Image 5.5, the spectral view of the information obtained after the 100% feedback amount set in Image 5.4 is shown for the first 30 seconds. When considering that feedback amount can be controlled with sudden drops and increases, it is also possible to visualize the 'human uncertainty' in the dynamics that will arise. In the next phase, the focus will be on executing the improvised dynamic control.

%100 Feedback Amount

---

[21] It should also be taken into consideration that this software allows for the feedback amount to be increased beyond 100%.

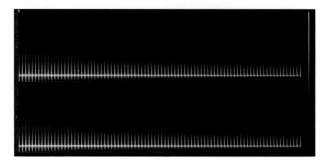

Image 5.5 : Spectrum image of %100 feedback amount

In the second phase, the focus is on spontaneous dynamic control of feedback amount, a fundamental characteristic of dub echo. In dub practices, the feedback amount is known to be a value that fluctuates spontaneously, as previously discussed. In this stage, this improvisational behavior is explored by creating a chain in which the feedback amount value located on the leftmost[22] of the echo panel[23] is controlled by an LFO on its right. Two adjustments made on the LFO are of importance: the first being the rate set to a non-synchronized value of 4.26 Hz, and the second being the selection of a 'random waveshape' instead of predictable options such as sine or square wave (as shown in Image 5.6). These adjustments aim to achieve a dynamic outcome of the feedback knob in the echo panel, through the spur-of-the-moment aspect of non-synchronization provided by the LFO with random movements-which represent human influence[24]. Additionally, as shown in Image 5.6, on the rightmost a low-pass filter modulated by a sine LFO with a rate of 0.11 Hz is used, this creates a sense of dynamic and non-synchronous change in the balance of presence and depth.

---

[22] The sequence of processing is denoted in the left-to-right progression in the image beginning with pre-FX and concluding with post-FX.

[23] On the echo panel, a high-pass filter with a Q value of 0.13 and a cutoff frequency of 271 Hz, as well as a low-pass filter with a Q value of 0.21 and a cutoff frequency of 1.87 kHz, were applied to the dry signal of the echo (see Image 5.6). This was done to selectively attenuate certain frequency ranges in the signal to enhance the desired spectral characteristics of the final output. The use of these specific filter types and values were considered to be an optimal approach to sculpting the tonal quality of the echo effect.

[24] As values such as feedback amount and filter cutoff frequency are manipulated manually, through knobs, in an improvised manner in dub music.

Image 5.6 : Dynamic feedback amount and LPF cutoff frequency

In Image 5.7, the spectral representation of how the use of LFO affects both the echo feedback amount and the LPF cutoff frequency with a pure sine signal is shown. At this stage, the sine wave sample is looped in a 4/4 time signature. The spectrum in Image 5.7 shows two peak forms where the feedback amount is increasing and the signal is overlapping. The sole factor that causes the peak forms is the LPF cutoff frequency being lowered and raised. Using a Q value of 57% in the LPF has characterized the perception at certain intervals. These movements can be said to have spontaneously changed the presence feeling in the echo output between 500 Hz and 5 kHz with the amplitude decrease and increase. The increase in the frequency of the peaks in the rising peak forms is a result of the effect created by the feedback amount, which is shown more simply in Image 5.5. Filter or linear or non-linear effects can be used to make the output's perception reach more different characteristics along with these increases and decreases in the feedback amount. The increases and decreases can be applied to all instruments that play a role in the dub music context. The manipulation of parameters such as feedback, stereo offset, timing, cutoff frequency, and Q value of LPF by using knobs and faders, can be utilized in various forms to shape transitions within the structure of dub music, impart distinct sensations to sections, imbue a sense of harmony, and inform instrumentation practices.

Modulated Feedback Amount and LPF Cutoff Frequency

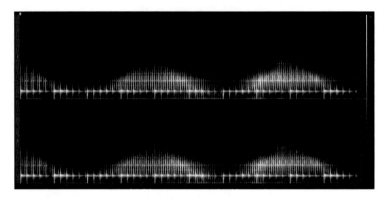

Image 5.7 : Spectrum image of the sudden changes in dynamics[25]

Timing differences between the left and right channels can be implemented in relation with the adjustments made in the previous example. The delay offset between the left and right channels can enhance the stereo feeling and produce a non-mechanical, 'flawed' human perception of timing. As an example, in Image 5.8, a delay offset value of 8% for the right channel and -8% for the left channel has been set. The change in delay offset has resulted in a small difference in the left and right sections of the plug-in interface's spatial illustration, which represents stereo-phonic information-as shown in Image 5.8. Other time parameters have been left at their default settings.

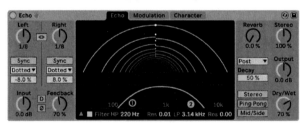

Image 5.8 : A spatial representation of delay offset on the interface

In this example, what is intended to be represented is the independence of the timing between the right and left channels. In the spectral representation of Image 5.9, the discrepancy created by the delay offset is visible between the right and left channels. The discrepancy, without modulating the panning, has made it possible to emphasize the stereo feeling as a result of a more straightforward outcome. It should be noted that setting a delay offset is just a method among

_____

[25] In this example, sudden variations were implemented in the echo feedback knob and the LPF's cutoff frequency.

numerous techniques to create a dynamic feeling through small timing differences.

Delay Offset

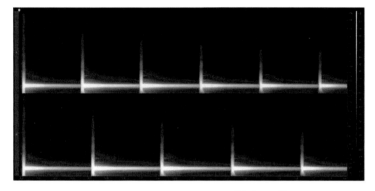

Image 5.9 : Spectrum image of delay offset

In this example, sudden modifications were made on the echo feedback knob and the LPF's cutoff frequency. These changes, which were primarily aimed at improvising the feedback amount, can also be applied to the delay time. As shown in Image 5.10, a 90% feedback amount, a 200 Hz HPF, a 5 kHz LPF filter, and a delay offset value of %8L and -%8R have been applied on the echo panel. Unlike previous examples, in this case, the delay mode is used in a time-based manner, rather than synchronizing with a specific beat. The time knob is mapped to the LFO with random waveshape, ¼ rate, and 100% smooth settings. The use of LFO with minimum and maximum values of 40% and 80%, respectively, has prevented the occurrence of extreme time changes. As can be seen in Image 5.10, the values of the left and right channels are linked. Using a time-based delay mode can cause eccentric pitch changes when sudden movements are made on the delay time knob, especially when used in conjunction with the correct echo feedback amount. These sudden pitch changes can be considered as a distinguishing element for the sound of dub music.

Image 5.10 : Delay time modulation

In Image 5.11, the spectrum illustrates the effect of spontaneously altering the delay time. It is clear that the initial frequency has changed in each repetitive beat. Furthermore, in contrast to other examples, the negative spaces between beats are not symmetrical. Considering that the negative spaces represent the delay time, the spectrum suggests a relatively free-form and unregulated timing. The sudden increase in the frequency of beats between seconds 8 and 11 can be considered as a fair example of the aforementioned pitch change at the spectral level. As with the other examples, it should be noted that the LFO represents human influence and all the values controlled by mechanical tools such as knobs or faders in authentic production and performances.

Modulated Delay Time

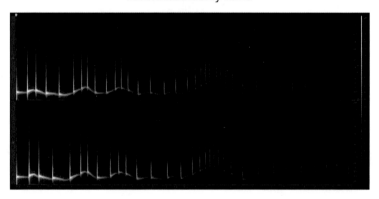

Image 5.11 : Spectrum image of modulated delay time

The above experiments were carried out on a sine wave. However, a sawtooth wave, which has a more harmonically rich nature, can produce a more dynamic auditory result, particularly when filter modulation is applied. Thus, rather than leaving the examples solely with a sine wave, the subject of the experiments, a pure sine, is switched to a sawtooth wave before carrying it out in a musical context. As shown in Image 5.12, the wavetable plugin is used again, the waveshape is set to sawtooth wave, and adjustments are made on the main panel. Additionally, modulation adjustments are made on the echo plugin's matrix panel to provide randomity, but these are not discussed to avoid unnecessary prolongation of the section. In short, a sawtooth wave is selected to create this example, an LPF process is applied, determined by a random waveshape with a 0.88 Hz rate via LFO1, and the LPF's Q value is set to 59%. An echo is used immediately after the signal-generating plugin, and all values in the interface are left almost at default. Also, four voices are used and set to a 30% amount in unison to add even more harmonics to the signal. The purpose of this example is to represent how filtering plays a role in creating a fluctuation between two contrasting auditory qualities, presence and deepness when the input signal is harmonically rich.

Image 5.12 : Primary adjustments made during the generation of the sawtooth wave

Filtering A Harmonically Rich Signal

In Image 5.13, the spectrum representation illustrates the effect of an LPF with a cutoff value randomly modulated on a sawtooth wave. The grid pattern emerged due to the richness of harmonic information that can be clearly seen on the spectrum. It is also easily observable that the modulated filter rolls off the high frequencies spontaneously on each sawtooth beat. The spectral image in Image 5.13 shows how an input signal with a good level of harmonics can produce a rich output even after the most basic echo process. The idea discussed here is not to subject basic waveforms to the echo process as exemplified above, but to apply the same process to live recorded instrument tracks in the paradigm of functional harmony, which will lead to a final analysis in this section. The progressive processes carried out below aim to examine how dub echo behaves within the musical context in question.

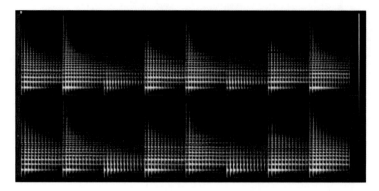

Image 5.13 : Spectrum image of the sawtooth sample's response

The musical aspect

In this section, the use of echo style which is examined in the technical aspect in the previous section is exemplified[26] in the dub music structure, by analyzing the second track on the B-side of the record released by King Tubby and Augustus Pablo in 1976, called *King Tubby Meets Rockers Uptown* and the second track on the A-side of the record released by Linton Kwesi Johnson in 1980, called *Reality Dub*. From the aforementioned two tracks, eight measure sections where the echo effect is applied have been sampled, notated, described, and analyzed through the spectrum images by the author.

In Image 5.14, several parts on the notation of the 5th to 12th measures of the track *King Tubby Meets Rockers Uptown* are highlighted to indicate the presence of the echo effect.

Measures 5-12 of 'King Tubby Meets Rockers Uptown'

---

[26] While the selection of only two examples may appear restrictive, it is deemed sufficient for the purposes of this study to develop an understanding of how the echo practice in question is employed within the musical structure. Of course, echo can serve a variety of objectives and outcomes, however, it is worth noting that this study entails a limited analysis. Additionally, albums such as *Total Dub* by Vital Dub (1976), *I'm All Right* by Keith Hudson (1975), *Curly Dub* by Lee Scratch Perry (1976), Dub Three by Joe Gibbs & The Professionals (1977), *My Island Dub* by Burning Spear (1999), *High Grade Dub* by The Heptones (2009), *Merciful Dub* by The Revolutionaries (1976), *Crofs* by Gregory Isaacs (1983), and *Rainbow Country Dub* by Augustus Pablo (1979) could be considered other examples in terms of their similar of echo practices.

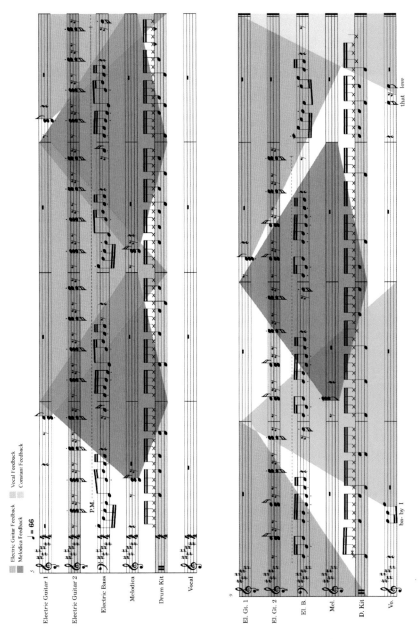

Image 5.14 : Echo practice between the 5th to 12th measures of King Tubby Meets Rockers Uptown

In Image 5.14, specific sections of the first electric guitar, melodica, and vocals have been marked with different colors to indicate the application of echo effects. The expanding colored areas signify the points in the multi-track composition where individual instrument tracks were exposed to echo effects. These colored markings also suggest assumptions regarding the stylization of echo within a specific harmonic and rhythmic context. It is also noteworthy that in the example, the use of echo in off-beat staccato electric guitar and melodica chords, and the increase of echo feedback amount creates a sort of motion in highlighted six moments. The echo effect feeds itself back for approximately two measures for both the electric guitar and the melodica tracks. Then the feedback amount decreases by creating a soft decay effect.

In the 9th measure, the second electric guitar deviates from the chord progression pattern established in previous measures-which is reinforced with a high amount of feedback. The high feedback amount also reinforces the syncopation feeling embraced especially in the drum partition. Echo-applied partitions bleed into the perception of other partitions and create areas of intersection with other tracks' echo outputs (Image 5.14). The notion that the intersection of the color assigned to the echo output of each section with the color of another section creates a distinct shade illustrates the idea that the intersecting dominant frequencies alternate the harmonic context compared to what is depicted in the written notation during the performance. Additionally a consistent echo feedback level is favored in the drum kit track (Image 5.14). Echo can be applied selectively in certain sections to produce a subtle effect without modifying a specific feedback and timing value. Additionally, it would be inaccurate to assert that the improvisation of the feedback amount is an inherent rule of dub music. Indeed, in the majority of dub tracks listened to for this research, arrangements were also encountered in which the echo parameters were not altered in any way[27].

There are a number of conclusions that can be drawn concerning the usage of echo and the arranging style in the 5th to 12th measure part of *King Tubby Meets Rockers Uptown*: First, the 'groove' created by the bass and drums provides a 'dry' backcloth for the 'wet' output of the electric guitar, melodica, and vocals to be heard within the form. This is because the hi-hats in the drum kit partition make complementary references to the bass partition and the relatively stable

---

[27] *Drifting Dub Plate* by The Heptones (2006), *Underground Roots* by Lee Scratch Perry (1976), *Jungle Fever* by The Upsetters (1973), *White Rice Dub* by Jah Thomas (1997), *Blackboard Jungle Dub Version 2* by The Upsetters (1981), *Black Out* by The Hardy Boys (1975), *Riding with Mr. Lee* by Earl China Smith (1971), *Michael Talbot Affair* by Keith Hudson (1994), *Herbal Weed Dub* by Augustus Pablo (1981), *Chanting Home* by Burning Spear (1997) can be seen as other examples where there are no radical echo feedback changes and instead, a subtle echo processing is preferred.

melody being played on the second electric guitar. This serves as a specific illustration of how the musical structure employs the riddim technique. This particular example has a spontaneous character because of the consistency of the beat, pattern, and pace as well as the non-constant nature of the echo feedback amount, which occasionally lowers or rises. The amount of echo feedback being increased is thought to be a key component in enabling distinctive transitions between measures. Special moments where the harmonic context temporarily changes, rhythms, patterns, and most importantly, the overall sense is alternated can be found in the sections where a particular partition's echo feedback amount, represented by colored areas, expands and spreads to other partitions and even intersects[28] with them. In conclusion, the most important consequence to take into account is that echo may produce changes, alternations and non-constant dynamism in both musical and spatial settings.

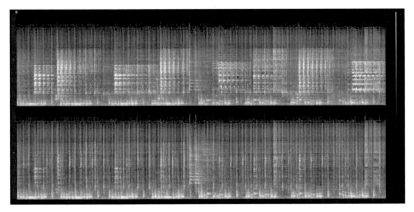

Image 5.15 : Spectrum image of the echo practice between 5th to 12th measures of *King Tubby Meets Rockers Uptown*[29]

---

[28] For instance, in the 5th measure, the melodica track's echo output—represented by the dark brown color—intersects with the first electric guitar's 6th measure's echo output—represented by the light brown color—, creating an orange hue. Similarly, a yellow hue initially appears in the 12th measure, as the vocal track's echo output—represented by the green color—collides with the first electric guitar's echo output (see Image 5.14). As it is the technique of using high echo feedback amounts in dub music that makes these unusual instances conceivable, these moments of intersection should be understood as special instances in which both the harmonic context and the sense of rhythm are briefly and alternatively transformed.

[29] The strong prominence of the echo output in the left channel is the most noticeable aspect of the spectrum that can be seen. This suggests that the echo's output has been purposefully adjusted to be dominant in the left channel. The regions of the spectrum where the echo effect is prevalent are highlighted along with amplitude and frequency values, whereas the sections of the spectrum where the echo effect is not significant are

In Image 5.16, a section between the 21st and 28th measures of the track *Reality Dub* is shown on staff to exhibit a distinct application of the same method. The impact of the echo processing can be observed in the spectrum in Image 5.15.

Measures 21-28 of 'Reality Dub'

In this example, echo is applied to the trumpet track first. The trumpet track is muted right after the D4 note is heard, and exposed to a large level of feedback, breaking the pattern that can be heard in the preceding measures. In the 25th measure, the trumpet's echo feedback, which was applied in the 23rd measure, starts to fade off, and in the 26th measure, it fully vanishes. The echo output in Image 5.16, indicated by two distinct colors, has also extended to other partitions, as was described in the first instance. In contrast to the other example, this section's application of the echo effect is more restrained, and there are no numerous and intersecting outputs. The echo effect's ability to reinforce the change from the 25th to the 26th measure is what stands out in this case. A new section starts when the crash cymbal plays on the first beat of the 26th measure of the drum kit partition; the closed hi-hat rhythmically accompanies the bass riff. Furthermore, the echo effect is used to emphasize this particular moment of transition, which obviously marks the start of the new segment. Furthermore, we can assume that the arrangement continues to evolve after the 28th measure as the echo effect, emphasizing the change, is introduced right after the E minor guitar strum in the 27th measure.

_____

shown in grayscale. The emphasized areas stand for the echo effect's recurring patterns, which are audible periodically and then become less loud. From left to right, it is possible to determine which piece corresponds to which partition by following the marks in Image 5.14.

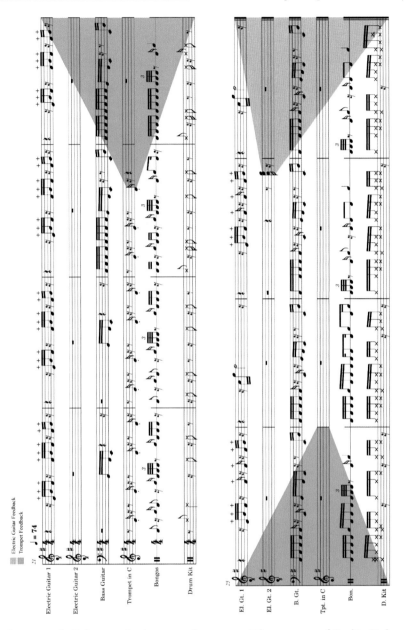

Image 5.16 : Echo practice between the 21st to 28th measures of *Reality Dub*

In Image 5.16, the closed hi-hat pattern creates a backcloth that may frame the dynamic fluidity brought on by the echo effect. It also clearly rhythmically accompanies the bass and the first electric guitar riffs with a set pattern from the 25th measure. It is also clear from this section that the echo effect has been applied exclusively to chords or notes that are audible off-beat - which is considered a common method.

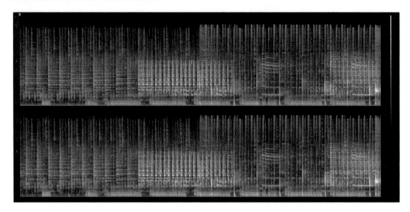

Image 5.17 : Spectrum image of the echo practice between 21st to 28th measures of *Reality Dub*[30]

When considering the first section on the left in Image 5.17, which is highlighted in color, the echo effect is structured to accompany the section change in question, as the information above 5 kHz in the spectrum becomes more strong towards the end of the highlighted section.

In conclusion, when considering the examples of the echo effect illustrated in the 8-measure sections of the tracks titled *King Tubby Meets Rockers Uptown* and *Reality Dub* which were deconstructed in the previous heading, and the musical aspects were discussed at a fundamental level, it appears to be possible to make various inferences:

- When using the echo effect, the fundamental parameters that may be altered include time, panning, LPF/HPF cutoff frequency, and feedback amount. In today's digital technology, it is important to remember that characteristics like timing and panning, as well as artifacts like wobble

---

[30] While the areas where the echo effect is not visible are depicted in grayscale, the areas where the echo effect is visible are highlighted in certain regions of the spectrum, along with amplitude and frequency numbers. In contrast to the preceding case, an echo effect is noticed in both the left and right channels. The highlighted sections of the spectrum show the repeated patterns formed by the echo effect. From left to right, it is possible to determine which piece corresponds to which partition by following the marks in Image 5.17.

and noise, may all be tweaked to get the same effect as the analog equipment used in the early dub versions.

- In the instances of _King Tubby Meets Rockers Uptown_ and _Reality Dub_, raising the amount of echo feedback at specific times momentarily affects both the harmonic and rhythmic setting.
- It should be noted that in the framework of dub music, any parameter of a signal processor may occasionally be altered abruptly or gradually by utilizing knobs or faders.
- Increasing the amount of feedback to a given degree, as seen in the relevant instances, is a dominating notion for reinforcing, embellishing, or organizing the transition from one part or measure to the next, as well as from one chord progression to another. Increasing the amount of feedback or changing other factors might be regarded as authentic articulation for transitions and alterations.
- In dub music, the echo effect generates a dynamic and unpredictable spatial effect, and it stylizes the narration by combining almost set melodic or rhythmic motifs.
- It may be claimed that the rhythmic pattern concretized by the bass and percussion partitions and reinforced by other instruments functions as a frame, preventing the output from deviating from the overall form of rhythm as the feedback amount increases. If this viewpoint is embraced, it may be argued that the rhythm not only structures the accompaniment of other instruments, but also serves as a reference value that increases the dynamism of drastically applied effects, particularly the echo effect, by constraining it.
- It is beneficial to consider that echo is not the sole effect utilized in dub music. Similarly, many parameters may be improved in addition to the feedback parameter. Advanced delay techniques, reverb, phaser, flanger, chorus, distortion, low-bit or filter, and a plethora of linear and non-linear processors are all stylistically crucial for dub music creation.

6

Pioneering the Future
The Birth and Growth of Techno Music

Techno, which is often viewed by researchers as a subcultural phenomenon, offers a wealth of material for cultural studies due to its historical development, "immanently ritualistic dimension," and "theatrical setting" (Becker et al., 1999, p. 59). During this study, it was observed that revisiting ideas put forth about techno decades ago can lead to a change in perspective in a thought-provoking manner. Simon Reynolds, who has made extensive analyses of the historicity of techno, claims that the genre was born in Detroit in the early 1980s and shaped by young, intellectual individuals. On the one hand, he asserts that it arose as a reaction against the mainstream entertainment industry of the time (1999, pp. 219-220). On the other hand, according to the IMS Business Report, it was the most popular music genre until the end of 2021 (Reis, 2022). It is interesting to consider that techno has become a crucial part of the mainstream entertainment industry over time. This drastic transformation can provide insight into the nature of change and the paradigm shift that has occurred within about twenty years, leading us to reflect on how musical genres should be approached. While there is an ongoing debate about the origins of techno, Botond Vitos (2014) argues that it emerged in Detroit and developed in Berlin, influenced by the political atmosphere. He suggests that techno should be understood as a culture that promised liberation from ideologies and attracted enthusiasts in this way. It is essential to keep in mind that techno, in all its forms, cannot be understood in isolation from the context in which it emerged.

A Concise Approach to the Style

A researcher conducting exploratory research on the history of techno may encounter the Detroit and Berlin debate, regardless of the scope or depth of their study. The central issue of this debate is not which city techno originated in, but rather the changes it underwent and whether it lost any of its essence as it spread across continents. It is asserted that techno emerged in Detroit in the mid-1980s under the influence of several pioneering electronic music artists such as Kraftwerk (Gamberini, 2019, p. 1). In addition to serving as an inspiration for the pioneers who created the first examples of techno, Kraftwerk should also be seen as a band that musically symbolized the "man and machine" debates that arose after modernity (Becker et al., 1999, p. 63). The band's unique, intellectually diverse music and choreographic stage show, which emphasized computer-based perfection, imbued the first examples of techno with philosophical depth. Some researchers argue that Kraftwerk's influence alone is evidence that techno originated with white Europeans, who artistically expressed the nature of the industrial revolution-rather than with black middle-class citizens of Detroit (Becker et al., 1999, p. 63). From another perspective, it could be argued that the philosophical value of techno emerged from a European-based expression and that the elements of musical style developed with the influence of black music that flourished in the United States. According to Albiez, "it is clearly the product of a post-soul moment peculiar to the post-industrial late twentieth century" (2005, p. 16).

The first examples of the genre in a certain form were realized by the trio named *Belleville Three* with the prominent role of Juan Atkins accompanied by Derrick May and Kevin Saunderson (Ching, 2022). "Atkins is revered as the 'godfather of techno' for being the sound's originator, while May is credited with taking the Detroit sound to sophisticated levels and Saunderson for bringing techno to the masses with Billboard dance hits" (The Associated Press, 2003). These first examples had a specific sound, and enthusiasts refer to it as 'Detroit techno'. So much so that Detroit's economic collapse is said to have played a role in the emergence of techno in the mid-1980s. Techno emerged in Detroit as a reaction to the social conjuncture, economic situation, and political constellations (Schaub, 2011, p. 188). Some researchers claimed that the tumbledown look of Detroit inspired pioneering artists such as Juan Atkins (Gamberini, 2019, p. 2). According to Schaub, quoting from Haraway (2011, p. 189), the social and cultural structure of Detroit which is also affected by the limitations has prepared the cyclical ground for the first examples of techno. In this direction, it seems that techno accommodates a subcultural nature in the context mentioned above, and it is somehow associated with the low class. On the other hand, some emphasize the opposite. Beverly May, for instance, clearly states that techno "is not about [the] hard times. It's about these middle-class kids who never starved" (May, 2015, p. 348). Albiez also emphasizes that techno is created by the black middle-class subculture (as cited in Schaub, 2011, p. 190). However, Albiez mentions that techno has "hybrid origins" and is complex when it comes to ethnic issues (2005, p. 15). According to this view, it is not possible to determine the ethnic identity of the genre. In light of all these ideas, the emphasis of Gaillot, citing Stiegler (1998, p. 40), seems crucial to summarize the ethnic identity issues of techno. Accordingly, the expansion of techno to different continents over time has led to linking various ethnic identities. As a result, techno has undergone deterritorialization. This situation also reveals the drawbacks of considering techno concerning a single ethnic identity today.

Although some experts have interpreted techno as a music genre that fills the void at the point where Rock 'n' Roll lost its popularity, it had a completely divergent structure in terms of its marketing approach. Gamberini highlights that techno is underground "by essence". In this context, "techno at its beginnings directed attention only to its music-putting live performance challenges, DJ groupies and the star-system aside. The fans do not have lyrics to memorize or personalities to follow" (2019, p. 1). The sense of entertainment of high school students, who are in search of new and original tastes, should also be considered among the factors that shaped the first form of techno music (Sicko, 1999, pp. 32-51). However, at this point, it should be emphasized that techno has reached distant continents with underground distribution methods created away from the concern of being mainstream. In light of these ideas, it would not be wrong to state that techno spread to a wide audience with the contributions of small labels and pioneering names in the early days. In the early Detroit scene, as Albiez recounts, "the subject of this music" was a subculture framed largely by black people and defined strictly (2005, p. 14). But the spread to other cities of the world after the 80s naturally attracted new communities to the field and developed the network. The influence of these new techno communities blended the genre with the rave experience, bringing it together with a kind of collective thought and socially perceived experience (Becker et al., 1999, p. 70).

It has been claimed that the process of change and redefinition that Europe underwent between 1989 and 1990 as it absorbed the effects of the Cold War gave rise to a new underground music scene formed by the youth in Berlin (Gamberini, 2019, p. 8). Techno's journey from Detroit to Berlin infused it with new stylistic elements in the 1990s. In other words, techno in Berlin was transformed through formal changes, which included a minimal and "harsh" sound, fewer vocal integrations, and more "in-your-face" basslines (Gamberini, 2019, p. 8). It is stated that with these new qualities added to its production arsenal, techno's status as a mainstream music genre is called into question upon its arrival in Berlin (Gamberini, 2019, p. 8). It is not incorrect to claim that techno's popularity has increased with the proliferation of digital music platforms in its evolution from the 1990s to the present. However, as a result of techno spreading to various countries in Europe from the 1980s to the 1990s,

69

subgenres emerged due to the unique touches of independent artists living in different countries (Ching, 2022). In summary, it may be vital to recognize that techno was not originally created as a mainstream music genre, and it flourished within the underground culture.

From Studio to the Dancefloor

This section includes the classification, intersection, and interpretation of data synthesized from various electronic sources. In other words, this section aims to provide a comprehensive understanding of the phenomenon of techno production and consumption, rather than offering a cookie-cutter approach[31].

Twenty-two years after Jerrentrup's study, in which he discussed the didactic introduction of techno music into the field of music education (see Jerrentrup, 2000), the proliferation of internet access has undoubtedly facilitated the dissemination of information about the genre. For example, the sound system culture discussed in the dub music section, while not widely known in its authentic Jamaican form, gained significant attention when it reached the UK scene, thanks in part to the awareness created by the internet (Fintoni and McLauchlan, 2018, p. 3). Techno, on the other hand, is a genre that emerged in a world where internet access is increasingly global, and it has certainly been influenced by the speed and reach of online information. As mentioned above, the internet has also transformed techno from an anti-mainstream genre into a mainstream genre within a few decades. Given this, it would seem logical to assume the benefits of internet resources in understanding techno production. It is worth noting that, in line with this testable assumption, the data discussed in this section is also mostly drawn from popular educational internet sources that are commonly utilized by today's techno music producers.

According to James Wiltshire, "techno is as much about sound design as it is about creating grooves that will work in clubs" (Point Blank Music School, 2016). Jerrentrup, on the other hand, suggests that techno should be handled not with the "time distribution of different impulse sounds into patterns and layering of

---

[31] Rather than providing compiled information about techno music production, this section examines three specific sub genres of techno: Detroit techno, acid techno, and minimal techno, with two opuses analyzed for each. The fundamental premise for selecting these opuses is that they represent the first examples in the respective genre's form. A total of six pieces were analyzed for their structural patterns, with specific melodic or harmonic sequences notated and sequencer images created, and the pieces were narrated linearly. The effects used in the pieces, their structuring qualities, transitional embellishments, and the electronic music instruments employed in their production were all directly addressed. Therefore, the compiled information, proposed ideas, and approaches in this section ultimately intersect with the analyses performed. Approaching this topic from this perspective will strengthen the scientific function of this research.

the patterns", but with the formation centered on "percussivity" and therefore the style's unique sound (2000, p. 74). Thus, the researcher emphasizes the necessity of thinking of techno in a quite different framework from the idea of music in the canonical sense. In the Studio Slave platform, which includes numerous tutorial content, it has been mentioned that techno mostly lacks melodic information, and this gap is filled with the use of various effects stylistically (Studio Slave, 2020). This indicates that we are far from the field of acoustic music for several reasons. Indeed, processors come to the fore in techno production by contributing to the style of narration. Thus, such basic and complex signal processors adhere to a particular paradigm (Tool Room Academy, 2021). The use of effects seems to give clues about the concept of spatiality. For instance, in techno music, delay and echo effects are often used to create a sense of space and depth and "add depth and dimension to sounds" (Studio Slave, 2020) within the music. They can also be used to create rhythmic patterns and add textural elements to the mix. Delay effects involve the repetition of a sound at a later time, while echo effects involve the repetition of a sound at a later time with a decay in volume. These effects can be used to create a sense of movement and progression within the music, as well as to add layers of complexity and interest. They are often used in conjunction with other effects, such as reverb, to create a sense of space and atmosphere within the music. However, in this context, the depth and dimension mentioned may not have the purpose of reaching a hyper-realistic result. For instance, in some cases "using reverb and delay on field recordings takes natural sounds and completely twists and mangles them" (Russell, 2022). Typically, it is recommended that the delay applied to any element of techno music be set to ¼ time, the mix level is kept low, and the feedback parameter is set by half (Loopmasters, 2020). This setting is seen as a basic starting point and it should be noted that parameters, including those not mentioned here, can be rearranged depending on the style of the production. Using tape echo is also among the options for the signal processors to provide a classic result as in the era when techno music was produced with analog hardware (Russell, 2022).

Like in most other electronic music genres, reverb, or reverberation, is utilized in techno music to imbue a sense of spatiality to the individual elements or overall musical structure. In other words, reverb is a vital effect in techno that imparts a feeling of space and depth within a mix. It can be used to create a sense of distance or proximity between different elements in the mix, such as vocals or drums. It can also be employed to create a sense of movement within a mix, as the reverb tail of a sound can be made to fade in and out over time. In a non-canonical context, reverb can be divided into three categories: "real-world, analog, and digital" (Hyperbits, 2022). According to the Hyperbits website (2022), real-world reverb is created by sound waves reflecting off physical surfaces in a physical space and is often considered the most natural and authentic, as it is generated through the same physical processes that occur in the real world. Analog reverb, on the other hand, is created using analog hardware or software and involves the use of filters, delays, and other processing techniques to emulate the effect of real-world reverb. Digital reverb, meanwhile, is created using digital algorithms and processing techniques and can offer a wide range of options and customization for sound designers and music producers. Ultimately, the choice between these different types of reverb will depend on the specific needs and preferences of the user, as well as the context in which the reverb is being used. In techno music, reverb is often used in combination with other effects such as delay and echo to create complex, layered soundscapes that can be both immersive and disorienting. Reverb can also be used to create a sense of unity within a mix, as it can help to blend different elements together and create a cohesive sound. Overall, the role of reverb in techno music is to create a sense of space and depth within the mix, and to help create a sense of unity and cohesiveness within the music.

Effects can be considered as aesthetic tools that are crucial for the sound design process of techno music, while another element of techno music that holds similar importance is undoubtedly the kick drum. In light of the numerous tutorials and discussions surrounding the specific design and production of kick drums in techno music, it may seem evident to one that the kick drum is a significant element. To be able to examine this, a survey was conducted. The opinions of 35 anonymous participants consisting of electronic music producers, performers, and listeners were gathered to determine the significance of the kick drum in EDM. The kick drum in EDM is regarded as a crucial component by many of the participants. It is often seen as the driving force that sets the rhythm and provides the foundation for the rest of the music. According to one participant, "The kick drum plays a central role in the beat of a techno track, providing the foundation for the rest of the music. It is typically the most prominent element in the mix, driving the track forward and helping to create a sense of momentum." Another participant describes the kick drum as the "spine that connects the body parts of the techno beast" (Appendix A.1), emphasizing its fundamental role in establishing the pulse and momentum of the music.

The significance of the kick drum in EDM is also attributed to its ability to create a physical and visceral impact on the listener. As one participant notes, "It's both the rhythm and has bass frequencies which can be felt through your body if listening to the music on a large sound system. The kick mimics the rhythm of walking" (Appendix A.1). The physical sensation created by the kick drum, particularly in genres like techno, is seen as an essential element in driving the dancefloor experience and energizing the audience.

While the importance of the kick drum is widely acknowledged, some participants point out that its significance may vary depending on the genre or style of EDM. For example, in ambient or chill-out music, the kick drum may not be as crucial as in genres like techno or house. One participant states, *"In the techno genre, we often come across songs without a kick drum, and it is usually referred to as experimental. It may not be essential in subgenres or new styles of techno"* (Appendix A.1) However, for many participants, the kick drum remains a fundamental element that defines the essence of techno music, with its absence potentially resulting in a track feeling incomplete or lacking the groove.

It's worth noting that some participants express differing opinions on the indispensability of the kick drum in EDM. While many see it as essential, others believe that it can be substituted with other elements or sounds to achieve similar effects. One participant states, *"I don't think it's essential, as you can fill its place with other elements or sounds, but kick usage is prevalent in a significant portion of techno music."* Another participant mentions, *"No, it's not essential. We can achieve the groove effect created by the kick drum with various synths and percussive sounds by manipulating them"* (Appendix A.1). This suggests that the significance of the kick drum may be subjective and dependent on individual artistic preferences and styles.

In conclusion, the kick drum is often considered a crucial element in EDM, particularly in genres like techno, where it sets the rhythm, provides the foundation, and creates a physical impact on the listener. Its absence or presence may vary depending on the genre or style of EDM, and opinions on its indispensability may differ among producers, performers, and listeners. Nevertheless, for many, the kick drum remains a fundamental element that contributes to the overall energy, groove, and momentum of EDM music.

Based on the responses of the 35 anonymous participants, the following key findings can be concluded:

- The kick drum is crucial in EDM, setting the rhythm and providing a foundation.
- The kick drum is the backbone of techno, contributing to its unique feeling and energy.
- Opinions vary on the kick drum's significance depending on subgenre and style.
- Balancing all elements is essential for a well-produced track, including the kick drum.
- There are differing opinions on whether the kick drum is indispensable or replaceable.
- The kick drum's impact is associated with physical and emotional responses in the listener.

- Perspectives on the kick drum's importance vary among participants based on genre and style.

Overall, there is no unanimous consensus among the participants, with some expressing that the kick drum is indispensable, while others feel it is not necessary or can be replaced by other elements. Perspectives vary based on personal preferences, genres, and production styles.

The use of sampling, on the other hand, is widely adopted in the production of various electronic music genres, including techno music. Sampling is a practice that involves taking a sound from one context and repositioning it in another, effectively recontextualizing the sound by giving it a different meaning or political background (Rodgers, 2003, p. 318). According to John (2017), sampling practices have endowed techno music with transformative, reprogramming, and synthesizing power, and therefore samplers have been the cornerstone of techno music since its inception (p. 281). Sample practices have been surrounded by copyright infringement issues, and scholars participating in these debates often overlook the musical and political objectives of samplists or the nuances in their expression forms (Rodgers, 2003, p. 313). From another perspective, the central issue in sampling debates is whether producers who create music using samples are committing plagiarism. On the other hand, Johannesen (2009) defines plagiarism as "a communication norm deeply imbedded in the Euro-American tradition of print orientation, individual originality, ideas as private property, and capitalistic commodification" (p. 185). Along with this definition, Johannesen points out that in contrast to Euro-American tradition, plagiarism is "natural, accepted, and ethical" in African-American oral culture and folk-preaching traditions. In African-American culture, words and ideas are seen as "communal resources" (Johannesen, 2009, p. 185). As Johannesen points out, while the tendency to view words and ideas as something that can be owned or marketed is present in Western traditions, it is important to also consider the existence of other traditions that find this tendency morally wrong. Therefore, it is clear that bringing in the concept of plagiarism to understand the sampling method observed in a music genre with African roots would lead to a Western-centric and one-sided perspective. Perhaps, as Rodgers suggests (2003), the function of sampling should be considered "a postmodern process of musical appropriation and pastiche" which is "often filtered through modernist conceptions of authorship and authenticity" (p. 313). Taking this perspective into account, it would not be wrong to think that it would be more appropriate to consider the concept of sampling as a stylistic element of narration, especially in music genres such as techno and sub-genres such as dub techno, which will be examined in the next section. In his article *Digital Sampling: A Cultural Perspective*, Henry Self (2002) also mentions that in non-Western societies, there is a cultural structure that is the opposite of the originality paradigm seen in Europe and America, which considers copyright infringement as an ethical and legal problem (pp. 355-357). Self (2002) talks about how, in these non-Western societies, the collective voice of the group is prioritized over the individuality of the individual and quotes Hebdige (p. 357):

> "What Westerners largely fail to understand is that originality was simply not a concern among performers in folk societies, as there was no framework within which they could even conceive of such a concept. Indeed, no single person could lay claim to a group of words or notes because they belonged to the entire group and descend in various incarnations and iterations through the generations. This implies that no one has the final say. Everybody has a chance to make a contribution. And no one's version is treated as the Holy Writ."

Although Self specifically addresses folk societies, his definition can be understood as a reminder that concepts such as belonging and originality can vary sharply across cultures. The same example also seems to be applicable to the different cultures generated by different genres. With this point indicated by Self, considering the sampling method commonly encountered in techno music beyond concepts such as artistic originality or labor theft creates a more objective perspective. Because, when considering its cultural development, it is difficult to speak of the existence of a framework where the above-mentioned concepts are also applicable in techno music. As a result, sampling, which is a characteristic part of Afro-diasporic music practices that have spread to electronic music practices (Rose, 1994, pp. 74-75) and is a hallmark for some techno sub-genres, can be evaluated as a narrative element that has legitimized its own paradigm over the years, rather than appearing as a concept that leaves behind the originality of the music creator. It rather recalls a postmodern, and possibly deconstructive, idea of composition.

Based on the responses of 17 anonymous participants, consisting of electronic music producers, and performers the vital rules for mixing techno music for clubs can be interpreted in several key ways. First, the importance of achieving a high-quality sound that is suitable for the club environment is emphasized. This includes considerations such as sound clarity, bass levels, loudness, and mono compatibility, as well as DJ-friendly arrangement and tracks with at least 320 kbps or WAV format. As one participant noted, *"Enough bass, general loudness, mono compatibility, and DJ-friendly arrangement. This is due to the design of sound systems, except obviously the last one"* (Appendix A.1). Additionally, attention to stereo width and controlling it to ensure optimal playback on club systems, which are often in mono, is highlighted. Another participant stated, *"Stereo width has to be controlled otherwise sounds will not be played as most club systems are in mono. Other than that as long as the track sounds good, there are no rules"* (Appendix A.1). Furthermore, the importance of capturing the preferences of the club's general audience and creating a high-energy, dance-inducing atmosphere is emphasized, while also maintaining

75

consistency with the genre's usual tones and rhythms. As one participant stated, *"A well-arranged composition with clear high-end, punchy low-end, and powerful mids... Not straying too far from the usual tones in productions that gave birth to EDM"* (Appendix A.1). The significance of transitions, beat matching, and phrasing to ensure a smooth flow of the music set is also emphasized, as well as the use of live effects to keep the performance entertaining for the crowd. Finally, the role of the creator's vision and the importance of a *"creative mix"* (Appendix A.1) phase before the final mix and mastering is noted, as it allows the artist to maintain artistic integrity and avoid conflicts with the mixer's ideas. As one participant mentioned, *"The best perception is in the hands of the creator of the piece. This way, the professional who does the mix and mastering won't have to struggle with their own ideas"* (Appendix A.1).

Overall, these interpretations highlight the shared importance of achieving a high-quality, dance-inducing sound, while also maintaining consistency with the genre's characteristics, considering club sound systems, and allowing for creative expression by the artist during the mixing process.

In conclusion, the following key ideas can be extracted from the responses of 17 anonymous participants regarding the vital rules for mixing techno music for clubs:

- Sound quality is crucial, including considerations such as sound clarity, bass levels, loudness, and mono compatibility, as well as DJ-friendly arrangement and tracks with at least 320 kbps or WAV format.
- Attention to stereo width and controlling it to ensure optimal playback on club systems, which are often in mono, is important to consider.
- Capturing the preferences of the club's general audience and creating a high-energy, dance-inducing atmosphere, while maintaining consistency with the genre's usual tones and rhythms, is essential.
- Transitions, beat matching, and phrasing are critical for ensuring a smooth flow of the music set, along with the use of live effects to keep the performance entertaining for the crowd.
- The creator's vision and the importance of a "creative mix" (Appendix A.1) phase before the final mix and mastering should be considered, allowing the artist to maintain artistic integrity and avoid conflicts with the mixer's ideas.

These ideas highlight the shared emphasis on sound quality, club audience preferences, transitions, and creative expression during the mixing process, while also considering technical aspects such as mono compatibility and stereo width for optimal playback on club systems.

Jerrentrup, on the other hand, emphasizes that dance music cannot be separated from rhythmic patterns. According to him, a "mindless repetition" is present, especially in genres such as techno. Repetition is considered one of the most characteristic auditory qualities of techno music. Repetition, on the other hand, existed within a framework of formality, thanks to the new possibilities offered by new hardware, such as drum machines used in the early stages of techno (Jerrentrup, 2000, p. 71). Takahashi explains the existence of high-tempo drum patterns reaching 150-160 BPM, especially in genres like hardcore techno, when computers went beyond human performance capability (as cited in John, 2017, p. 283). Therefore, just like repetition, high tempo can be considered as a style element within the framework of a cause-effect relationship with the devices produced thanks to the developing technology. On the other hand, speaking of repetition, Jerrentrup argues that it did not arise as a fruit of electronic dance music and that its use dates back to earlier times. According to Jerrentrup, especially with Steve Reich's minimal style, repetition is an element of musical narrative that has been used since 1965 (2000, p. 72). Therefore, to think that the element of repetition comes into question with the development of techno music leads to an erroneous inference in Jerrentrup's opinion. Also, Henriques' ideas on repetition (2010) seem to have the quality to make the discussion fruitful, even though it is related to the sound system issue that was discussed in the dub. Henriques considers repetition as a branch of the concept of 'vibrations of affects'. Henriques conceives vibration as a semi-abstract concept that is released into the atmosphere of the dancefloor when the content of a musical performance is harmonized in a sensory context, affecting the audience (Henriques, 2010, pp. 64-70). The fact that the 'crowd' on the dance floor feels good enough is defined as 'vibesy' in the sound system culture, enabling Henriques to make an intricate connection between repeating vibrations and affect (Henriques, 2010, p. 77). This connection that Henriques made in the dub was also valid for techno in this study due to the similarity of the contexts. The indoor events that came into question (Fintoni and McLauchlan, 2018, p. 12-13) after the dub became visible in the United Kingdom, also give ideas about the techno scene in many respects. It is undeniable that repetition, loudness, and ceremonial dance accompaniment are observable issues for Techno as well. Henriques emphasizes the notability of repetition, arguing that it is related to an affect on a visceral background (2010, p. 77). According to him, this repetition stimulates an ancient mechanism that has taken place in different guises at most points in human life: habits. So much so that, the researcher proposes to think about the repetition created by the music played in the dancefloor, concerning circadian monthly cycles, routines and rituals, obsessive-compulsive disorder, and more (Henriques, 2010, p. 77). In light of these considerations, it is possible to talk about the existence of a ceremonial context on the dance floor thanks to a primitive impulse evoked by repetition.

According to Jerrentrup, techno tracks are not intended for passive listening or singing along, but rather to provide a multidimensional experience on the dancefloor. In order to understand the genre, it is crucial to consider techno as part of a multi-sensory stimulus for prolonged dancing (Jerrentrup, 2000, p. 69). Jerrentrup roughly categorizes the content of these multi-sensory stimuli as auditory, visual, physical, social, and mental (2000, p. 70). The auditory stimuli of the techno scene consist primarily of the music itself and external audio. Visual stimuli include flashing strobes and other elements related to light, color, and contrast. Physical stimuli encompass elements related to the physical space and its integrity. Social stimuli pertain to the nature of relationality and communicativeness, while mental stimuli are associated with drug use[32]. Jerrentrup's view of the electronic dance music scene as multi-sensory stimuli (as shown in Figure 6.1) was found to be significant and useful for this research.

In addition, this approach leads one to think of electronic dance music in general as closely related to spatiality. Ultimately, for Jerrentrup, supporting or expanding the euphoric experience of ravers by providing an intense aural atmosphere is one of the basic functions of techno (2000, p. 68). This indicates the close relationship between electronic dance music and sociability. The insights gleaned from the diverse perspectives of 15 anonymous participants, consisting of electronic music producers, performers, and listeners, shed light

---

[32] As can be seen in the Figure 6.1, mental stimuli allow the dancefloor experience to be shaped by internal and subjective factors, rather than external and objective ones. Drug use is noteworthy among the stimuli classified by Jerrentrup, as it is the most intrinsic factor shaping the dance floor. In his thesis, *A Brief History of Drug Taking in Popular Music and the Influence of Drugs on the Creation of Music*, Beklenoglu thoroughly examines the history of the relationship between music creation, performance, and listening practices and drug use from the early 20th century to the present day in various aspects (see 1997). According to Beklenoglu (1997), "mind-alteration" (p.7) or "expanded sense of time" (p. 53) achieved through drug use are underlying factors in the philosophy of many music genres. Although the relationship between music and psychoactive substances dates back thousands of years and expresses various specificities for each music culture, this issue can be addressed in a narrower context for techno music. Considering the political and cultural background of the production and consumption practices of techno music, drug use has different meanings and qualities for producers/creators and consumers/listeners. While individuals producing music may use drugs in relation to issues such as creativity, self-concerns, or performance anxiety, listeners may hold onto reasons such as altering their perception and experience of music or enhancing feelings of kinship or loneliness (Beklenoglu, 1997, p. 7). Especially in this study's specific sections, the relationship between techno sub-genres and drugs has been emphasized. Furthermore, beyond techno music, advanced research is needed on the effect of psychoactive substances on experiences in both the production and consumption phases of texture-based electronic music genres.

on the multifaceted nature of the atmosphere in techno music. As a cornerstone of the genre, the atmosphere is meticulously crafted through a skillful interplay of various sonic elements, such as lead, pad, and FX, intricately woven together within the framework of a 4/4 rhythm. These elements persistently linger in the background of the track, subtly asserting their presence while creating a rich tapestry of sound that envelops the listener.

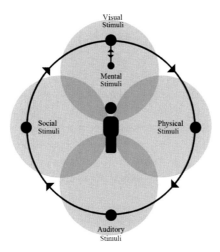

Figure 6.1 : Jerrentrup's multi-sensory stimuli on the dancefloor

The utilization of ambient sounds, often enriched with copious amounts of reverb on pads and other sonic elements, emerges as a prominent feature in shaping the atmosphere. These reverberant soundscapes create an immersive environment that is both expansive and captivating, evoking a sense of depth and space within the music. As one participant keenly observed, *"Atmospheric sound can be achieved with a reasonable level of reverb and depth, complemented by atmospheric pad chords"* (Appendix A.1). This underscores the deliberate intentionality in crafting the atmosphere, with an acute awareness of the role that reverberation and spatialization play in creating a sense of ambiance.

Furthermore, the participants elucidate that the atmosphere in techno music serves as the catalyst for storytelling, setting the stage for the unfolding of a narrative. It is the starting point, the canvas upon which the musical journey begins to unfurl, creating a sense of intrigue and mystery. As one participant eloquently remarked, *"The atmosphere is the element that draws the listener into the story of the track. It should be more than just filling the background"* (Appendix A.1). This sentiment is echoed by others who highlight that the atmosphere adds emotion and sentiment to the track, imbuing it with a sense of intrigue and captivation that keeps the listener engaged.

Additionally, the notion of filling in gaps in the arrangement and creating a sense of depth resonates with the participants. Pads and drones, often categorized as atmospheric sounds, are recognized as integral components in shaping the atmosphere. These elements interweave with the rhythmic and melodic elements of the music, creating a sonic landscape that is immersive and otherworldly. As one participant insightfully expressed, *"Sounds that are outside the rhythmic and melodic elements of the music, which can be categorized as pads and drones, create the atmosphere"* (Appendix A.1). This further underscores the holistic approach in crafting the atmosphere, where every element contributes to the overall sonic experience.

Moreover, the unique advantage of atmospheric sound in techno music is highlighted by the participants. It has the ability to transport the listener beyond the earthly realm, creating a sense of detachment and taking them on a profound and introspective journey. As one participant aptly pointed out, *"You feel like it's playing all over the planet"* (Appendix A.1). This illuminates the transformative power of the atmosphere in techno music, transcending traditional musical boundaries and evoking a deeply emotional and immersive experience for the listener.

In conclusion, the interpretations of the anonymous participants reveal that the atmosphere in techno music is a complex interplay of lead, pad, and FX elements shaped by a 4/4 rhythm, enriched with reverberant soundscapes, and meticulously crafted to create a sense of depth, emotion, and storytelling. It serves as the foundation upon which the musical journey unfolds, drawing the listener into a captivating narrative. The atmospheric sound, often achieved through the use of pads and drones, plays a pivotal role in creating an immersive and otherworldly sonic landscape. Furthermore, the unique advantage of the atmospheric sound in techno music lies in its ability to transcend traditional musical boundaries, transporting the listener to a realm that is beyond the ordinary, and evoking a profound and introspective experience.

Based on the insights gathered from the responses of the anonymous participants, the following key essences can be concluded:

- Techno music's atmosphere is meticulously crafted through a skillful interplay of various sonic elements, such as lead, pad, and FX, within a 4/4 rhythm.
- Ambient sounds, enriched with reverberation, play a prominent role in shaping the atmosphere, creating an immersive environment that is expansive and captivating.
- The atmosphere serves as the foundation for storytelling in techno music, setting the stage for the unfolding of a narrative and adding emotion and intrigue to the track.

- Pads and drones, categorized as atmospheric sounds, are integral components in shaping the atmosphere, filling in gaps in the arrangement, and creating a sense of depth.
- The unique advantage of atmospheric sound in techno music is its ability to transport the listener beyond the earthly realm, evoking a sense of detachment and taking them on a profound and introspective journey.

On the other hand, examining various intertwined ceremonial phenomena on the electronic music dance floor, St. John recommends a different perspective. According to his way of framing, one will experience a 'liminal aesthetic' on the dance floor by attending a rave event (2017, p. 284). If we charily reinterpret St. John's approach, which also falls within several related fields, we should mention the palpable presence of liminality on the dancefloor. The notion of liminal seems like a key to making sense of the trance state at rave events. To understand the liminal aspects of the techno dance floor, it is necessary to examine the term 'liminal' more closely.

The term liminal arose from Arnold Van Gennep's ethnological studies on tribal ceremonies. Later, it was found remarkable by Victor Turner and brought to the literature through his work (Andrews and Roberts, 2015, pp. 131-132). By analyzing the patterns that take place in the initiation ceremony, Van Gennep discovered three different stages: preliminal, liminal, and post-liminal. In the pre-liminal stage, there is a physical separation of the person from normal life and comfort. In the liminal stage which Turner found crucial, the participant is "literally and symbolically" marginalized. In the post-liminal stage, the participant reconnects with the community after overcoming the challenges (Andrews and Roberts, 2015, pp. 132-133). While St. John mentions the existence of a liminal aesthetic on the dance floor, he seems to emphasize that there is a ceremonial side of dancing *en masse* to techno music. "In an ever-individualizing world, it is possible that techno could be at the core of new forms of community, sending us back to the way of functioning of tribal communities" (Gamberini, 2019, p. 16). Turner, who conducted advanced research on Van Gennep's work, speaks of a sense he calls 'communitas' which is a kind of consociation that develops with the feeling of togetherness that arises among the participants who are in the focus of the ceremony (1977, p. 94-99). Individuals marginalized in the liminal stage seem to be connected to the challenging nature of the ceremony. In summary, in Turner's perspective, liminality is associated with being without status and indefinite, in a transitional phase between two social statuses, while moving from one social status to another. Liminal beings experience nothingness between two different social statuses. Other members of the community treat them as if they never existed until they acquire their new social status. In his work *From Ritual to Play*, Turner argues that the concept, which is defined as liminal with its archaic aspects, has undergone a contextual change with the conditions accompanying modernity. This change has created the 'liminoid', which is different from the notion of liminal (Turner, 1982, pp. 20-59). According to Turner, modern "play, creativity, drama, and other associated art forms" have created liminoid experiences (as cited in Andrews and Roberts, 2015, pp. 135-136). So somehow we still may experience the marginalizing liminality and the mentioned eccentric comradeship, albeit in a different state. It is possible to interpret the liminal experience as realized on the techno dancefloor. Thus, St. John (2017) interprets the trance state with this perspective in the narrative he developed through psytrance events. According to him, the event in which the person is involved has a ceremonial nature. The individual may participate in this pseudo-ceremony to "escape from [him/herself]" or to "potentiate the discovery or affirmation [of his/her] relationship in the web of life." (p. 281). Richie Hawtin describes an insider experience that depicts the state of existence or non-existence when he says "when you go to a techno club, you forget where you are, what time it is, who you are" (Gamberini, 2019, p. 9). It is here that Turner's 'liminoid' reveals itself. One may consider non-verbal communication which accompanies the camaraderie on the dance floor. Thereby, techno is the main element of the atmosphere in which the rave takes place with the guidance of its "sound-specific characteristics of signals and rhythmic pulsation" (Becker et al., 1999, p. 68). Accordingly, rave happens in the dark. Indeed, darkness filters a large — and undesirable — part of visual stimuli and prioritizes music (Fintoni and McLauchlan, 2018, p. 13). Perhaps the prioritization of music through darkness can be thought of as a preliminary stage of directing individuals to the kind of introversion mentioned by St. John.

When we interpret Van Gennep's and Turner's comments concerning liminality together with Jerrentrup's definition of multi-sensory stimuli, it would not be wrong to say that the dancefloor surrounds the person with the accompaniment of various and layered stimuli and creates a kind of liminal context. In this point of view, while stepping on the dance floor, one is somewhat alienated from the coded flow of everyday life, just like a participant in a tribal ceremony. At this stage of the discussion, DJ's presence ought to be pondered. DJ can be considered as an "operator" on the dance floor, where all the above-mentioned stimuli come together and create an indisputable effect (Becker et al., 1999, p. 59). The same authors allegorize the collective dance on the techno dance floor with archaic ceremonies. Hence, they choose to perceive the DJ as a "modern shaman". (Becker et al., 1999, p. 64). This allegorical nomenclature reveals that the DJ has a side that affects the dancing crowds. The DJ "is the personification of 'groove' as a God-like creator who takes possession of dancing human bodies" (Becker et al., 1999, p. 59) which "must be open to actively dealing with the gathered dancers" (Jerrentrup, 2000, p. 68).

The depictions of DJs by Becker et al. (1999, p. 64) and Jerrentrup (2000, p. 68) give rise to the idea of a hierarchy between DJs and listeners on the techno dancefloor. Both Becker et al. and Jerrentrup's descriptions place the audience in a passive position, subject to affect. It is important to consider the notion of hierarchy on the dancefloor, as it can distort and redefine the function of music and be seen as a socio-political factor that intervenes externally. To shed light on the phenomenon of hierarchy, interviews was conducted in this study. The answers provided by 33 anonymous participants, consisting of electronic music producers, performers, and listeners, regarding the hierarchy between the DJ and the listener in the club are varied. Some participants believe that there is a clear hierarchy, with the DJ being seen as the leader or conductor, while others feel that there is more of a collaboration or equal relationship between the DJ and the audience.

One participant described the DJ as the "king" and the listeners as "slaves", emphasizing a power dynamic where the DJ has control over the audience. Another participant mentioned that DJs often see themselves as "manipulating a crowd" and leading it, suggesting a sense of authority or dominance (Appendix A.1). Some participants also mentioned the physical positioning of the DJ, often elevated on a stage or designated area, which creates a visual separation between the DJ and the audience and may contribute to a perceived hierarchy.

On the other hand, some participants mentioned that the DJ and the audience are both in the club for fun and that the club environment should be free from hierarchy. They highlighted that the energy and enjoyment of the audience are essential in creating the atmosphere of the club, and the DJ's role is to entertain the audience.

There were also mentions of interaction and collaboration between the DJ and the audience, rather than a strict hierarchy. Some participants mentioned that the DJ determines the flow of the night and sets the tone for the party, but it's more like a collaboration with the audience, as they let themselves go and have fun with the DJ's music.

The physical conditions of the venue and the architecture were also mentioned as factors that shape the interaction between the DJ and the audience. In smaller nightclubs where the DJ and the audience are in the same area, participants felt less of a hierarchy compared to larger stages where the DJ is physically elevated and separated from the audience. Some participants also mentioned the concept of VIP areas or backstage areas behind the DJ, where higher-priced tickets are sold, creating a perceived hierarchy. The DJ's role as a performer or artist, and the idolization of DJs due to their focus on music, was also mentioned by some participants as a factor contributing to the perceived hierarchy.

However, there were also participants who did not feel or notice any hierarchy between the DJ and the listener in the club, and some who believed that the opinions and individuality of the listeners are important in the overall club experience.

In conclusion, the answers provided by the anonymous participants reflect a range of perspectives on the hierarchy between the DJ and the listener in the club. While some participants perceive a clear hierarchy with the DJ as the leader or conductor, others see it as more of a collaboration or equal relationship. Factors such as the physical positioning of the DJ, the presence of VIP or backstage areas, and the role of the DJ as a performer or artist may contribute to the perception of hierarchy. However, there are also participants who do not feel or notice any hierarchy and believe in the importance of the audience's opinions and individuality in the club environment.

In conclusion, the dynamics of hierarchy in a club setting can be complex and subjective, with varying perspectives and factors at play. Here are some concise points that can be inferred from the findings:

- Opinions vary on the presence of a hierarchy between the DJ and listeners in a club.
- Some perceive a clear hierarchy with the DJ as dominant, while others see more collaboration.
- Physical positioning, role as conductor, and special treatment can contribute to the perception of a hierarchy.
- Venue size and VIP areas can also influence the perception of hierarchy.
- Some participants do not believe in or pay much attention to the hierarchy, focusing on music and overall enjoyment.

According to St. John, dancing to techno is a performance fueled by what he called "modern maladie" (2017, pp. 281-282). In the perspective of St. John, modern maladie can be considered as a profound state of mind that, if analyzed, leads to numerous existentialism-related questions, and it seems that the disciplinary interpretivism of fields such as anthropology, sociology, and psychology is needed to reveal its origins. On the other hand, Rietveld (2018) emphasizes, drawing from Savage (p. 117), that the uninterrupted and relentless flow of electronic information is also crucial to the aesthetics of techno music. According to Rietveld (2018), electronic dance music is a "texture-dominated" genre that seriously utilizes electronic music technologies, and one of the greatest features of electronic music is that it constitutes a "DJ-friendly" musical structure (p. 113). This perspective seems to allow for various inferences:

Firstly, the musical structure of electronic dance music, which is integrated with the DJ phenomenon, homogenizes it with the dancefloor context, and therefore the entire aesthetic paradigm is based on 'functioning' on the dancefloor. The DJ-friendly musical structure can be considered a decisive aesthetic rule in the context of electronic dance music. An electronic dance music track takes shape by enabling a seamless transition to another piece in a live DJ set or allowing for an uninterrupted listening experience. Secondly, the transformative power of electronification that affected various fields of life brought updates also to the collective entertainment phenomenon that led to changes in the social fabric. When Rietveld says "the dancer can enter the musical experience by embodying its electronic sound," he talks about the dance community producing a "cyborg subjectivity" by coming together (2018, p. 133). Indeed, the techno aesthetics, which have been approached in some ways in a post-human framework by the author, are shaped by the dynamics of repetition, automation, electronification, and relentless flow of information.

The formation of techno aesthetics through machine-like repetition, the absence of human error, and the exaltation of cyclical data flow may be connected to modernity's potential to optimally modify its tools, social classes, desires, and dynamics. While it may be seen as an inspiration, it also looks to be the outcome of the digital age's transformational influence. In any event, technology has enabled technoculture in an era when electrical and digital perfection is central to everyday existence. The techno dancefloor as a consumption domain of the musical products generated by this phenomenon urges individuals to "dance to the technoculture," as Rietveld described it (2018, p. 117). It is worth noting that all of these ideas were born within a process initiated by modernity. Techno may be one of the reactive - or perhaps ordinary and natural consequences of the decentralization of production phenomena, in which automations continue to output as long as they are not deliberately stopped or malfunction. Relatedly, Rietveld associates techno music with post-Fordism when discussing production and consumption "dynamics (2018, p. 120). In the end, the dance floor can also be considered as a space of consumption shaped by the impact of the production process, in which St. John's "modern maladie" (2017, pp. 281-282) resurfaces. With its "relatively abstract machine aesthetic" (Rietvelt, 2018, p. 134), techno has transformed the first examples spreading from Detroit, Berlin, and London into a supranational language, which is developed, restructured, and aestheticized with new perspectives on a global scale. The spread has become a phenomenon through the influence of the rapidly increasing dissemination power with the development of global networks (Rietvelt, 2018, p. 134). The techno dance floor invites neoliberal selves (Hagood, 2019, pp. 178-180) who suffer from St. John's *maladie*. In this context, modern communal entertainment is adorned with Jerrentrup's multi-sensory stimulus (2000, p. 69) (see Figure 6.1). The individual internalizes the abstract machine aesthetic on the dancefloor and recreates it. This aesthetic is also "liminal" (John, 2017, p. 284). Ultimately, techno, on the dancefloor, provides individuals with an opportunity to perceive themselves and each other differently - and in some respects, ceremoniously from what is experienced in everyday life. The dance floor appears to be vital for examining techno as its default context.

In the context of this section, it is deemed sufficient to point out that techno mediates a whole slew of fields. Along the same line, it might be inspirational to highlight Reynold's illuminating way of thinking: techno is "not about what music means but how it works" (1999, p. 9). It is hoped that the interpretation of these approaches at a fundamental level will give clues about the perception of the techno dance floor in this research. Up to this point, seeing various meandering approaches in the literature gives clues about the multi-faceted nature of the dancefloor issue. This provides insights into how dance-focused genres can be interpreted in terms of relevant aspects. More importantly, it was assumed that it would be useful to address the aforementioned approaches to give clues about the motives of techno music production.

Although numerous sub-genres of techno that have emerged from the early 80s to the present could be discussed in this section, it was foreseen that it would be sufficient for the scope of this study to briefly tackle three specific styles: Detroit techno, acid techno, and minimal techno. Hence, they were found to be prominent to get a preliminary impression of how the music changed dynamically on other continents during its developmental stage.

Detroit techno

Juan Atkins, Kevin Saunderson, and Derrick May introduced the genre to the music scene by producing characteristic examples of Detroit techno as the *Belleville Three* (Hanf, 2010). While talking about his memories, May talks about a specific kind of listening which is noteworthy (as cited in Reynolds, 1999, p. 15):

> "We perceived the music differently than you would if you encountered it in dance clubs. We'd sit back with the lights off and listen to records by Bootsy and Yellow Magic Orchestra. We never took it as just entertainment, we took it as a serious philosophy."

This attitude summarizes the mood on which Detroit techno is based. May's recounting that techno "is not just about entertainment" seems to indicate profound premises in the nature of the genre. It is noteworthy to refer to the use of electronic equipment used by European electro-pop bands after the 1970s as a source of inspiration. Similarly, Chicago house has influenced Detroit techno, especially with its common time signature and danceable groove (Masterclass, 2021). On the other hand, while talking about the origins of Detroit techno, Albiez claims that the inspirations of Afro-futurism also played a crucial role in the emergence of Detroit techno in the early-80s (2005, p. 7-11). In this respect, it would not be wrong to consider Detroit techno as a musical genre shaped by the influence of funk and futurism. In the technical aspect, the originator artists "used whatever technology they could get their hands on to pioneer a cutting-edge sound made up of growling synths and driving dance beats" (Glasspiegel and Bishop, 2011). Since the 1980s when Detroit techno emerged, the primary drum machine of both old-school and today's producers has been considered the Roland TR-909 (see Image 6.1) (Allen, 2021). The characteristic recordings that emerged in the early stages of techno music were created as a result of creatively utilizing technological devices to create formal elements. Detroit techno is one of the main examples of techno styles with its philosophy influenced by the social, political, economic, and psychological conditions of the period.

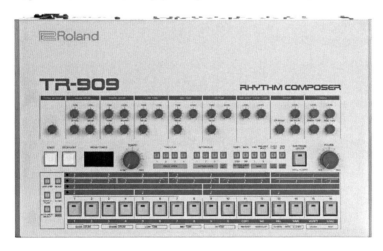

Image 6.1 : Roland TR-909[33]

---

[33] The TR-909 features an intuitive interface with 16 buttons arranged in a 4x4 grid that can be used to program and sequence drum patterns. Each button corresponds to a specific drum sound, such as kick, snare, hi-hat, and cymbals. The machine also includes various controls for adjusting the volume, tuning, and decay of each drum sound. One of the most unique features of the TR-909 is its ability to create the characteristic 'accent' sound that is commonly heard in techno music. This is achieved by adjusting the level of the accent control for each drum sound, which adds a louder and more pronounced hit to that particular sound. The TR-909 also features a built-in sequencer that allows users to program and sequence complex drum patterns with ease. The machine can store up to 96 patterns, and these patterns can be chained together to create longer and more intricate arrangements. In addition to its sequencing capabilities, the TR-909 can also be used as a sound source for creating techno basslines and other synth sounds. By using the machine's

In sum, Detroit techno is a genre of EDM that originated in Detroit, Michigan in the 1980s. Characterized by the use of electronic instruments and computer-generated sounds, Detroit techno has a strong emphasis on repetitive rhythms and melodies. Some of the hallmark tracks and producers of this genre include Strings of Life by Derrick May, released in 1987 and considered a classic of the genre; No UFOs by Model 500, also released in 1987 and featuring a repetitive beat and spoken-word vocals; Good Life by Inner City, released in 1988 and incorporating elements of soul and house music; and Big Fun by Inner City, also released in 1988 and featuring a memorable synth melody and vocals by Paris Grey. These tracks, along with the work of producers such as Carl Craig, Jeff Mills, and Eddie Fowlkes, have played a key role in shaping the sound and style of Detroit techno and continue to be influential in the genre.

Under the following two subtitles, the tracks *No UFOs* by Model 500 and *Strings of Life* by Derrick May have been reviewed in various aspects in order to comprehend their structural and sonic qualities more closely.

Model 500's *No UFOs*

No UFOs[34], produced by Juan 'Model 500' Atkins[35], symbolizes a watershed event in the evolution of electronic dance music. This classic piece, released in

---

onboard controls for tuning and filtering, users can create a wide range of unique and interesting sounds that can be used to add depth and texture to their productions.

[34] In this section, the A2 of the *No UFOs* album, which consists of five pieces released in 1985 and produced by Model 500, has been subjected to track analysis. For further information, see https://www.discogs.com/release/3113-Model-500-No-UFOs.

[35] Atkins is widely regarded as the "godfather" (The Associated Press, 2003) of techno: "[...]Atkins made significant contributions as part of the Belleville Three and as a solo artist" (Masterclass, 2021). "[...]Atkins, came out of Detroit to spearhead the techno genre" (Bein, 2020). "Detroit techno pioneer Juan Atkins[...]" (Resident Advisor, 2021c). "Considered to be the creator of techno, that person is Juan Atkins" (Hiphop Electronic, 2022). He relied on a wide range of musical and technological elements. These included the synthesizer-based electronic music produced by German acts such as Kraftwerk (Becker et al., 1999, p. 63) and the funk and R&B sounds that dominated Detroit's musical landscape. The resulting piece is distinguished by its minimalist style, characterized by the scant usage of melodic parts and an emphasis on their interplay However, the significance of *No UFOs* goes well beyond its musical qualities. It is generally considered a cultural touchstone reflecting the social, economic, and technical transformations in Detroit in the 1980s. This era of tremendous transformation in the city was marked by deindustrialization and economic deterioration. Against this backdrop, the birth of techno provided a form of artistic expression and cultural creation for the city's citizens, as well as contributing to the city's status as a center for electronic music production (see Reynold, 1999; Albiez, 2005; Allen, 2021; Glasspiegel and Bishop, 2011). It is possible to claim that the track represents a pivotal moment in the development of electronic dance music and serves as a testament to the enduring impact of Juan Atkins and his pioneering vision. The track

1985, is widely considered a seminal example of early Detroit techno and is largely regarded as one of the genre's defining compositions. The song represents the musical advances that evolved from Detroit's developing electronic music scene in the 1980s, with a modest yet dramatic usage of synthesizers and drum machines.

Below, the fundamental elements of *No UFOs* will be analyzed in a linear and concise manner, accompanied by a narrative. Through this analysis, the dominant layers and effects present in the arrangement and sound will be indicated, and an effort will be made to illuminate the structure's design.

No UFOs

The piece's structure has been identified as having 25 sections as its core blocks (Image 6.2) (Chart 6.1).

continues to influence new generations of electronic musicians and is widely regarded as a classic example of early Detroit techno.

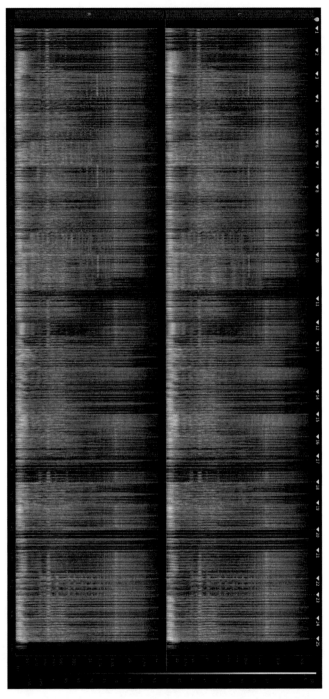

Image 6.2 : A spectral representation of 25 core blocks of *No UFOs*

Section	1	2	3	4	5	6	7	8	9	10	11	12
Time	00:05	00:21	00:37	00:52	01:15	01:23	01:38	01:54	02:24	02:40	03:10	03:26
Occurrence	The main TR-808 pattern introduces the rhythmic foundation (Fig. 6.1).	A fill that utilizes delay FX on the drum line. This section increases the suspense, leaving the listener in anticipation.	The main bass riff (Fig. 6.3) and the rhythmic accompaniment (Fig. 6.5) are introduced.	The transition patterns and the chopped spoken-word vocals are introduced.	A short hi-hat fill transition.	The bassline is muted. Square synth chords are introduced with the spoken accompaniment of the word.	The bassline becomes audible with the rhythmic accompaniment.	The rhythmic accompaniment is replaced by a transition pattern.	The bass riff slurred up two semitones. The echo effect is applied to the word 'fly' on the last beat of the section to reinforce the feeling of transition.	The echo output of the word 'fly' is heard as a looped two-beat sample for the entire section, resembling a dub feedback transition effect.	The hi-hat pattern is muted.	The bass line is muted and a radical tom fill loop is used.

Section	13	14	15	16	17	18	19	20	21	22	23	24	25
Time	03:41	04:13	04:27	04:43	04:56	05:13	05:28	05:44	06:00	06:19	06:30	06:46	06:59
Occurrence	A beatbox layer, tom fill and tops are heard without the drum pattern, with all elements blended with an echo effect, accompanied by an African drumming feel.	The echo effect is reduced and the bass riff becomes audible again.	A more radically intense tom fill and a dominant echo effect.	Spoken word, bass riff, and drum pattern culminates and resolution in the arrangement.	All components except the drum layer are muted and the arrangement breathes for the first time.	The primary spoken-word layer appears and is repeated twice. The word 'fly' is stressed, as it has been in previous parts.	The same structure as in Section 3 is applied: the bass and drum combination.	Only kicks and claps can be heard. In addition, the tom fill is heard momentarily at intervals, interrupting the calm state	The drum pattern is assembled and the groove is built again.	A brief bridge consists of the drum layer and a transition pattern.	Only the drum pattern remains. However, it is a voluminous section owing to the echo effect.	The final section where the main combination of the drum and bass layers is introduced once again.	Instant outro.

Chart 6.1 : The structure scheme of *No UFOs*

Section 1 - Begins with an impactful reverse FX, the main drum layer created with TR-808 which serves as a determining factor in introducing the tracks' rhythmic foundation (Figure 6.2 and Figure 6.3).

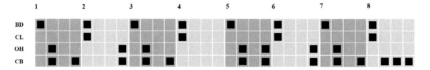

Figure 6.2 : The main TR-808 drumline of *No UFOs* on the sequencer[36]

Figure 6.3 : The notation of the main TR-808 drum line of *No UFOs*

Section 2 - A fill that utilizes delay FX on the drum line. This section increases suspense, setting the stage for the third section and leaving the listener in anticipation. Section 3 - One of the core sections where the main bass riff (Figure 6.4 and Figure 6.5) and the rhythmic accompaniment (Figure 6.6) are first heard in conjunction with the main drum layer.

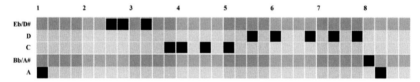

Figure 6.4 : Folded view of the main bassline of *No UFOs* on the sequencer (A2-Eb3)

Figure 6.5 : The notation of the main bass riff of *No UFOs*

---

[36] Given the idea that the drum pattern of *No UFOs* and other Detroit techno examples are made using drum machines and sequencers, it might be argued that the sequencer representation in this figure gives a more suitable visualization than notation.

Figure 6.6 : The notation of the rhythmic accompaniment[37]

Section 4 - a transition pattern is introduced with various alternatives. This is also the first section where the chopped versions of the spoken-word that will later be heard in full are introduced. This can be considered an arranging strategy that teases the full spoken word partition that will be heard in later sections. Section 5 - A short hi-hat fill transition. Section 6 - The bass line is muted. The sustaining and dynamically pitch-modulated saw-square synth chords are introduced with the accompaniment of spoken-word:

> They say there is no hope,
> They say no UFOs,
> Why is no head hung high?
> Maybe you'll see them fly.

The second repetition of the word 'fly' is used complementarily as a sudden transition with the help of the delay processor and the high-pitched accent in the spoken word. Section 7 - The bassline becomes audible with the rhythmic accompaniment. Section 8 - Begins with reverse FX and the rhythmic accompaniment is replaced by a transition pattern. The seventh and eighth sections should be considered as a moderate climax after the sixth section. Section 9 - The bass riff shifted up two semitones. The echo effect is applied to the word 'fly' on the last beat of the ninth section to reinforce the feeling of transition[38]. Section 10 - The echo output of the word 'fly' is heard as a looped two-beat sample for the entire section, resembling a dub feedback transition effect. This effect ends abruptly. Section 11 - The hi-hat pattern is unmuted. Section 12 - The bass line is muted and a radical tom fill loop is used. Section 13 - A beatbox layer, tom fill, and tops are heard without the drum pattern, with all elements blended with an echo effect[39], accompanied by an African drumming feel. Section 14 - The echo effect is reduced and the bass riff becomes audible

[37] This pattern can be heard in specific sections of the piece. Given the rhythmic qualities of the pattern, it would not be wrong to suggest that it provides melodic information to the drum layer.

[38] This can be considered as major a stylistic articulation through knob tweaking of multiple echo parameterswhich has been discussed in detail under the title of dub music. Although conceptualized with dub music, this effect has also been used in early examples of techno music.

[39] It would not be wrong to posit that one of the most important aspects of No UFOs is the ample use of echo. Indeed, the echo effect has enabled the development of the sensation of transition between parts and the enhancement of the drum pattern to become more voluminous and energetic.

again. Section 15 - A more radically intense tom fill and a dominant echo effect are heard. Section 16 - Consists of elements that are spoken word, bass riff, and drum pattern and should be considered as a section of calmness and resolution in the arrangement. Section 17 - A brief bridge in which all components except the drum layer are muted and the arrangement breathes for the first time. Section 18 - The primary spoken-word layer appears and is repeated twice. The word 'fly' is stressed, as it has been in previous parts, to emphasize the transition to the following section. Section 19 - The same structure as in Section 3 is applied: the bass and drum combination[40]. Section 20 - Only kicks and claps can be heard. In addition, the tom fill is heard momentarily at intervals, interrupting the calm state. Section 21 - The drum pattern is assembled and the groove is built again. Section 22 - A brief bridge consists of the drum layer and a transition pattern. Section 23 - Only the drum pattern remains. However, it is a voluminous section owing to the echo effect. Section 24 - The final section where the main combination of the drum and bass layers is introduced once again. Section 25 - Instant outro.

In summary, *No UFOs* can be regarded as a track that consists of a limited number of layers[41] but is dynamically amplified through the echo effect characterized by rapid transitions, fade-outs, and intensifications. Echo is an obvious stylistic element in the structure *No UFOs*. Additionally, it is clear that the bassline and drum layers are vital in determining the groove. The other layers can reasonably be considered as elements that accompany and embellish the blend of the bass and drum layers in a rhythmic or harmonic manner, enhancing their unity. The frequent increase and decrease of the number of elements, the erratic rise and fall movements, and the way of design to not lead build-ups to a big climax, have transformed *No UFOs* into a highly dynamic example, consisting of multiple bridge sections and minuscule climax points.

---

[40] It appears that this combination is the piece's default state and that all other sections are meant to meet the satisfaction of returning to this combination. On the other hand, when considering the experimental nature of the techno examples produced during that time, it may be incorrect to say that a 'satisfaction' of the type discussed existed during the period when No UFOs was released.

[41] Bass, main drum, synth, tom fill, reverse FX, and spoken-word can be considered as the complete stem palette of *No UFOs*.

Derrick May's *Strings of Life*

Derrick May's[42] *Strings of Life*[43], released in 1987, may be regarded as another pivotal track in the history of electronic dance music. With its several qualifications, the track became an immediate hit and is now regarded as one of the genre's defining tunes. So, it is possible to claim that May's *Strings of Life* is a pivotal and iconic track in Detroit techno[44], noted for its effect on the creation of the genre and its ongoing cultural relevance.

Below, the fundamental elements of *Strings of Life* will be analyzed in a linear and concise manner, accompanied by a narrative. Through this analysis, the dominant layers and effects present in the arrangement and sound will be indicated, and an effort will be made to illuminate the structure design.

Strings of Life

The piece's structure has been identified as having 24 sections as its core blocks (Image 6.3) (Chart 6.2).

---

[42] May is widely considered one of the genre's original founders in the Detroit techno music scene and has gained international acclaim for his contributions to the genre: "May was pivotal in organizing the parties and producing the songs that would later congeal into[...]techno" (Schlein, 2020). "May and his friends were once at the center of a creative universe" (Bein, 2020). "Derrick May is a true living legend" (Schmidt, 2006). "May's reputation as an originator remained intact despite more than a decade of recording inactivity" (Resident Advisor, 2021a). His work is considered particularwhich became emblematic within the genre, shaped its sound and style, and influenced other producers.

[43] In this section, the second track of the Strings of Life album, which consists of five pieces released in 1987 and produced by Derrick May, has been subjected to a track analysis. For further information, see https://www.discogs.com/master/695-Rhythim-Is-Rhythim-Strings-Of-Life.

[44] "More than 30 years after Derrick May's "Strings of Life" saw release, techno remains a pillar of the modern dance community" (Bein, 2020).

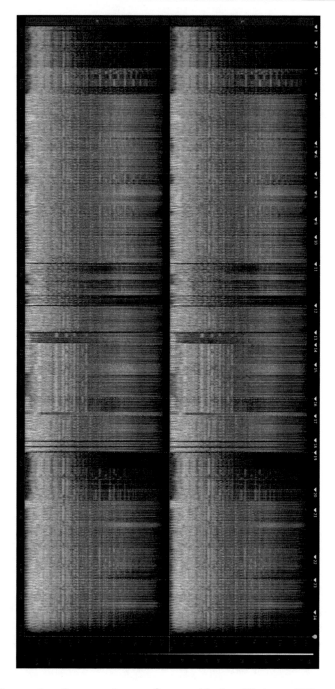

Image 6.3 : Spectrum image of 24 core blocks of *Strings of Life*

Section	1	2	3	4	5	6	7	8	9	10	11	12
Time	00:00	00:12	00:32	00:51	01:27	01:34	01:50	02:14	02:24	02:37	02:57	03:28
Occurrence	Commences with a variation of the piano sequence that was composed by May's then-friend Michael James".	The very first section that the piano and the marcato synth strings blend.	The strings acquire almost a plucked quality and the dynamics increase, marking the conclusion of the introduction.	The drum pattern created with the TR-909 (Image 6.2) is blended with a string layer that carries staccato qualifications (Fig. 6.6).	Brief pause and simplification.	Features the string section becoming more intense and playful with the addition of new notes, creating a scherzo-like narrative.	Introduction of sustained strings, with the drum track silenced for a 4-bar period.	The first climax - marks the full formation with the reunion of String 1, String 2, TR-909, and Piano layers, serving as the first climax.	A continuation section where the snare drum is heard and a variation of the previous section is displayed.	A soft cutback, kick drums are reduced and the transition is strengthened immediately afterward by muting the entire drum pattern on the last beat.	The piano melody transitions to an impetuous call-and-response pattern consisting of rises and falls within the scale.	Returning to the core block (Fig. 6.7) which was first heard in Section 8.

Section	13	14	15	16	17	18	19	20	21	22	23	24
Time	03:48	03:57	04:12	04:37	04:50	05:08	05:17	05:45	06:00	06:35	06:52	07:16
Occurrence	A new conga pattern introduced (Fig. 6.10).	The combination of the congas and the sustained strings accompanying the ostinato piano motif can be perceived as a new variation that creates a groove.	A transitional moment where the snare drum patterns are added and the tension is increased.	The congas are muted which points out that the piece will return to the core block.	The piece returns to the core block once again.	A variant of the form in Section 17 is heard with a sharp mute alternating every two bars.	Solo piano, which nearly leads the narration into the initial form.	The common time is emphasized with staccato strings.	By muting the kick drum and utilizing drum fills variations, the track is diluted in terms of the dominance of low frequencies.	The strings enrich the form in volume.	The second strings accompany the 16th staccato notes, thereby re-varying the narrative.	The outro takes place with a slow fade out.

Chart 6.2 : *The structure scheme of* Strings of Life

Section 1 - Commences with a variation of the piano sequence that was composed by May's "then-friend Michael James" (Discogs, n.d.). This section can be considered as the exposition of both the harmonic aspect and the mood of the track. Section 2 - The very first section that the piano and the marcato synth strings blend. Section 3 - The strings acquire almost a plucked quality and the dynamics increase, marking the conclusion of the introduction. Section 4 - The drum pattern created with the TR-909 (Figure 6.7) is blended with a string layer that carries staccato qualifications (Figure 6.8).

Figure 6.7 : The main TR-909 drumline of *No UFOs*

The fourth section can be considered as the core block which will be heard repeatedly with different variations later in the track (Figure 6.8).

Figure 6.8 : The notation of the core block

Additionally, the fourth section features simple drum fills (Figure 6.9) to enhance the section's dynamics. Drum fills are a frequent movement element in this piece.

Figure 6.9 : The notation of one of the fills utilized in the composition

Section 5 - is considered a brief pause and simplification, with the drum layer temporarily muted and a drum fill providing the transition. Section 6 - features the string section becoming more intense and playful with the addition of new notes, creating a scherzo-like narrative. Section 7 - is the introduction of sustained strings, with the drum track silenced for a 4-bar period to highlight the added string layer and create a small negative space. Section 8 - marks the full formation with the reunion of String 1, String 2, TR-909, and Piano layers, serving as the first climax. Section 9 - can be considered as a continuation section where the snare drum is heard and a variation of the previous section is displayed. Section 10 - a soft cutback, kick drums are reduced and the transition is strengthened immediately afterward by muting the entire drum pattern on the last beat. Section 11 - can be regarded as an 'eccentric twist' of the track. The piano melody transitions to an impetuous call-and-response pattern consisting of rises and falls within the scale. The staccato strings accompany and accentuate the piano's pattern on the first and third beats of each measure (Figure 6.10).

Figure 6.10 : The notation of the 'eccentric twist'

Also, the eleventh section is embellished with rewind FX and another drum fill, leading to an abrupt transition. Section 12 - Returning to the core block (Figure 6.8) which was first heard in Section 8. This section can be seen as a 'glue' that holds the whole form together, providing similarity, and avoiding the risk of disruption as the general arrangement will change in Section 14. Section 13 - A new pattern that includes conga drums is introduced shortly and informatively (Figure 6.11).

Figure 6.11 : The notation of the new pattern that includes conga drums

Section 14 - The combination of the congas and the sustained strings accompanying the ostinato piano motif can be perceived as a new variation that creates a groove. Although this section appears to be heard for the first time in the piece, it seems that the effect has been captured by altering the basic patterns to a very minor extent. Section 15 - A transitional moment where the snare drum patterns are added and the tension is increased. Section 16 - The congas are muted. The message seems to be conveyed that the piece will return to the center and that the core block will be heard again. Section 17 - The piece returns to the core block once again. Section 18 - A variant of the form in Section 17 is heard with a sharp mute alternating every two bars. Section 19 - solo piano, which nearly leads the narration into the initial form. Section 20 - The common time is emphasized with staccato strings. Section 21 - By muting the kick drum and utilizing drum fills variations, the track is diluted in terms of the dominance of low frequencies. This can be considered the first step of the outro. Section 22 - The strings enrich the form in volume. This makes the narrative rich in terms of melodic information. Section 23 - The second strings accompany the 16th staccato notes, thereby re-varying the narrative. Section 24 - The outro takes place with a slow fade out.

In conclusion, the most striking aspect of *Strings of Life* is the absence of a bassline which may be considered a surprising aspect from a biased listener's point of view. The piece has a soft layout and melodic characteristic that is complementary to its rhythmic quality. This situation can be attributed to two main reasons:

1.   The spontaneous muting of the string and drum tracks
2.   The systematic arrangements of transitions between three main sections[45] without resorting to any echo effect

Therefore, with its eccentric qualities such as the absence of a bassline[46] and echo effect, *Strings of Life* is seen as a quality example produced by Derrick May in 1987, characterized by the harmonization of sharp, flowing, and dynamic various piano and string patterns and instruments in a raw and rhythmic context, and is one of the *opus magnums* of techno music.

When two Detroit techno examples, *No UFOs* and *Strings of Life* is compared for their similarities in structure and musical elements, it is clear that both pieces have dynamic structures that are characterized by rapid transitions, intensifications, and fade-outs. Additionally, both pieces have elements that contribute to the overall rhythm and unity of the track, such as the bassline and drum layers in *No UFOs* and the harmonization of piano and string patterns in *Strings of Life*. Despite these similarities, it is important to note the differences between the two pieces. *No UFOs* relies heavily on echo effects and has a strong bassline, while *Strings of Life* lacks a bassline and focuses instead on the harmonization of various musical elements. This highlights the distinctiveness of each piece and showcases the different approaches taken by the producers.

---

[45] Section 8, Section 11, and Section 13

[46] "There's not a single drop of bass in the whole seven and a half minutes. Bottomless though it was, *Strings of Life* had no ceiling" (Bein, 2020).

Acid techno

Acid techno emerged in the early 1990s with the shaping influence of the British and German rave scenes (Ching, 2022). As with many subgenres, the emergence of acid techno has been linked to new technology and electronic music equipment. The hardware that gives acid techno its distinctive midrange bass characteristic, derived from erratic Q dynamics, is believed to be the TB-303 (see Image 6.4) produced by Roland. Acid techno has a sound that differs from others in this respect, and it is claimed that the TB-303 brought techno a new "squelchy" bass character (Ching, 2022). The creative pioneers of the acid techno style are credited as Richie Hawtin, Aphex Twin, Dave Clarke, and Damon Wilde (Sword, 2016). Acid techno is characterized by distorted and bright TB-303 sequences and the use of other drum machines, particularly the TR-909, which producers described as "pounding" and "filthy", also adding to the aesthetic of the genre (Sadoux, 2021, p. 63).

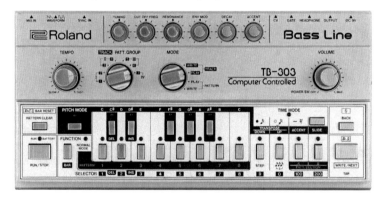

Image 6.4 : Roland TB-303[47]

Oriented towards the UK scene, acid techno "developed its very own unique network of underground acid raves" with its "short, fast-paced repetitions combined with a pounding, relentless beat" (Spruill, 2022). It is notable that acid

---

[47] The interface of the TB-303 features several knobs and buttons that allow for precise control over the synth's parameters. These include knobs for controlling the cutoff frequency and resonance of the low-pass filter, as well as knobs for adjusting the envelope settings and accent level. Additionally, the TB-303 features a distinctive slide function that allows for glissando effects between notes, giving the instrument its signature sound. In techno music, the TB-303 is primarily used for its ability to produce distinctive and highly resonant basslines that cut through the mix and provide a driving rhythmic pulse. By manipulating the filter cutoff and resonance controls, producers can create a range of tones that range from deep and subby to aggressive and abrasive. The slide function is also frequently used to create melodic riffs and sequences that lend a sense of urgency and tension to the music. Overall, the TB-303's unique interface and distinctive sound make it an essential tool for producers of techno and other electronic dance music genres.

techno represents a turning point where techno music meets rave culture. The underground rave network has shaped both the scene and the sound of acid techno. Spruill identifies acid techno culture with the participation of anti-heroes, punks, and rebels and emphasizes that the genre is associated with illegal activity (Spruill, 2022). When discussing acid techno culture, it is necessary to mention 'squatting', a form of accommodation in which financial necessity becomes a political attitude, that was brought to the scene. Squatting refers to actions such as illegally occupying urban spaces to host parties and living in unowned or unrented buildings (Sadoux, 2021, p. 62). Sadoux (2021) argues that the pioneers of acid techno lived by squatting and adds that "these artists, who met in marginal spaces, came from different backgrounds, they were drawn to the same type of rave music and felt out of place in what they call commercial events: they described themselves as "misfits"" (p. 62). Understanding acid techno as the sound of an illegal and dynamic social network may be beneficial in interpreting its quality.

Accordingly, the acid techno compilation album *It's Not Intelligent...And It's Not From Detroit...But It's F**king 'avin It!*, released by True Love Collective label in 1997, seems to carry various clues only in its title: On the one hand, the title denies the argument that techno was formed on an intellectual ground. On the other, it carries the message that acidifying techno brings it a new UK origin. With this aspect, the title initiates a conflict between Detroit and London, encouraged by 24 tracks. Although the word 'acid' is associated with a specific bass character produced by the TB-303, it should be kept in mind that some of the tracks in the discography have names[48] that allusively refer to the psychedelic compound lysergic acid diethylamide (LSD) and other substances. This allusion raises the unseen issue of drugs.

Under the following two subtitles, the tracks *Plasticine* by Plastikman and *Acid Phase* by Emmanuel Top have been reviewed in various aspects in order to comprehend their structural and sonic qualities more closely.

---

[48] *Two Lines of K...* produced by Kektex in 1997, *The 'E' Spot* produced by Cosmos Trigger in 1995, *Mushrooms on Daleks* produced by Sarcoblast in 1997, and *B.4.U. (Come Down)* produced by Trip Hazard in 1997 are some of the albums with the aforementioned allusion.

Plastikman's *Plasticine*

Richie 'Plastikman' Hawtin's[49] *Plasticine*[50] is an electronic dance music track from his album *Sheet One* released in 1993. The track exhibits Hawtin's acid techno practices[51]. *Plasticine*, with its relentless beats and emphasis on textures and atmosphere, also demonstrates Hawtin's minimal approach to production and sound design, which has served him to establish himself as a fundamental figure in the techno genre. The track exemplifies fusing experimental elements with driving rhythms to produce an immersive listening experience. Relatedly, Hawtin himself manifests his motif: "of me just trying to see how much I could drive people's mental state and physical states" (909 Originals, 2019).

Below, the fundamental elements of *Plasticine* will be analyzed in a linear and concise manner, accompanied by a narrative. Through this analysis, the dominant layers and effects present in the arrangement and sound will be indicated, and an effort will be made to illuminate the structure's design.

Plasticine

The piece's structure has been identified as having 22 sections as its core blocks (Image 6.5) (Chart 6.3).

---

[49] Canadian electronic music producer and performer Richie 'Plastikman' Hawtin is widely considered another pioneer of techno music: "The electronic music visionary and techno pioneer[...]" (Mixmag Caribbean, 2023). "No matter how early you came into electronic dance music, it always felt like Richie Hawtin had already been there for a lifetime" (Moayeri, 2022). "Hawtin created a unique techno sound, which is regarded as synonymous with the city of Detroit" (Resident Advisor, 2021a). Hawtin is noted for his creative approach to music production and sound design, which includes a minimalist style with sparse beats and a concentration on textures and ambience. His sound combines experimental elements with strong rhythms to produce immersive EDM.

[50] In this section, the seventh track of Plastikman's album, *Sheet One*, released in 1994, entitled *Plasticine*, has been analyzed. For further information, see https://www.discogs.com/master/37367-Plastikman-Sheet-One.

[51] If analyzed with the aim of uncovering its minimalistic features, *Plasticine* can be viewed as a representation of minimal techno as well. The choice of this piece as an acid techno sample serves to emphasize the presence of specific cross-overs between sub-genres and to encourage other scholars to steer clear of rigid divisions between sub-genres.

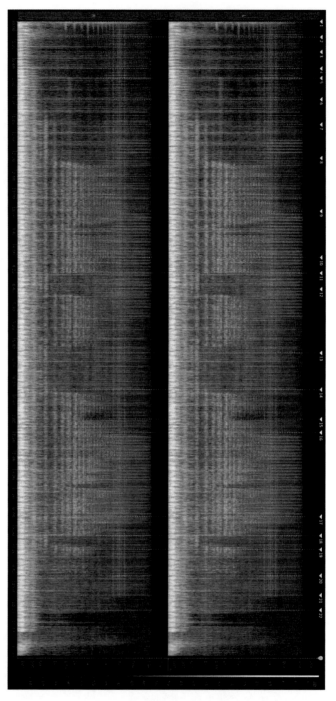

Image 6.5 : Spectrum image of 22 core blocks of *Plasticine*

Section	1	2	3	4	5	6	7	8	9	10	11	12
Time	00:00	00:17	00:33	00:51	01:01	01:24	01:51	02:27	03:24	04:13	04:30	04:47
Occurrence	Begins with a noise fall, introducing the main drum pattern created with the TR-606 (Fig. 6.11).	The kick drum 'drops', signalling a progression in the piece.	The groove elements of the composition begin to coalesce slowly.	The TB 303 bass riff fades in (Fig. 6.13).	The drum sequence is augmented with 16th rimshots. The groove is still being constructed through the merging of the drum tracks.	Main TB-303 melodic sequence (Fig. 6.14 and 6.15) gradually fades in.	The clap is added to the drum sequence on the second and fourth beats of each bar in the first half of the section. In the second half, open hi-hats heard on off-beats are introduced, adding movement to the piece.	The LPF cutoff value of the TB-303 sequence is increased.	The melodic sequence is alternated by adding a single note (G4) (see Fig. 6.16).	The kick drums are muted and the piece takes a short respite.	Introduces the whisper spoken word, with no other changes made.	Raising tension - The amplitude of the TB-303 sequence is reduced, leading to a clearer perception of the repetitive whispery spoken word vocal.

Section	13	14	15	16	17	18	19	20	21	22
Time	05:55	06:34	07:06	07:20	08:50	09:10	09:25	09:53	10:14	10:30
Occurrence	The TB-303 melodic sequence is made more stable through the LPF effect.	The kick drum is muted for 8 bars and then heard again, while the TB-303 is exposed to a dynamic LPF modulation.	Similar to the previous section but with the inclusion of the clap.	Showcases the same main block demonstrated in Section 9, embellished with elements such as the occasional open-hi-hat, whispery spoken word vocal, and rimshot fills to create an adorned narrative.	The TB-303 melodic sequence is at its most present and dynamic state.	Provides tranquility through the excessive filtering of the melodic sequence with the LPF.	Spontaneous sudden muting (amplitude gate modulation) is applied to the TB-303 melodic sequence.	Tension decreases - The TB-303 melodic sequence fades out, but the bass sequence remains present.	The bass is soloed alongside a slightly audible percussive element.	The piece comes to a conclusion.

Chart 6.3 : The structure scheme of *Plasticine*

Section 1 - begins with a noise fall, introducing the main drum pattern created with the TR-606 (Figure 6.12).

Figure 6.12 : The main TR-606 drumline of *Plasticine*

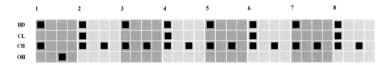

Figure 6.13 : The main TR-606 drumline of *Plasticine* on the sequencer

The drum sequence (Figure 6.13) is introduced without the inclusion of the kick and clap. The reverberation of the entire drum track is a significant stylistic element, allowing for a spatial introduction to be realized. Section 2 - the kick drum 'drops', signaling a progression in the piece. Section 3 - the clap drum with a reverb effect on the fourth beat of each bar becomes audible, as the groove elements of the composition begin to coalesce slowly. Section 4 - the TB-303 (Image 6.4) bass riff fades in (Figure 6.14).

Figure 6.14 : The notation of the main TB-303 bass riff of *Plasticine*

Although it appears to be a constant partition that only has E2, the bass is dynamically enhanced by the cutoff value of a high Q LPF being raised and lowered. This qualification is expressed on the note with crescendo and decrescendo lines (see Figure 6.14) but it should be pointed out that there is no consensus on a method of fully incorporating the filter practices into the notation. Section 5 - The drum sequence is augmented with 16th rimshots, and the groove is still being constructed through the merging of the drum tracks. Section 6 - Main TB-303 melodic sequence (Figure 6.15 and 6.16) gradually fades in.

Figure 6.15 : The notation of the main TB-303 melodic sequence of *Plasticine*

Figure 6.16 : Folded view of the main TB-303 melodic sequence of *Plasticine* on the sequencer (E1-C2)[52]

In the following sections, the dynamics of the main melodic sequence will be varied through filter cutoff tweaking techniques. Section 7 - the clap is added to the drum sequence on the second and fourth beats of each bar in the first half of the section. In the second half, open hi-hats heard on off-beats are introduced, adding movement to the piece. Section 8 - the LPF cutoff value of the TB-303 sequence is increased, making the saw character of the signal more pronounced in the higher frequencies, resulting in a more prominent and assertive sound. In Section 9 - the melodic sequence is alternated by adding a single note (G4) (see Figure 6.17). The alternated melody sequence is accompanied by open hi-hats heard on every off-beat (see Figure 6.18 and 6.19). In this section, the dynamic evolution that has been unfolding so far is taken one step further.

Figure 6.17 : The notation of the alternated TB-303 melodic sequence[53]

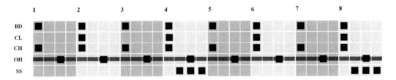

Figure 6.18 : The alternated TR-606 drum pattern on the sequencer

Figure 6.19 : The notation of the alternated TR-606 drum pattern

These minuscule touches appear to have sufficed to alter the repetitive arrangement. The idea of shaping the narrative and creating a climax by adding

---

[52] The curved lines represent glide movements.

[53] The alternations are highlighted in red color on Figure 6.17, Figure 6.18, and Figure 6.19.

a single note to the melodic pattern is also evident in this example, just as in the previous one. However, this section is emphasized as the first climax of the piece with the reintroduction of the open-hi-hat pattern heard in Section 7. Hence, this part can be considered the main block of the composition. Section 10 - the kick drums are muted and the piece takes a short respite. Section 11 - introduces the whisper spoken word, with no other changes made. Section 12 - the amplitude of the TB-303 sequence is reduced, leading to a clearer perception of the repetitive whispery spoken word vocal. A sense of build-up is created towards the end of the section. Section 13 - the TB-303 melodic sequence is made more subtle through the LPF effect. The whispery spoken word vocals are silenced at the end of this section. Section 14 - the kick drum is muted for 8 bars and then heard again, while the TB-303 is exposed to a dynamic LPF modulation. Section 15 - similar to the previous section but with the inclusion of the clap. Section 16 - showcases the same main block demonstrated in Section 9, embellished with elements such as the occasional open-hi-hat, whispery spoken word vocal, and rimshot fills to create an adorned narrative. Section 17 - is the moment where the TB-303 melodic sequence is at its most present and dynamic state. Section 18 - provides tranquility through the excessive filtering of the melodic sequence with the LPF. By the end of the section, the delay feedback ratio is increased to create the feeling of an imminent transition to the next section. Section 19 - spontaneous sudden muting (amplitude gate modulation) is applied to the TB-303 melodic sequence. The final melodic narrative is carried out through the utilization of the 'filling the gaps' aspect of the delay and reverberation effect. Section 20 - the TB-303 melodic sequence fades out, but the bass sequence remains present. The dynamic intensity decreases during this section. The beginning of the outro. Section 21 - the bass is soloed alongside a slightly audible percussive element. Section 22 - The piece comes to a conclusion.

The utilization of the Roland TB-303 Bassline synthesizer in *Plasticine* may initially suggest a categorization as acid techno. However, it is imperative to acknowledge the presence of other elements and arrangement practices that embody the characteristics of minimal techno, making the labeling of the piece as both acid and minimal techno justifiable. The dynamic nature of the single-note bassline which is achieved by modulating LPF's Q value, and emphasis on sound processing practices rather than the stability of melodic sequences highlights the acid-style techniques in close association with the fluxional knob settings. For *Plasticine*, it is crucial to note that the focus is on creating immersive and textured soundscapes.

With its repetitive nature, gentle transitions, subtle melodic variations, and central use of the Roland TB-303 Bassline synthesizer, *Plasticine* exemplify noteworthy viability. In tandem with the previously analyzed *Acid Phase*, the utilization of spatial effects, repetitive sequences, high tempo, and textures generated through filters and other linear or non-linear effects all play a crucial role in creating a 'rich' and engaging musical narrative.

Emmanuel Top's *Acid Phase*

Acid Phase[54] by Emmanuel Top[55] is a techno track published in 1994 that is widely recognized as a crucial piece in the creation of acid techno music. The tune is distinguished by its utilization of the Roland TB-303 (see Image 6.4) bassline synth, which generates a repetitive and pounding acid-style sound. *Acid Phase*'s unrelenting intensity and other stylistic qualities have made it a mainstay in techno and electronic dance music EDM circles, as well as a classic example of the genre.

Below, the fundamental elements of *Acid Phase* will be analyzed in a linear and concise manner, accompanied by a narrative. Through this analysis, the dominant layers and effects present in the arrangement and sound will be indicated, and an effort will be made to illuminate the structure design.

Acid Phase

The piece's structure has been identified as having 13 sections as its core blocks (Image 6.6) (Chart 6.4).

---

[54] In this section, the second track of Emmanuel Top's album, *This Is A...? / Acid Phase*, released in 1994, entitled *Acid Phase*, has been analyzed. For further information, see https://www.discogs.com/release/8310-Emmanuel-Top-This-Is-A-Acid-Phase..

[55] Emmanuel Top is a French DJ and producer who was at the forefront of the acid EDM movement in the 1990s: "One of the most successful French producers, Emmanuel Top[...]" (NTS Radio, 2020). "Acid pioneer Emmanuel Top is back" (Techno Station, 2017). He is also widely recognized as one of the pioneers of electronic music and is renowned for his innovative and distinctive production style.

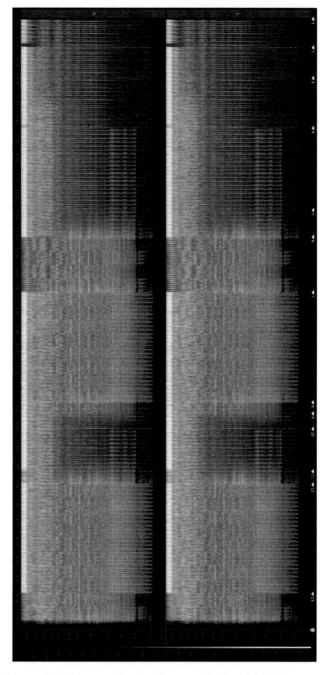

Image 6.6 : Spectrum image of 13 core blocks of *Acid Phase*

Section	1	2	3	4	5	6
Time	00:00	00:15	00:31	00:57	01:40	01:54
Occurence	Consists of a kick and rim shot. It showcases the tempo of the track in a 'DJ friendly' manner.	Side-chained single-note (C2) bassline is introduced in the off-beats. This enhances the low-frequency information and balances the mix (see Image 6.7).	Features the gradual fade-in of the TB-303 sequence (Fig. 6.19 and 6.20).	The gain of the TB-303 melodic sequence has reached a staged point. In conjunction with this, an off-beat tambourine drum pattern is included, forming the main drum pattern (Fig. 6.21 and 6.22).	16th open hi-hat fill that prominently dominates the frequency range between 5 kHz and 10 kHz (see Image 6.7 and (Fig. 6.23).	All elements are muted. The predominantly saw-characteristic melodic sequence (Fig. 6.24) is introduced in a solo fashion.

Section	7	8	9	10	11	12	13
Time	02:23	03:20	03:26	03:34	04:55	04:02	04:55
Occurence	The climax- the harmonic context introduced in the previous section acts as the backdrop for the TB-303 sequence, drum track, and bassline.	A sudden rest. The kick drum is left alone and other percussion elements are briefly muted.	The saw synth gradually fades out relatively quickly. The rimshots become prominent again.	The tambourines become part of the groove again.	The open-hi-hat fill is heard, the kick drums are muted, and the tension raises again.	A copy of Section 7. On the other hand, it can also be considered a continuation.	Only the TB-303 and saw sequence is left. All other elements are muted. The piece comes to an end with an open-hi-hat fill.

Chart 6.4 : The structure scheme of *Acid Phase*

Section 1 - consists of a kick and rim shot. It showcases the tempo of the track in a 'DJ friendly' manner. Section 2 - A side-chained single-note (C2) bassline is introduced in the off-beats. This enhances the low-frequency information and balances the mix (see Image 6.6). Section 3 - features the gradual fade-in of the TB-303 sequence (Figure 6.20 and 6.21). It should be considered as a build-up prior to the main block of the piece. A four-beat rest is made at the end of the section.

Figure 6.20 : The notation of the TB-303 sequence of *Acid Phase*[56]

Figure 6.21 : The TB-303 sequence of *Acid Phase* (C2)

Section 4 - The gain of the TB-303 melodic sequence has reached a staged point. In conjunction with this, an off-beat tambourine drum pattern is included, forming the main drum pattern (Figure 6.22 and 6.23).

Figure 6.22 : The main drumline of *Acid Phase*

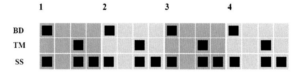

Figure 6.23 : The main TR-606 drumline of *Acid Phase* on the sequencer

Up until this section, the track has shown progressive development without any harsh transitions. In this section, it remains somewhat fixed for a prolonged period. Thus, this section can be considered as the first climax of the piece.

---

[56] The term 'emp.' used in Figures 6.20 and 6.21 refers to an abbreviation for 'emphasized'. So, the two eighth notes (C2) in the sequence are emphasized and accentuated by using these knobs. Emphasis is achieved by tweaking the topmost knobs on the TB-303 interface (see Image 6.4). In this particular example, the emphasis in question was created by dynamically using the cutoff and resonance knobs. Also, the six mentioned knobs are commonly used in TB-303 practices to achieve the acid bass sound.

Section 5 - A fill pattern consisting of 16th open hi-hats that prominently fill the frequency range between 5 kHz and 10 kHz (see Image 6.6) enters into play (Figure 6.24).

Figure 6.24 : The drum fill of *Acid Phase* on the sequencer[57]

The open hi-hat gradually fades in and reaches its highest amplitude at the end of the section. This creates anticipation for the transition to the next section. The suspense is allowed to build. Section 6 - All elements are muted. The predominantly saw-characteristic melodic sequence (Figure 6.25) is introduced in a solo fashion.

Figure 6.25 : The notation of the melodic sequence of *Acid Phase*

Figure 6.26 : Folded view of the saw the melodic sequence of Acid Phase on the sequencer (C4-Db5)

This section, where the idea of harmony is introduced, is crucial in determining the tonality of the track. Section 7 - the climax. The harmonic context introduced in the previous section acts as the backdrop for the TB-303 sequence, drum track, and bassline. The TB-303 sequence, which has been introduced progressively until this section, takes a harmonic context. The

---

[57] Although indicated as a measure, the drum fill in the piece is used with a gradual fade-in of the open hi-hat, in blocks of four bars.

tambourine heard on off-beats in previous sections is replaced by the open-hi-hat, altering the drum pattern. Section 8 - a sudden rest. The kick drum is left alone and other percussion elements are briefly muted. This lowers the tension and creates a short sensation of an alternation. Section 9 - The saw synth gradually fades out relatively quickly. The rimshots become prominent again. Section 10 - the tambourines become part of the groove again. Section 11 - the open-hi-hat fill is heard, the kick drums are muted, and the tension raises again. Section 12 - a copy of Section 7. On the other hand, it can also be considered a continuation. Either way, this section is the second longest section where the main block is heard again. Section 13 - only the TB-303 and saw sequence is left. All other elements are muted. The piece comes to an end with an open-hi-hat fill.

In conclusion, *Acid Phase* exemplifies acid techno's features with its distinctive 'emphasized' TB-303 bassline, relatively high tempo (135 BPM), and static drum machine rhythm. The track is progressive, developing gradually and remaining at its peak for an extended period. Examining the spectrum (Image 6.6), it is clear that the sub-frequencies are nearly exclusively audible throughout the track. This points to the power of the sub-frequency band to reduce intensity and tension when it is repressed[58]. Both *Acid Phase* and *Plasticine* are characterized by the use of the Roland TB-303 Bassline synthesizer and high-tempo beats. *Acid Phase* is noted for its progressive development and extended peak, while *Plasticine* has a much more dynamic quality with its sudden, repetitive transitions. Both tracks utilize various musical elements, such as spatial effects, repetitive sequences, and textures generated through filters, to create a rich and engaging musical experience. Overall, both pieces showcase the key features and impact of acid techno in creating a dynamic and engaging musical experience.

Minimal techno

Minimal techno, a subgenre of techno music, is characterized by its simplicity. It features a pared-down arrangement that typically comprises only drums, a bassline, and minimalistic essential elements, thereby fostering a grooving track. Nevertheless, as with all musical genres, minimal techno sound has undergone a metamorphosis since its inception (Ching, 2022). The term 'minimal techno' was popularized in the mid-1990s, specifically after the release of the *Minimal Nation* by Robert Hood. Since Hood's seminal release, minimal techno has been distinguished by an emphasis on rhythm instead of melody, harmony, or other elements (Ching, 2022). Another theory holds that early

---

[58] Section 6 can be taken as an example.

Detroit techno producers forwent the arrangement, texturing, instrumentation, and other production techniques that had previously been followed in the rock and pop tradition and stripped their music of extraneous embellishments by standing against the mainstream aesthetics (Sherburne, 2017, p. 319). The 'stripping' served as a turning point and since then EDM has established itself with a quite "limited set of sounds" (Sherburne, 2017, p. 319). Minimal techno possesses qualities as a result of being purified of excesses. From this perspective, the authentic sound was shaped with a loop and sequence-based, and fairly repetitive structuring approach. According to Simon Reynolds, compared to the UK's breakbeat and hardcore techno sound, the music created by the Detroit techno movement's forerunners was "elegantly minimalist" (as cited in Sherburne, 2017, p. 321). In Reynolds' perspective, techno already had a minimal aesthetic from its birth in Detroit before being given the epithet 'minimal'.

There is little doubt that the advent of minimal techno is largely anchored in technical breakthroughs that have altered techno music production techniques, notably in terms of software and hardware (Nicolas, 2013, p. 143). Technological tool interfaces actively shape the principles of techno music creation and consumption processes. Doran Eaton (2014) points out that merely linking minimalism with "in-human goal-directedness" is not totally adequate. He then gives a fresh set of alternative ideas for defining the relationship between music and minimalism (p. 6). By applying the suggested perspective to the subject, it is likely to identify some of the main qualifications of minimal techno:

- It primarily emphasizes repetition rather than melody.
- It possesses a steady pulse and devoids any radical rhythmic breaks.
- It embraces the auditory qualities of immutability and constant flow by keeping dynamic contrast to a minimal degree.
- Minimal techno emphasizes time and "gradually evolving rhythmic cycles" (Sherburne, 2017, p. 323).

Considering the aspect of technology in shaping, defining, and aligning with minimalism, which has nurtured minimal techno within a hardware and software-based paradigm, is crucial in developing an approach towards it. German restraint, rationalism, and exactitude are stereotypes linked with minimal music, which aspires to abstraction, reduction, and pure sound (Nye, 2013, p. 165). But it is non-negligible that the term represents many attitudes, artistic methods, and backgrounds.

According to Jacques Attali (as described in Nicolas, 2013, p. 143), music's connection with society will be subject to considerable and potentially unforeseen variations as long as it is allowed to evolve independently. Parallel to Attali's beliefs, Jerrentrup's (2000, p. 67) prediction that minimalist-technoid music forms will determine the future of techno appears to have been realized.

In this sense, minimal techno may be considered as just one-and surely not the last-stage in the evolution of techno music in connection to technology, as a result of its exploitation at the most recent and utmost degree of 'dexterity.' However, minimalism as an aesthetic concept was not limited to techno, it was also used to describe a broad range of practices in music and media across different locations in Germany (Nye, 2013, p. 154).

According to Sean Nye (2013), the minimal style in electronic music emerged as a movement in the 2000s and was quickly adopted by a slew of labels and artists. Nye claims that the aesthetic approach to the sound of techno music prior to 2000 saw a metamorphosis after 2004 in Berlin[59], specifically in the realms of sound and album artwork (p. 163). This minimalist disposition has brought a distinct new sound to techno music by generating a slower, less ornamented, and less forceful tone. However, it would be fair to say that the birth of minimal styles and the alteration of the 'embryonic' techno sound in EDM has a history. When examining the development of minimal music in Western geography from the 1890s to the present, it is feasible to conclude that significant repeated themes, diluted harmonic motion, and the enhancement of 'negative space' are common musical features, as is the "overall atmosphere of simplicity" (Nicolas, 2013, p. 143). These similar features are also concretely reflected in techno, which can be clearly identified when listening to the archetypes of minimal techno. It is suggested that the entrance of minimalism into the techno realm led to the birth of a polished and nearly polar opposite version of the 'harder/faster/louder' aesthetic[60] that had been synonymous with music's indiscriminate relation with partying. This scenario spawned the concept of 'functionless aesthetics,' which evolved as a clear and indisputable purpose of minimalism on the dance floor in the techno aesthetic. By abstracting techno from its function of having people dance, minimal techno established a "non-dancefloor" (Sherburne, 2017, pp. 322-323) kind; it set aside the utility by embracing the form of techno music as the foundation. According to this viewpoint, minimal techno emerged in reaction to the basic functionalities provided by early techno on the dance floor.

Minimalism in music is distinguished by its concentration on minuscule sounds and how these sounds are handled as the key ingredients that comprise the song. It cleanses the form by removing excesses and embellishments, and it promotes the ideal of attaining the best outcomes by using a restricted amount

---

[59] Nye (2013) used bold rhetoric to explain how minimalism sparked a Berlin-based transformative wind: "[...]the years 2003-2004 can be seen as Berlin's symbolic pivot into an international minimal mecca" (p. 163)

[60] In certain examples, minimal techno represents an aesthetic that is almost the complete opposite, boasting a 'softer/slower/quieter' quality.

of components in the sound palette (Nye, 2013, p. 165). The notion of the restricted amount of components might entail fewer sounds, fewer effects, fewer twists and surprises in the arrangement, fewer jarring transitions, and less 'refulgence' in minimal techno. In addition to all these qualities, minimal techno's emergence can be seen in relation to the desire to recreate the groovier vibe of early Detroit techno (Ching, 2022). According to a MusicRadar article, the utilization of shorter sounds is a more effective means of achieving the desired aesthetic in minimal techno. This can be achieved through the programming of synth patches with "short decay times and zero sustain", which results in the generation of a "series of blips". Additionally, the manipulation of decay time through automation can serve to enhance the melodic elements within specific segments of the track, and add an element of interest to the overall composition (Computer Music, 2020). While melodic elements are still vital, some tracks entirely forego them in favor of an exclusive focus on drums, requiring a re-evaluation of how they are perceived (Ching, 2022).

Furthermore, both in terms of techno music specifically and more generally in the context of a minimalized musical structure, the influence of West African Drumming has been widely discussed in various sources (see Nye, 2013, p. 160; Nicolas, 2013, p. 28; Sherburne, 2017, p. 321). These discussions imply that minimalism carries the African rhythm paradigm at its core as it spreads to EDM genres-which is crucial to consider both for future research and, more importantly, in the process of demystifying minimal EDM genres within listener consciousness. The "sort of temporal dislocation[61]" effect created by minimal electronic music is a result of prioritizing percussive sensation and foregrounding the groove alone (Sherburne, 2017, p. 320).

In summary, minimal techno is a subgenre of techno music that arose in the early 1990s and is distinguished by its repetitive, stripped-down sound. The use of basic, repetitive rhythms and melodies, frequently with an emphasis on a single, recurrent motif, characterizes minimal techno. This repetitive structure is frequently accomplished by using recurring percussion beats and loop-based production techniques. Minimal techno is also known for its sparse usage of melodic components, with a concentration on lengthy, sustained notes and minimalistic chord progressions. This minimalist approach to music production

---

[61] Sherburne does not consider the effect of temporal dislocation to be solely created by music on the dance floor. The author seems to view this effect as a part of the "multi-sensory stimulus" that envelops the crowd on the dance floor, as conceptualized by Ansgar Jerrentrup (2000, p. 69). Furthermore, the author examines the immersive effect created by the groove within the context of the dance floor's drug-influenced needs (Sherburne, 2017, p. 320)which is an issue that cannot be overlooked in the EDM field even though it has not been discussed in this research.

and arrangement has become a distinguishing feature of the genre, giving rise to its name.

When considered within the context of this research, minimal techno can be seen as fertile soil for the departure from the conventional techno function, in terms of form, narrative, production, and consumption style, specifically in terms of its non-dancefloor characteristics as seen in some examples. Multiple sources confirm that minimal techno has had a significant emergence, both directly and indirectly, on the structure, cultural codes, perception by listeners and producers, and most importantly, the introduction of unique formal elements into the techno realm. Taking the thought further, it is possible to argue that minimal techno can be defined as an 'intermediate genre' and that after facilitating the transition, it has completed its role by transforming into other genres[62].

Under the following two subtitles, the tracks *Minus* by Robert Hood and *Sweat* by John Tejada have been reviewed in various aspects in order to comprehend their structural and sonic qualities more closely.

Robert Hood's *Minus*

Minus[63] is a pivotal track released in 1994 by Detroit-based techno producer Robert Hood[64]. The track is a seminal work in the minimal techno genre, distinguished by its minimalist and repetitive musical components. The combination of a simple relentless melodic narrative, and a 'punchy' bass riff

---

[62] Furthermore, Sherburne (2017) explicitly states that "the very idea of minimalism has lost much of its specificity as variations on reductionist themes [...] have evolved into a staggering array of styles varying from Chain Rection's well-known ambient dub techno" (p. 324). Nye, on the other hand, suggests the 'minimal continuum' model to better describe the evolutionary changes of minimal EDM in Germany by referring to Reynolds' 'hardcore continuum' model used to describe the development and relationship of different genres within the UK's hardcore EDM (Nye, 2013, p. 165). Through this model, which seems worthy of attention, it is possible to make commentary on the linear transformation between minimal genres.

[63] In this section, the second track of Robert Hood's album, *Internal Empire*, released in 1994, entitled *Minus*, has been analyzed. For further information, see https://www.discogs.com/master/12446-Robert-Hood-Internal-Empire.

[64] Robert 'The Floorplan' Hood is a producer, DJ, and founder of the record label *M-Plant*. Hood is regarded as one of the pioneers of Detroit techno and a key figure in the development of minimal techno: "Someone who is as influential and integral to techno's success over the last two decades is Robert Hood" (Mixmag, 2017). "Hood, a Detroit producer widely credited for 'inventing' minimal techno" (Scaruffi, 2010). "Hood's legacy in the electronic music world is almost peerless" (Burns, 2015). He remains active in the techno scene by performing and releasing music regularly. His contributions to the genre seem to solidify his status as a pivotal artist in the history of electronic dance music.

provides an immersive aural experience. *Minus* is considered a mainstay of Hood's repertoire, influencing the techno sound.

Below, the fundamental elements of *Minus* will be analyzed in a linear and concise manner, accompanied by a narrative. Through this analysis, the dominant layers and effects present in the arrangement and sound will be indicated, and an effort will be made to illuminate the structure's design.

Minus

The piece's structure has been identified as having 7 sections as its core blocks (Image 6.7) (Chart 6.5).

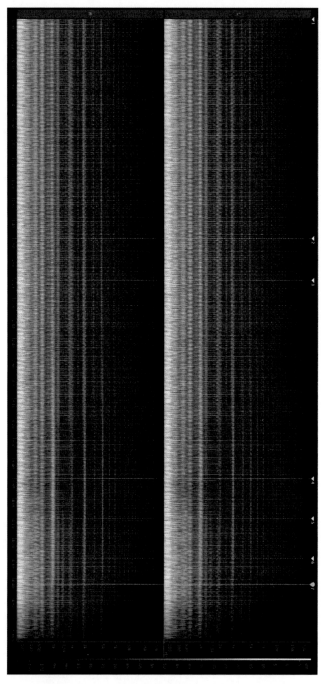

Image 6.7 : Spectrum image of 7 core blocks of *Minus*

Section	1	2	3
Time	00:00	01:50	02:11
Occurence	Instantly begins with a kick drum, a square synth sequence (Fig. 6.26) with a plucked-sounding ADSR quality, and a bassline consisting of two notes (Fig. 6.28). The combination of these three elements creates the core block of the piece (Fig. 6.29).	The introduction of a second square synth partition (Fig. 6.30). The defining characteristic of this section is a 16th-note square signal sequence that is heard twice per measure and changes its starting point every four measures.	The main form consisting of three tracks started to be subjected to an LPF with a gradually decreasing cutoff frequency until the next section. However, the application of LPF that excludes the second square synth partition, which is dominant in high frequencies, has made it more present. This minor movement alters the overall impression.

Section	4	5	6	7
Time	03:50	04:10	04:30	04:43
Occurence	The LPF process, which began in the previous section, comes to an end when the cutoff value reaches the lowest frequency set. Therefore, this section might be regarded as distinct, since the whole composition sounds more deeply than ever before.	The rising LPF cutoff value disambiguates the high frequencies of the first square synth sequence heard from the start and boosts the presence of the whole composition. This part might be thought of as a 'return' or repositioning.	The second square synth gradually exits the composition with the aid of an LPF modulation which makes this section short but significant that exclusively marks the process of filtering.	A soft conclusion is made possible through a slow fade-out of the master channel. This outro, by preventing a sudden end to the repetition, results in a smooth ending.

Chart 6.5 : The structure scheme of *Minus*

Upon examining the stillness and unchanging nature of the spectral representation in Image 6.7, the minimalist structure of the piece becomes quite apparent. In this five-minute track, only a single element, the second square synth is added and subtracted. The remaining three elements, the bassline, kick drum, and first square synth are looped at a constant pace from beginning to end. The structure of the piece aligns directly with the deductions made in the category of minimal techno, and as such, *Minus* has been deemed a crucial example in this section.

Section 1 - instantly begins[65] with a kick drum[66], a square synth sequence (Figure 6.27 and Figure 6.28) with a plucked-sounding ADSR quality, and a bassline consisting of two notes (Figure 6.29). The combination of these three elements creates the core block of the piece (Figure 6.30).

Figure 6.27 : The notation of the first square synth sequence of *Minus*

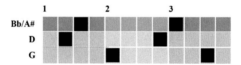

Figure 6.28 : Folded view of the first square synth sequence of *Minus* on the sequencer (G4-Bb5)

---

[65] Section 2, on the other hand, should not be considered as an intro typical in techno music. Moreover, the notion of viewing this section as an intro seems to be an inconsistent approach.

[66] Throughout the piece, no percussion element other than the kick drum has been used. This characteristic highlights the nature of minimal techno.

Figure 6.29 : The notation of the bass riff of *Minus*

Figure 6.30 : The notation of the core block of *Minus*

The three elements continue to sound at the same pace until the second section. The repetitive melody sequence creates a 'hypnotic' effect accompanied by a relatively high tempo (139 BPM). The 16-beat rests in the Sq. 1 partition (Figure 6.27) are perceived as if they are filled with a spatial plane through a reverb effect. Consequently, the reverb effect has brought a different sensation that is much more distinct from what is seen in the note. This section manifests an effect based on repetition and a low dynamic range. The simplicity of the elements, the uncomplicated harmony, and the fact that the entire piece consists of only three elements, highlight the significance of the mix. In short, this section exhibits the essence of minimal techno's 'employing as few components as possible and stressing repetition' in a consistent manner. Section 2 - commences approximately one minute and fifty seconds later with the introduction of a second square synth partition (Figure 6.31). The defining characteristic of this section is a 16th-note square signal sequence that is heard twice per measure and changes its starting point every four measures. To demonstrate this variation,

Figure 6.31 displays a color-coded 8-measure segment. The two distinct rhythmic patterns are represented by two different colors, namely pastel blue and pastel green.

Figure 6.31 : A representation of the second square synth variation

In the second square synth sequence, there is only one note (B5). On the other hand, the planning of this sequence is complex due to the addition of a dynamically changing layer of rhythmic information, which is distinct from the repetitive structure introduced in the previous section. Although the presence of the second square synth layer seems to place the track on a polyrhythmic ground, it is deemed unnecessary to complicate the analysis by attributing this qualification to looping practice. This section can be regarded as a significant section in which the second square synth is introduced. Figure 6.32 displays the notation of this section along with the second square synth partition in the piece.

Figure 6.32 : The notation of the second section of *Minus*[67]

Section 3 - the main form consisting of three tracks started to be subjected to an LPF with a gradually decreasing cutoff frequency until the next section. However, the application of LPF that excludes the second square synth partition, which is dominant in high frequencies, has made it more present. This minor movement alters the overall impression. Therefore, in this section, a major movement is created essentially just by utilizing the cutoff knob of the LPF. Apart from filter processing, there has been no other major or minor change and the track continues to exhibit the same rhythmic and melodic form.

Section 4 - The LPF process, which began in the previous section, comes to an end when the cutoff value reaches the lowest frequency set. Therefore, this

---

[67] In Figure 6.32, the underlying idea behind the change in the piece is illustrated only on an 8-measure segment. The second square synth is sustained through a forward-backward shifting operation between 16th beats every four bars from Section 2 to Section 6, as shown in the notation.

section might be regarded as distinct, since the whole composition sounds more deeply than ever before. On the contrary, the second square synth sounds prominent. The LPF cutoff value begins to rise toward the end of the section. Section 5 - The rising LPF cutoff value disambiguates the high frequencies of the first square synth sequence heard from the start and boosts the presence of the whole composition. This part might be thought of as a 'return' or repositioning. Section 6 - The second square synth gradually exits the composition with the aid of an LPF modulation which makes this section short but significant that exclusively marks the process of filtering. Section 7 - a soft conclusion is made possible through a slow fade-out of the master channel. This outro, by preventing a sudden end to the repetition, results in a smooth ending.

Minus can be considered a well-rounded example of minimal techno, featuring three fundamental elements in its sound palette, a deliberate lack of sudden rises and falls with the use of subtle effects, and unassuming melodic and rhythmic patterns. One of the track's most notable characteristics is the ¾ time signature, with the kick drum being perceived in quarter notes, which can initially give the illusion of the common time signature - often called the four-on-the-floor in EDM. With regard to creating a sense of repetition and hypnotism. The second key aspect is the effect of repetition and the way in which the second square synth modulates the harmony by shifting to another hit every four measures. In summary, nothing appears to change in *Minus* yet many changes. In conclusion, *Minus* can be considered a good stylistic manifesto has given in the context of minimal music's fundamental principle.

Daniel Bell's *Baby Judy*

Baby Judy[68] by Daniel Bell[69] is a techno track that exemplifies the minimalist approach to electronic music production. Characterized by its stripped-down, percussive groove, and sparse melodic elements, the track embodies the ethos of the minimalist techno movement that emerged in the early 1990s. Bell's focus

---

[68] In this section, the B1 of Daniel Bell's album, *Rare and Unreleased*, released in 2000, entitled *Baby Judy*, has been analyzed. The piece is featured in three different albums, and an identical version has been utilized in all of them. However, since the earliest dated release in the Discogs database is associated with this album, it has been favored as the primary choice. See https://www.discogs.com/release/22637-DBX-Rare-And-Unreleased for further information.

[69] Daniel Bell is a techno producer and DJ from the United States who has been active since the late 1980s. His work under various aliases, notably DBX, has had a significant effect on the development of techno music: "[...]a sound that changed the course of electronic music" (Fabric London, n.d.). Bell's work is distinguished by a stripped-down, percussive sound that stresses rhythmic intricacy and timbre.

on timbral experimentation creates a hypnotic and engaging sonic experience that defies traditional dance music conventions.

Below, the fundamental elements of *Baby Judy* will be analyzed in a linear and concise manner, accompanied by a narrative. Through this analysis, the dominant layers and effects present in the arrangement and sound will be indicated, and an effort will be made to illuminate the structure design.

Baby Judy

The piece's structure has been identified as having 15 sections as its core blocks (Image 6.8) (Chart 6.6).

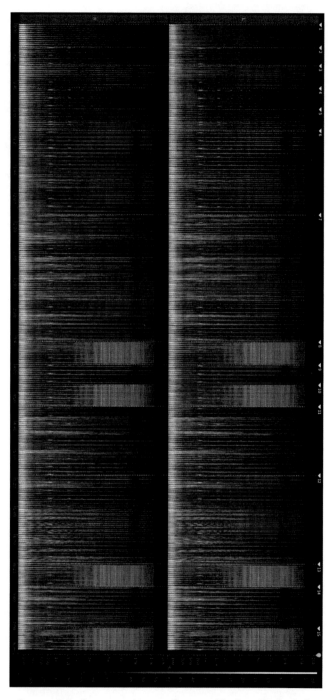

Image 6.8 : Spectrum image of 15 core blocks of *Baby Judy*

Section	1	2	3	4	5	6	7
Time	00:00	00:15	00:30	00:45	01:00	01:15	02:14
Occurrence	The first variation (V1) of the drum pattern (Fig. 6.32) and the bass sequence (Fig. 6.33 and 6.34) in C minor, is introduced. This section could be considered a concise intro.	The blip (Fig. 6.35 and 6.36) that fills the negative space on the final beat of the bass partition, making it a part of the groove's repetitiveness, is introduced. It resonates on the fifth of the C minor chord by engaging a minimal call-and-response relationship with the bass partition.	The V2 drum pattern is introduced (Fig. 6.32), where only closed hi-hats come into play on the offbeats.	The closed hi-hats are muted, and the tension drops.	The closed hi-hats are reintroduced.	Claps are added to the drum pattern which builds the third variation (V3). Apart from the fill, is the most "complex" pattern that the drums achieve in the rest of the track (Fig. 6.32).	The closed hi-hats are muted. The pitch-downed spoken word is introduced: "[...]nobody is asking about Baby Judy[...]".

Section	8	9	10	11	12	13	14	15
Time	03:44	03:59	04:14	04:29	05:19	06:20	06:36	07:06
Occurrence	The fill pattern (Fig. 6.32) is introduced. However, the rising tension does not reinforce the transition to a different and more intense section compared to the previous ones.	After the fill the V3 drum pattern, bass, and blip are heard.	The fill pattern is reintroduced.	A copy of Section 9, but only the closed hi-hat is muted. The spoken word continues to narrate.	The closed hi-hat is heard again. The length of the previous section creates a sense of renewed movement in this section. In the second half of the section, the pitch of the spoken word is raised.	The fill pattern is reintroduced.	The tension raised with the fill pattern drops again, and the track transitions to the V3 drum pattern. The spoken word continues: "Nobody, but nobody is asking about Baby Judy[...]".	The fill is heard for the last time, and the track suddenly ends.

Chart 6.6 : The structure scheme of *Baby Judy*

129

Section 1 - The first variation (V1) of the drum pattern (Figure 6.33) and the bass sequence (Figure 6.34 and 6.35) in C minor, is introduced. This section could be considered a concise intro.

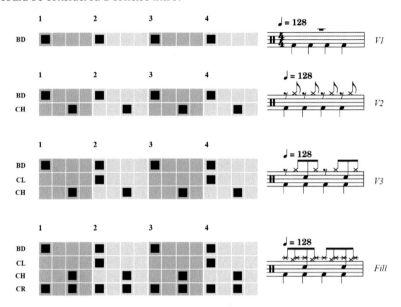

Figure 6.33 : Four drum pattern variations of *Baby Judy*[70]

Figure 6.34 : The notation of the bassline of *Baby Judy*

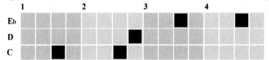

Figure 6.35 : The bassline of *Baby Judy* on the sequencer (C2-Eb2)

Section 2 - The blip sound (Figure 6.36 and 6.37) that fills the negative space on the final beat of the bass partition, making it a part of the groove's repetitiveness, is introduced. It resonates on the fifth of the C minor chord by engaging a minimal call-and-response relationship with the bass partition.

---

[70] The V letter in the labeling on the far right of the figure indicates 'variation'.

Figure 6.36 : The notation of the blip sound

Figure 6.37 : The blip sound on the sequencer (G5)

Section 3 - The V2 drum pattern is introduced (Figure 6.33), where only closed hi-hats come into play on the offbeats. Section 4 - The closed hi-hats are muted, and the tension drops. Section 5 - The closed hi-hats are reintroduced. Section 6 - Claps are added to the drum pattern which builds the third variation (V3). Apart from the fill, is the most complex pattern that the drums achieve in the rest of the track (Figure 6.33). Section 7 - The closed hi-hats are muted. The pitch-downed spoken word is introduced:

[...]nobody is asking about Baby Judy[...]

Section 8 - The fill pattern (Figure 6.33) is introduced. However, the rising tension does not reinforce the transition to a different and more intense section compared to the previous ones. Section 9 - After the fill, the V3 drum pattern, bass, and blip are heard. Section 10 - The fill pattern is reintroduced. Section 11 - is a copy of Section 9, but only the closed hi-hat is muted. The spoken word continues to narrate. Section 12 - The closed hi-hat is heard again. The length of the previous section creates a sense of renewed movement in this section. In the second half of the section, the pitch of the spoken word is raised. Section 13 - The fill pattern is reintroduced. Section 14 - The tension raised with the fill pattern drops again, and the track transitions to the V3 drum pattern. The spoken word continues:

Nobody, but nobody is asking about Baby Judy[...]

Section 15 - The fill is heard for the last time, and the track suddenly ends.

Upon this concise approach, *Baby Judy* serves as a prime and extreme example of how the arrangement can be simplified and how simplicity can be taken to advanced levels within the boundaries of minimal techno. The track also exemplifies how sound processing-based embellishments or knob tweaking are virtually non-existent, with the exception of the three-note bass partition. Aside from these qualities, the track lacks almost any harmonic sequences and all elements are percussive in nature - including the bass which is reminiscent of the tom. In light of this, the track solely emphasizes a percussive nature and does not provide the listener with an abundance of information in a harmonic context. As mentioned under the relevant heading, this validates the notion that 'techno is essentially an auditory stimulus generated with the aim of being played on the dancefloor by the aid of percussive emphasis'. Furthermore, the kick drum is never suppressed in the record, and conventional four-on-the-floor drum patterns are constructed in key areas to accentuate a constant rhythm. The entire narrative of the track is constructed by blending only the bassline that accompanies the drum pattern and the syncopated blip sound[71], almost completely abstracted from any harmonic considerations. Additionally, the spoken word with its raised and lowered pitch must be regarded as a separate element that changes the context of the track. The track's relentless structure, lack of abrupt transitions, and circular flow are significant factors that have been determined. All these aspects are taken into consideration, *Baby Judy* can be categorized among the initial and primitive examples of minimal techno.

In conclusion, the two pieces, *Minus* and *Baby Judy* are both examples of minimal techno with several similarities. Both tracks feature a deliberate lack of sudden rises and falls, unassuming melodic and rhythmic patterns, and a focus on repetition and hypnotism. *Minus* uses a ¾ time signature and incorporates a second square synth to modulate the harmony, while *Baby Judy* is characterized by its simplicity, percussive nature, and emphasis on a constant rhythm through conventional four-on-the-floor drum patterns. Both tracks also demonstrate the use of repetition to create a circular flow and the absence of sound processing-based embellishments. Overall, both pieces can be considered valid examples of minimal techno that showcase the genre's principles of simplicity and repetition.

---

[71] The title of another album from 2003 that features the same track, 'Blip Blurp Bleep', seems to manifest this approach. Therefore, it is important to consider the blip sound as a stylistic element adopted for a concept created by Daniel Bell. For further information, see https://www.discogs.com/release/218814-Daniel-Bell-Blip-Blurp-Bleep-EP.

7

The Fusion
A Brief History and Analysis of Dub Techno

Dub techno as the main objective of this study, can be considered as a techno sub-genre and deep techno sub-variation in which dub and techno genres are combined with a significant formula, as mentioned in the study with their historical and cultural content until this part. Dub techno has a distinctive sound, which, if subjected to scrutiny, is expected to yield various fruitful results, as will be described in the following paragraphs. In its most general form, dub techno sound has come into existence with the legacy of dub music, which is a derivative of Jamaican reggae, various sub-genres of techno, and also the sound, technique, paradigm, and cultural structure of other electronic dance music genres (Dub Monitor, 2020). Discussions on the historical development, cultural domain, and stylistic foundations of dub and techno genres in the previous two chapters above were aimed at nothing but illuminating the field of dub techno. It seems safe to say that dub techno still maintains its stance in the catalogs as a niche music genre with its sound, which has been subjected to various experiments as a result of the harmony of various stylistic elements and has been constructed by a cascade of trial and error if it is pondered from a historical perspective.

The Invention Phase

From an isolated perspective, it is quite possible to get the impression that, unlike most music genres, dub techno was not a consequential result of a slow-burning historical, political, or cultural development process, at first glance. After reviewing a diversified amount of internet-based sources, it can be venturesomely inferred that it seems to be accepted by the vast majority of dub techno communities that Moritz von Oswald and Mark Ernestus are the originators of the genre. So much so that dub techno seems to be 'invented' on a specific procedure of mixing thanks to the experimental efforts of von Oswald and Ernestus in the early 90s (Baines, 2015). Thus, electronic music producer and music journalist Dub Monitor[72] claims that von Oswald's friendship with Ernestus in Berlin is "the point of origin for what we call dub techno nowadays" (Dub Monitor, 2020). Von Oswald himself also states that he found the inspiration needed to shape the sonic features of dub techno while working in a record shop in the early 80s. He depicts his memories in which he often listened to reggae records, imported from the United Kingdom at that time-and mentions Lee Perry's recordings specifically (Schmidt, 2008). Talking about the times when he enthusiastically listened to imported reggae recordings, "every time a record came in, it was something we sat down and discussed, listen to it at that time because [the recordings] were so hard to get" (Red Bull Music Academy, 2018) says von Oswald by explaining how the interest prompted him to a sort of critical listening tendency. As he mentioned, von Oswald's interest in reggae, which emerged in the early 80s, reappears more strongly in the early 90s. Von Oswald states that it was Mark Ernestus, who was more deeply involved in reggae music, that triggered the 're-engagement' process. He also mentions Ernestus as his partner, with whom he co-founded Basic Channel, the cornerstone dub techno record label (Schmidt, 2008). Although Basic Channel seems to be the most decisive for establishing dub techno sound among the projects created by Oswald in creative collaboration with Ernestus, it should be emphasized that there are other music projects created before and after its establishment (see Figure 7.1).

---

[72] One-on-one interviews were held with the creator of the Dub Monitor project and he requested that his name be withheld. Therefore, in this research, it was refrained from using the real name of the content creator.

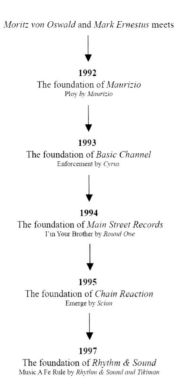

Moritz von Oswald and *Mark Ernestus* meets

1992
The foundation of *Maurizio*
Ploy *by Maurizio*

1993
The foundation of *Basic Channel*
Enforcement by *Cyrus*

1994
The foundation of *Main Street Records*
I'm Your Brother by *Round One*

1995
The foundation of *Chain Reaction*
Emerge by *Scion*

1997
The foundation of *Rhythm & Sound*
Music A Fe Rule by *Rhythm & Sound and Tikiman*

Figure 7.1 : The labels founded by Moritz von Oswald and Mark Ernestus until 1997

Figure 7.1, which was created based on the data obtained as a result of the classification of the records recorded in the Discogs database, represents the chronological order of the labels established by von Oswald and Ernestus from 1992 to 1997 and the first albums released by each label. Established in 1992, Maurizio was known for a long time as a project carried out by von Oswald alone, but later on, von Oswald stated that behind this project was the effort of a team including Ernestus (Dub Monitor, 2021). After Maurizio was founded in 1992, the duo founded the *Basic Channel* in 1993, *Main Street Records* in 1994, *Chain Reaction* in 1995, and *Rhythm & Sound* in 1997. All these labels paved the way for new recordings, careers, and styles with nuance differences to come together under the umbrella of von Oswald and Ernestus. Throughout this process, vinyl has been the main medium. Ansgar Jerrentrup especially emphasizes the place vinyl holds for techno culture as a medium where music is structured, distributed, listened and performed by writing "whoever approaches techno music should know that it is fundamentally produced from vinyl" (Jerrentrup, 2000, p. 67). If we consider vinyl as Jerrentrup emphasizes, it seems possible to think of the various labels that von Oswald and Ernestus founded several years apart after 1993, perhaps beyond commercial reasons, as various forms of expression adopted to emit the sound of dub techno they originated which evolved in due course. Although, as mentioned above, it seems widely accepted that the process of recognition of dub techno by catalogs and listeners as a musical genre solidified with its characteristic features is based on the work of von Oswald and Ernestus, Dub Monitor makes another point: the phrase 'dub techno' seems to have first become legitimate in 2001 (Dub Monitor, 2020). He claims that dub techno, created by von Oswald and Ernestus in 1993, was known as the 'sound of the Basic Channel' until the early 2000s, but was defined as 'dub techno' after the 2000s (2020):

> "It was not, actually, until 2001 that they started using the phrase dub techno. In fact, the first time they used it was in a single issue they reviewed two dub techno albums one was by Jan Jelinek, called *Loop-Finding-Jazz-Records* and the other was an album called Anima by *Vladislav Delay*. So, while the sound that we now call dub techno was invented in 1993, it seems like around the turn of the millennium was probably when most people started viewing it as dub techno rather than just as Basic Channel."

Above, Dub Monitor seems to appeal to the demonstrative nature of literature by predicting that the process of dub techno becoming legitimate as a sub-genre begins with the first use of the phrase by The Wire Magazine. When retrospective research is undertaken in The Wire internet archive, Dub Monitor's claim has a scientificness, but on the other hand, it seems possible for this claim to be fully verifiable only by scanning other journals and making the necessary determinations in a chronological context. However, even shying away from accepting this claim as verified, one seems to think that dub techno was first born as a sound and was then qualitatively revised and named. On the other hand, this claim also protects dub techno from reducing it to the efforts of von Oswald and Ernestus, warns the researcher to consider other producers, and seems to contribute to a relatively more objective perspective.

When the cascade of foundations is taken into account chronologically, it seems doable to sum the process roughly as follows: von Oswald moves from Hamburg to Berlin and meets Ernestus. The duo's overlapping musical tastes led to the founding of a minimal techno duo named Maurizio circa 1992 (Dub Monitor, 2020). Although Maurizio's recordings until 1993 carry clues about the origins of dub techno, the main breaking point was the foundation of Basic Channel-which was a duo project launched by von Oswald and Ernestus as a record label in 1993 (Dub Monitor, 2020). It is a matter of debate that Maurizio's first recordings, which were established just before the Basic Channel, were not heard as dub techno as it has become known today (Dub Monitor, 2021). However, it is claimed that von Oswald and Ernestus founded the Basic Channel in 1993 and blended Jamaica-originated dub sound with Detroit-originated techno sound, and released the first examples of dub techno (Dub Monitor,

2021). In other words, they "gave birth to a new subgenre" (Spruill, 2022). Chain Reaction is another notable label founded by Oswald and Ernestus after Basic Channel, which carries significant importance for dub techno (Spruill, 2022). The records released by Chain Reaction, which "emerged from the ashes" of Basic Channel, can be considered as the first distinct examples of the dub techno sound that has now gained acceptance aesthetically (Baines, 2015). Finally, Rhythm & Sound, founded by the same duo in 1997, was "a label strictly dedicated for dub techno and dub reggae," taking inspiration entirely from dub roots and developing its approach to Jamaican sound system culture (Spruill, 2022). Thus, the label "pulled inspiration directly from the roots of dub as it presented their own renditions of Jamaican sound system culture" (Spruill, 2022). The sound and structure proposed by the Rhythm & Sound label have been approached as "smoked-out," and everything related to this sound has been described as "half-remembered, half-there" and "half-real" (Baines, 2015) from a perceptual standpoint.

On the other hand, the friendship between Lloyd "Bullwackie" Barnes and von Oswald, which has been mentioned several times under the dub title above, started in New York, and shaped von Oswald's perspective on the field of production (Schmidt, 2008). It would not be wrong to infer that von Oswald was aware of the dub *version* culture, which was one of the hallmarks of dub music. Von Oswald describes how he created several remix projects within the borders of the Jamaican dub tradition. He specifically mentions one of these projects that was included in the album Mango Walk, created by *The Chosen Brothers* and *Rhythm&Sound* in 1998, in which von Oswald followed the B-side method and created a remix version of the original track printed on the back side of the record (Schmidt, 2008). While answering a question that ponders how he thought outside the boundaries of Berlin techno culture and incorporated mixing paradigm and aesthetics of dub music into his production field, von Oswald highlights Ernestus' interest in dub music, and points out Bullwackie as a figure of the inspirational catalyst of dub music's influential existence of the duo's sound (Red Bull Music Academy, 2018):

> "We realized [Bullwackie] was one of our favorite producers and tried to link up with him and get into his world. We were going to New York anyway, seeking out old cellars and basements for records, and, at some point, we met him in the South Bronx. Another thing that came up, which I've put on the player; there was a guy from London, who also had a connection with him and he said it would be great if we could do a remix of this track he wanted to release called Mango Walk, produced by [Bull]Wackies, which hadn't been released before. We had the original tapes, we released it and we did a remix."

In the same interview, von Oswald describes the distinctive low-frequency feel of the New York dub sound, citing Bullwackie's mixing style as an example. According to von Oswald, in the New York dub sound, low frequencies are heard "more like a pulse" rather than a conventional bass (Schmidt, 2008). Considering the full context, it is quite clear that von Oswald was intrigued by the role of low frequencies characterized by dub music, as has been covered above under the dub title.

The Sound

Alessio Kolioulis argues that in the eyes of von Oswald and Ernestus, the seemingly cankered popularization of the Berlin club techno scene triggered the duo's dissatisfaction between 1993 and 1995, and eventually the duo attempted to search for "new, revolutionary sounds" (Kolioulis, 2015, p. 78). Kolioulis' inference seems to emphasize the fact that dub techno is somewhat separated and isolated from the techno phenomenon in its inclusive sense, from the stage culture that was getting stronger with the 'fuel' of popularism at that time-more importantly, from the Berlin or Detroit techno sound with its sonic feel. Although von Oswald lived in Detroit, joined the Detroit techno network, and released his recordings in the USA to be in contact with the techno culture more closely, he expressed in 2008 that he did not think that the music he produced had the Detroit techno sound (Red Bull Music Academy, 2018). The incident in which von Oswald himself made this sharp distinction is seen as a clue to think that the sound paradigm of the music he produced is slightly separated from the authentic techno vein which contributes to the definition of dub techno sound. It would not be incorrect to suggest that dub techno carries impressions from the mixing nature of dub music, and indeed, the phrasing of dub techno itself seems to have been created with this expectation in mind. When it comes to the dub techno sound, it is evident that the recordings released through the labels established by von Oswald and Ernestus carry a hallmark quality. Thus, "from 1993 to 1995, Ernestus and von Oswald operated as 'Basic Channel' revitalizing Oswald's passion for dub" (Kolioulis, 2015, p. 77). Considering various examples of dub techno, the nature of the sound that deviates from the techno umbrella raises a significant question, which is seen as one of the fundamental problems of this study: how does the alteration of some aspects of the dub techno sound from 'raw' techno genres affect the dub techno scene? Moreover, does the dub techno scene, as an area of listening that the techno culture has left as a legacy over the years, render clubs obsolete? After recalling these questions, it is almost necessary to make some interpretations about the auditory aesthetics of dub techno.

Dub and techno, two distinct music genres that emerged independently in different countries, were fused together and sampled in the pot of dub techno in the early 1990s. The stylistic nature of the fusion of dub and techno is often attributed to the groundwork of minimalism. Dub techno has a minimalist structure, which gives it an atmospheric, ethereal, and spacey feel that is similar to ambient music (Spruill, 2022). To frame dub techno correctly, it is important to recognize its direct or indirect relationship with ambient music (Baines, 2015). According to Kolioulis (2015), "the tension between minimalism and dub produced the prototypical dub techno genre" (p. 77). Jerrentrup (2000, p. 67), who predicted that minimalist-technoid music structures could shape the future of techno with his various conclusions in 2000, seems to have been proven right, as evidenced by the section on minimal techno.

According to Kolioulis (2015, p. 65), dub techno produces a sense of "futuristic melancholy." This sense is generated by integrating the soundscape of urban areas into electronic dub music form, in other words, fusing it with other elements of the form. (Kolioulis, 2015, p. 65). According to Baines, this fusion has been achieved through the "reciprocal relationship" between the "convergences and disparities" of the two music genres (Baines, 2015). In other words, von Oswald and Ernestus fused the "warmth and humanity" of dub music with the "precise, mechanistic iciness" of techno music (Baines, 2015). Spruill, on the other hand, suggests that dub techno takes classic dub elements, gives them a "dub techno twist," and blends them with techno elements within a four-on-the-floor format at a tempo of around 120-130 BPM (2022). It would not be incorrect to argue that the rules of dub techno are the driving force behind this blending process. Dub techno has inherited a considerable portion of its auditory aesthetic from dub music. "Dub techno [is] the accumulation and stratification of dub sounds' techniques into techno's rhythmic components" (Kolioulis, 2015, p. 65). At this point, it is evident that an 'aesthetic adaptation' has taken place, and the most fundamental proof of this adaptation is the specific delay style that has been characterized by dub music and adapted to techno music (Dub Monitor, 2022). The self-sustaining echo effect with a high feedback amount can be applied to any track in music. However, the high-feedback echo alone may not produce characteristic results. The parameters on the effects processor, such as delay time, feedback amount, high-pass and low-pass values, panning, etc., are "live improvised" by the producer to give the dub echo its fundamental characteristics (Dub Monitor, 2022). In the early examples of Oswald and Ernestus, echo usage was characterized by Roland's RE201 Space Echo. However, the vital role played by the TB-303 in acid techno is not as prevalent in dub techno with the RE-201 (Dub Monitor, 2022). This specific echo effect can certainly be achieved with other devices or software. These parameters are not limited to those mentioned, and it should be noted that numerous parameters can be controlled through live improvisation techniques, especially with the production process becoming software-based.

The Attack Magazine has published a fundamental 'manual' for dub techno, which contains methodological written information on how to produce multiple dance music genres. According to the article titled *Basic Channel-Style Dub*

Techno, the use of "distorted" and "noise-driven" musical elements is vital for dub techno (Esen, 2021). The article, starting with the snare drum design, suggests that the snare drum should have a "snappy" character and should not contain low-end frequencies (20-250 Hz). Additionally, the snare drum should be pitch-uped, subjected to bit crushing and downsampling processes, and high-passed by reducing the 150 Hz range after these processes (Esen, 2021). The article emphasizes that the echo character of dub music is essential for a dub techno track. In creating this character, the effect chain for the stab layer is clearly described. Following the guidelines, the resolution of the stab sound should be lowered and made more 'jagged', a bandpass-modeled filter's cutoff value should be randomized with a low Hz LFO to eliminate 'harshness'. The resulting sound will be described as 'soft' due to its weakened high-end information. Lastly, the use of an ⅛ dotted Filter Delay[73] is recommended (Esen, 2021).

It can be argued that the concept of 'live improvisation' in dub techno production, as discussed under the relevant heading in this work, has been inherited from the console usage observed in the production and performance process of dub music. The production style that incorporates live performance in dub music has resulted in the transformation of mixing engineers into "creative engineers" (Vendryes, 2015, p. 12), and the practices they apply are among the characteristics of dub techno. Oswald, for example, responds to the question "When you dealing with especially echoes and delays, it is so easy to over-cloud the track. How do you open up the wide spaces and keep them in a box at the same time?" with "live mixing" (Red Bull Music Academy, 2018), drawing attention to the humanistic aspect of electronic music and dub techno in particular. Taking into account the idea of live mixing or the dynamic improvisation of certain parameters specific to effects also opens up the concept of 'spontaneous recording' in dub techno mixes. Oswald explains in his works that he does not consider certain situations that most music producers would regard as mistakes, saying "I like to finish stuff also really quickly. If it is done, it's done. If there are mistakes, there are mistakes" and adds: "If the vibe is right, let's go for it" (Schmidt, 2008). On the other hand, Oswald emphasizes the need for a dub techno producer to be aware of other people listening to the outcome while live mixing. According to him, being aware of "both what is happening technically in the mixing process and what is not" is key (Redbull Music Academy, 2008). Oswald describes this as the "ability to listen to the music with other people's ears" (Red Bull Music Academy, 2018). Oswald's view summarizes

---

[73] Filter Delay is one of the stock plug-ins in the Ableton Live software, which enables separate control over three different regions of the spectrum, filter type, cutoff value, Q value, feedback amount, amplitude, and panning information.

issues specific to dub techno, such as why music is produced, what its essence is, and whether hardware-based thinking is problematic.

The association of noise as a narrative, stylistic, or evocative element with the sound of dub techno is of significant importance in framing the genre. Spruill (2022) argues that considering its focus on "micro" or "tiniest hints of hiss and fuzz", one can gather insights about the spatiality of dub techno. According to Spruill, "minuscule swatches of sounds" reverberate in the sonic space created by dub techno, thereby announcing its spatiality (2022). In the same context, Spruill draws attention to the power of spatiality, stating that "every element in the mix is given breathing space and, accordingly, takes on a sense of the organic" (2022). Oswald, discussing the element of noise in dub techno, explains its place in the music through the use of analog hardware as a characteristic element of the genre. He expresses that he does not view noise as a defect in his own work, and even asserts that it often contributes to the vibe, emphasizing that noise is an integral part of the music (Red Bull Music Academy, 2008).

The tendency to describe dub techno by comparison with other genres with close aural qualities seems to be quite common. Dub techno meets electronic ambient music on a common production denominator. In addition, some emphasize that ambient music and dub techno music often have intersecting parts in a stylistic context (Dub Monitor, 2022). On the other hand, Oswald has expressed his preference for not making rigid categorizations when thinking about music genres (Schmidt, 2008). Additionally, he states that he does not attach much importance to how the music will be perceived in the club when producing it. According to him, although there is a significant dub inspiration in dub techno, the idea of differentiating between dub and techno by using the criterion of 'whether they are club music or not' is rejected (Schmidt, 2008). Similarly, he criticizes the attitude of techno listeners who find Western classical music 'old' (Schmidt, 2008). This attitude provides clues about Oswald's musical perspective. Accordingly, Dub Monitor (2021), a critic who advocates avoiding sharp distinctions in the categorization of techno genres, argues that there is overlap between techno sub-genres and predicts that definitions will vary significantly among listeners who use sensory impact as a criterion when defining techno sub-genres. In addition to sensory impact, according to Dub Monitor (2021), considering three basic criteria, namely "energy level, stylistic choices (effects, etc.), and point of origins (or inspirations)," is quite reasonable, especially when classifying deep techno sub-genres. Deep techno is an "umbrella" genre, with a relatively low tempo, soft sound, and distinct "subtlety," lacking sharp rises and falls in its structure, unlike hard techno (Dub Monitor, 2021). Dub techno, which shares these qualities with deep techno, with its use of echo and reverb, minimalist structure, and prominent noise layer, is considered by the critic as a sub-genre of deep techno (2021). Figure 7.2 is designed with inspiration from the idea of overlapping.

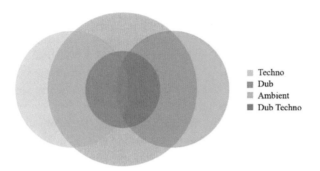

Techno
Dub
Ambient
Dub Techno

Figure 7.2 : A representation of dub techno's intersectional nature

Figure 7.2 illustrates the intersectional nature of dub techno, which is a sub-genre under the techno umbrella. Dub techno sound is heavily influenced by spatial design practices such as echo, delay, and reverb, which have shaped its form to a significant extent. This shaping has led to an intersection between dub techno and dub music, as well as other genres under the techno umbrella. Similarly, it is evident that dub techno has a stylistic intersection with ambient music (specifically electronic ambient). This intersection is perceivable in the structural design of dub techno. As discussed earlier, dub techno has a relatively less variable structure, which refers to its interaction with ambient music that has a fixed and unassertive structure. In the same context, some albums[74] produced without any percussion layer, sometimes at a tempo below 100 BPM, but released by dub techno labels, have led to dub techno being regarded as a variety of ambient techno in some sources. Recordings that use dub techno production techniques, prioritize atmosphere, and are designed to be listened to with headphones (Dub Monitor, 2022) can be considered within the category of ambient dub techno. Likewise, ambient practices legitimized by dub techno's structure have, in a broad perspective, influenced the entire techno umbrella to some extent. Ultimately, the point that needs to be emphasized in Figure 7.2 is the center point where techno, dub, ambient, and dub techno intersect. The sound that occurs at this point fully reflects the intersectional nature of dub techno.

---

[74] The *Round Series* (1994-1999), *Fremd* by Pole (1999), *UR* by Cio D'or (2012), *Standing Still* by CV313 (2011), and the *Sol* produced by Fluxion (2021) are among the numerous albums that fall under this categorization.

Dub techno is a combination of these three genres, combining dub-style effects and instrumental focus, techno's computerized production techniques, and ambient music's atmospheric characteristics. It is frequently distinguished by the use of repetitive, hypnotic rhythms, as well as a concentration on sound manipulation and experimentation. In this sense, dub techno is a confluence of the 'kinesis' of dub; the 'mechanical' quality of techno; and the soothing, atmospheric aspects of ambient music.

Based on the responses of the 18 anonymous participants, consisting of electronic music producers, performers, and listeners, a diverse array of perspectives and descriptions emerge when attempting to define the dub techno sound. Some participants emphasize the genre's historical roots in Jamaica, noting how it builds upon the foundation of dub music, a genre characterized by its innovative use of effects, such as delays and echoes, to create spatial and immersive soundscapes. These effects are also highlighted by some participants in their descriptions of dub techno, with mentions of *"a lot of delay effects"* and *"dub effects like echoes very obviously"* (Appendix A.1). This suggests that the use of effects is a prominent characteristic of dub techno, contributing to its atmospheric and immersive qualities.

Furthermore, participants also highlighted the role of rhythm and tempo in dub techno. Several participants describe dub techno as having a slower tempo compared to general techno, with references to *"low BPM,"* *"slower than normal techno,"* and *"deep, rhythmic, hypnotic"* qualities (Appendix A.1). This slower tempo, combined with a repetitive kick and melody sequences, is mentioned by some participants as defining features of dub techno. This suggests that the genre's rhythmic and repetitive elements contribute to its hypnotic and mesmerizing nature.

In addition, there are mentions of the minimalistic nature of dub techno, with participants using terms like *"chilled progressive,"* *"minimal techno,"* and *"repetitive chords, ambient atmospheres, small and subtle grooves"* to describe the genre (Appendix A.1). This suggests that the genre's minimalistic approach to composition and arrangement, characterized by repetitive elements and subtle grooves, is a distinguishing feature of dub techno.

Moreover, participants use various descriptors to convey the mood and character of dub techno, such as *"dark"*, *"atmospheric,"* *"calming,"* *"mystic,"* and *"sharp and edgy"* (Appendix A.1). These descriptions highlight the genre's emotive and evocative nature, suggesting that dub techno elicits a range of emotional responses from listeners, from introspection to stimulation.

In conclusion, the responses from the anonymous participants illustrate the complex and nuanced nature of dub techno as a music genre. Combining elements of dub and techno, dub techno is characterized by its atmospheric, immersive, and rhythmic qualities, often featuring minimalistic arrangements, slower tempos, and repetitive elements. The genre's emotive and evocative nature is also evident, as participants use various terms to convey the mood and character of dub techno. Overall, the interpretations from the participants highlight the diverse and multifaceted nature of dub techno, contributing to its rich and evolving musical landscape.

Based on the responses from 18 anonymous participants, the following key essences can be concluded about the dub techno sound:

- Dub techno incorporates elements such as dub effects (e.g., delays, echoes) to create expansive and immersive sonic landscapes.
- Dub techno is characterized by a deliberately slower tempo compared to conventional techno, often with repetitive kick and melody sequences, resulting in a deep, rhythmic, and hypnotic quality.
- Minimalism is a prominent aesthetic in dub techno, featuring repetitive chords, ambient atmospheres, and subtle grooves.
- Dub techno elicits diverse emotional responses, ranging from dark, atmospheric, and sharp to calming, mystic, and edgy.
- Dub techno can fit various moods and settings, allowing for comfortable listening, danceable grooves, and performance on stage.
- Effects play a significant role in shaping the unique sound of dub techno, with the deliberate use of delays, echoes, and other effects contributing to its atmospheric and immersive auditory aesthetics.

A hauntological approach to noise

In 1983, Jacques Derrida foresaw that ghosts would play an "integral" role in the future with his statement, "I believe that ghosts are a part of the future" (Coverley, 2021, p. 8). He established the term 'hauntology' in literary discourse through a clever wordplay on 'ontology' in his work, *Specters of Marx*[75],

---

[75] According to Miller (2015), in *Spectres of Marx*, "Derrida confines Marx to a realization that he was haunted by iterations of spectres of the future and the past" (p. 9). Derrida used the concept of hauntology as a tool to create a distinction between Marx's ontological approach and historical materialism. The book suggests that the concept of hauntology creates this distinction through the gaps opened up between closed conceptualizations such as class antagonisms in Marx's ontology (Miller, 2015, p. 5). The first element that triggered the emergence of the concept of 'hauntology' was Derrida's critique of Marx, but later the term was made to be used in other areas due to the influence of Mark Fisher and Simon Reynolds. In this section, when 'hauntology in music' is mentioned, the definition of Mark Fisher is adopted first, and the conceptual framework that he outlines in his critique of the "failure of future" (2012, p. 16), specifically in the lack of futurism and the 'stale' retro-futurism in post-millennium art works, is utilized.

published in 1993 (Coverley, 2021, p. 10). As a result of the influence of writers such as Mark Fisher, hauntology studies gained widespread popularity and the term gained currency. In the conceptual framework he formulated, Derrida used the term *spectre* to describe instances in which the past exerts its influence on the future and 'haunts' it in various ways. In this sense, Derrida's *spectres* are seen as symbols of a kind of unity between the past and the future that is elusive and challenging to comprehend.

It appears that the concept of hauntology gained popularity in the field of music criticism and analysis with the use of the term in a music blog by Simon Reynolds in 2005 (Coverley, 2021, p. 9). Thus, the use of words such as 'haunting' and 'haunted' can be stumbled upon in many canonical and non-canonical sources that aim to define dub techno's sonic qualities. In order to approach dub techno from a hauntological perspective, the boundary drawn by Mark Fisher seems important. According to Fisher (2012), the term hauntology can be used to describe a world where the present can only be experienced as "a sum of its pasts" (p. 16). In Fisher's perspective, electronic music, in particular, has not produced anything that will truly shape the future since 2005. In other words, post-millennium electronic music has not come up with any futuristic yields like those given in the past (Fisher, 2012, p. 16). Fisher (2015) clearly claims that electronic music in the 21st century has not been able to go beyond music recorded in the previous century (p. 16). Accordingly, he enounces "practically anything produced in the 2000s could have been recorded in the 1990s" and "electronic music had succumbed to its own inertia and retrospection" (Fisher, 2012, p. 16). As the electronic music genre has become increasingly mired in retrospection, it has concomitantly lost its impetus and the inherent capacity to be a pioneering voice of the future. Fisher asserts that at some juncture, humanity lost its social imagination. In this context, Fisher discusses the concept of the 'end of history', which refers to Fukuyama's belief that the global proliferation of liberal democracy and free market capitalism marks the terminal point of humanity's social and political evolution (2012, p. 16). In a similar vein, Fisher posits that electronic music no longer has any pertinence to the future, despite the technological advancements that allow for the creation of the voice of the future. Rather, the inclination and capability to generate music that is conceptually linked to the future are gradually dissipating. This perception, that electronic music can no longer engender a connection to the future and that the very notion of creating such music is waning, has become the predominant viewpoint. At this point, every 'new' musical creation in electronic music reworks, evokes, references, or imitates original music produced in the past that may have once purely reflected the future, as a result of which it is haunted by the past (Fisher, 2012, p. 17). This is the point where Fisher's hauntology comes into play. According to Coverley, Fisher believes that in the first decade of the

21st century, the imagination of the future has become so useless as to be unable to output. This has led to the "cultural time" becoming distorted, slowed, stalled, and regressed (2021, p. 9). According to Fisher's hauntological approach, the inability of the future imagination to produce results has led contemporary music practices to repeat past patterns and stifle humanity's collective musical imagination. Therefore, hauntology highlights the current time's lack of originality in music creation and the failure of recent political, intellectual, and material developments to offer any promise for the future. The conceptuality of hauntology brings to light moments when an alternative path, distinct from that previously taken, may be pursued (Coverley, 2021, p. 10). For Fisher, the beginning of the 1970s saw the decline of the revolutionary quality of counterculture, leading to the creation of the neoliberal world that is now fully familiar. The culmination of this long-term change is the widespread "deadly" proliferation of late capitalism (Coverley, 2010, p. 10). Fisher sought to challenge this proliferation by attempting to revive the lost potential of a time marked by the widespread emergence of neoliberalism.

It must be acknowledged that Fisher explicitly states that electronic music has "failed" (2012, p. 16). It has failed because, rather than generating the new and discovering the unknown, electronic music, which has possessed a futuristic nature for a considerable amount of time and ranges from 'high culture' composers to popular music groups, has fallen into a retrospective impasse and constantly re-invented the wheel. This tendency has been explained by being based on a broad political background, as previously mentioned. In other words, the fact that nothing but the sound of the past can be produced and, furthermore, the sounds of the past are served up anew in a period when the sounds of the past are the only ones that can be produced is one of the side effects of the transition to a neoliberal world from the hauntological perspective. When the relationship between Fisher's thought-provoking discussions and electronic music is considered, it is seen that this relationship provides an eccentric perspective for approaching the idea of 'noise in music production'. This perspective can also be adopted for dub techno. While discussing the production foundations of dub techno, Oswald contemplates the idea that noise has become an undesirable element since technological advancements have enabled the creation of 'crystal-clear' sounds (Red Bull Music Academy, 2018). According to him, noise is a form of auditory information produced by the hardware used in the production of the early dub techno examples-as analog equipment can generate noise. Oswald implies that noise does not necessarily have to be disturbing, that music should not be stripped of noise, and that in some cases, noise can serve as a valuable narrative element in the dub techno structure, enabling the genre to manifest a unique narration style (Red Bull Music Academy, 2018). Therefore, noise is considered a characteristic layer within a dub techno composition for Oswald. In other words, Oswald's "if the vibe's right[...]let's go for it" (Schmidt, 2008) attitude, which rejects the idea of disregarding noise, has established noise as a complementary element of the dub techno sound for producers who follow this attitude. The presence of a stylistic noise layer can be observed in numerous tracks produced in the paradigm of dub techno sound (see Chart 7.1). The frequent use of noise as a compositional element in dub techno is worth noting.

Chart 7.1 : List of 50 different dub techno tracks with identified noise[76]

	Producer	Track Title	Release	Noise Type
1	Susumu Yokota	Kinoko	1994	Forest
2	burger/ink	Elvism	1996	Static
3	Alex Cortex	Nachtariff - Original	1996	Vinyl Crackle
4	Pole	Rondell Eins	1998	Static
5	Maurizio	Mo4.5a	1997	Static
6	Pole	Stadt	1999	Vinyl Crackle
7	Fluxion	Largo	1999	Vinyl Crackle
8	Rhythm & Sound	Carrier	2001	Static
9	Jan Jelinek	Rock In the Video Age	2001	Vinyl Crackle
10	Rod Modell	Kingston	2003	Static
11	Biosphere	Fall In Fall Out	2006	Vinyl Crackle
12	STL	Loop 006	2007	Static
13	Quantec	Deliberate	2008	Static
14	Pulshar	Nospheratu	2008	Vinyl Crackle
15	Intrusion	Montego Bay	2009	Static
16	Dainel Stefanik	Reactivity 8	2009	Indoor
17	Intrusion	Intrusion Dub	2009	Static
18	Leo Cavallo	Null 01	2010	Vinyl Crackle
19	Gunnar Jonsson	Morgonanga	2010	Static
20	Marko Furstenberg	Site 312	2010	Static
21	Dublicator	Elasticity	2011	Static
22	Djorvin Clain	Fragile Care	2010	Static
23	Shinsuke Matsumoto	Iantern	2011	Rain
24	Martin Schulte	Urban Wind	2011	Vinyl Crackle
25	Dublicator	Compact Impulse	2011	Static
26	Yagya	The Salt On Her Cheeks	2012	Rain
27	Sensual Physics	Dust Mite No.56 - Original	2012	Vinyl Crackle
28	Tomas Rubeck	Factions	2012	Static

---

[76] The criteria for selecting the 50 tracks were that they either carry the 'dub techno' label or a closely related one in the Discogs database (to access the relevant section in the database, see https://www.discogs.com/search/?q=dub+techno&type=all&style_exact=Dub+Techno, retrieved January 6, 2023) or that they heavily incorporate stylistic elements of the related genre. No other criteria were taken into consideration. The tracks were subjected to spectrum analysis. The list could potentially be expanded by adding more examples. It is believed that these 50 tracks will demonstrate how noise is commonly utilized in the structure of dub techno. The tracks in the list are arranged chronologically, with those produced between 1994 and 2022. In these 50 tracks, three types of noise were identified: static, vinyl crackle, and found sound. Each type was marked using three shades of gray.

29	Terekke	Amaze	2013	Static
30	Dub Taylor	Urban Silence III	2013	Static
31	Stephen Hitchell	For Convextion	2014	Static
32	Aris Kindt	Embers	2015	Vinyl Crackle
33	Yagya	The Great Attractor	2016	Static
34	Federsen	Oz	2016	Vinyl Crackle
35	Jon Fay	1271	2016	Static
36	Ben Bitendijk	Near Mint	2016	Vinyl Crackle
37	Upwellings	Slow Lane	2017	Static
38	Sebastian Mullaert	Wings of Remembrance	2017	Static
39	Deepchord	Point Reyes	2017	Static
40	Patricia	Shiba Inu Dub	2017	Static
41	Shinichi Atobe	First Plate 3	2017	Vinyl Crackle
42	Christopher Rau	Virologen	2018	Static
43	Vakula	New Sensations	2018	Static
44	Roman Poncet	Gypsophila	2018	Static
45	Yagya	Mountain Story	2020	Rain
46	Babe Roots	Over Babylon	2020	Vinyl Crackle
47	Forest Drive West	Creation Dub	2020	Static
48	Heavenchord	Lunar Dub	2020	Static
49	Mohlao	Cut	2021	Static
50	Milian Mori	I Listen 1	2022	Static

At this point, the presence of noise can be associated with a fascination with analog technology[77] in electronic music production. However, on a smaller scale, the fact that noise serves as a stylistic element in the dub techno sound and is utilized may not have such a simple explanation as simply a fascination with analog technology. Nonetheless, as mentioned previously, according to Oswald, the reason for the initial noisy examples of dub techno was, as previously mentioned, due to the use of analog hardware. This situation sets the foundation for Fisher's concept of hauntology in the music industry. In fact, the trend of fascination with analog technology in music production in recent years can be considered in the framework of hauntology "as we contrast the imperfections of earlier recording techniques with the timeless anonymity of the digital" (Coverley, 2021, p. 12). Fisher believed that the desire to imitate the sound of the era when analog equipment was used reached its peak with the emergence of internet technology. The recording of the past, the creation of an ever-growing archive of the recorded past, and the effortless access to this archive brought hauntology back to the forefront. According to Coverley (2021), Fisher depicted an "atemporal" current time that portrays the past not as lost or forgotten, but as "technological uncanny" (p. 12).

---

[77] In the section discussing dub music, it was mentioned that the fascination with analog technology has created a wave in the field of music production. It was also emphasized that the emulation of echo equipment used in the analog era is preferred by many producers because it creates an analog feeling and the desire to capture the 'flawed' output of devices used in the past is prevalent in the contemporary music production.

"It was in cyberspace that the ever-growing archive of the recorded past first became instantaneously accessible, releasing a seemingly endless deluge of recorded time from which it seemed no aspect of the past, however trivial, was able to escape. According to Fisher, it was directly as a result of this technological revolution in the early years of the twenty-first century that hauntology re-emerged, as a cultural and political response to the atemporality of a present in which the past no longer dies."

The proliferation of nostalgia in many art forms has caused the meaning of the concept itself to be lost. It could be said that the retro trend revives the ghosts of the past, that these ghosts create post-nostalgia and shape the world in a way that imprisons the present in the past.

When approaching dub techno from a hauntological perspective, one of the first fruits might be skepticism toward the existence and stylistic significance of noise. In the context of dub techno sound, noise can be considered in three different types: static, vinyl crackle, and soundscape[78]. Static noise can be thought of as auditory information created by the flow of electricity within the hardware. The presence of static noise in the structures of tracks produced even in 2022, when hardware noise has almost disappeared, suggests that noise was intentionally shaped by producers as a stylistic element of the tracks. Similarly, vinyl crackle noises, which are created by the needle rubbing against the record, may also be considered a decisive aspect of the dub techno structure, despite being considered undesirable sounds at one time. Additionally, it is clear that various soundscapes recorded in urban, indoor, rural, and natural environments also have a certain 'drone' sound quality in some dub techno tracks. When considering these three different types of noise, it becomes apparent that the relationship between dub techno and noise is clear and multifaceted.

Sampling practices in electronic music, on the other hand, perhaps attract more attention than the intentional use of noise[79]. Sampling practices in dub techno tend to create examples that perpetuate the *Clicks & Cuts*[80] sound.

---

[78] In this study, the concept of soundscape has been understood as a type of noise, rather than using the multiple definitions it has acquired since R. Murray Schafer's work. In this context, the concept of noise is considered as an unprocessed sound that obscures the main information, interferes with it, and makes it difficult to understand. The issue is the use of noise, which normally damages the clarity of the information and the smoothness of the transmission process, with a completely embracing intention in a musical structure.

[79] In the section on "sound design in style," the use of sampling practices and their ongoing significance in shaping the meaning and direction of techno music was discussed. It should be noted that sampling practices have played a crucial role in the development of techno music and have closely influenced the ideas that have given rise to its sub-genres.

[80] The Clicks & Cuts series was a seminal collection of electronic music compilations released by Mille Plateaux label in the late 1990s and early 2000s. Characterized by the use

However, if we consider electronic music genres that are entirely sample-based, such as vaporwave, which have a political manifestation quality, outside the framework of dub techno, then we would be dealing with a better example that fits into the context of hauntology in terms of sampling practices. Therefore, dub techno has not been subject to discussion in this heading in terms of sampling practices.

In summary, the integration of noise in the sound palette of dub techno creates a sensory recollection of the past. Additionally, the continued use of dub echo and reverb techniques developed by 'creative engineers' in Kingston, Jamaica in the 1960s, largely unchanged in their parametric design, also contributes to the haunting of new dub techno recordings by elements of the past. The replication of the hardware-generated noise present in the early examples of dub techno through sampling and plug-ins also offers a perspective on how the past can linger in the present. From a hauntological perspective, it is possible to feel the post-nostalgic phase signaled by Fisher at this very point. The technological inadequacies of the past are still evident in today's high technology. Of course, discussing the specific reasons that neoliberalism or the post-capitalism atmosphere affects this field falls outside the scope of this study. Nonetheless, within the framework created by Derrida, Fisher's technological uncanny reveals itself. While noise is an attractive aesthetic element for producers in dub techno (see Chart 7.1), the hauntological perspective allows for the consideration that the dub techno 'invention' brought by Oswald and Ernestus has been repeating itself for approximately forty years and that a new artistic creation attitude has not been developed.

When it comes to electronic music, hauntology can be seen as the multifaceted manifestation of various ways in which the past is restructured and repeated, shaping the sound, structure, and even medium of the genre. When considering the dub techno discography, it is clear that the static noise produced by past hardware haunts the present-day form of dub techno.

The Right Room Issue

It is evident that the ambiance in which dub techno music is listened to is considered as a criterion that can alter the listening experience or the manifestation of the music itself. In other words, the spatiality that dub techno music acquires during the arrangement, mixing, and mastering processes, as

---

of 'microsound', a style utilizing short sound samples manipulated through digital audio processing, the series garnered critical acclaim for its innovative approach to electronic music production. The name 'Clicks & Cuts' refers to the editing software and techniques employed in the creation of music. The series has had a lasting impact on the evolution of electronic music.

well as the environment in which a dub techno record is ultimately listened to, is regarded as a strictly determining factor that shapes the spatial perception of the listener and ultimately determines their experience. For example, Oswald emphasizes the crucial importance of playing records in the "right room" or "right environment" by referring to reggae and dubstep parties (Schmidt, 2008). On the other hand, it has been identified that the consumption of music individually through personal technological devices rather than collectively is also a format of experiencing music. Dub Monitor (2022) distinguishes between two experiences, 'headphone listening' and 'dancefloor listening'. While making this distinction, Dub Monitor (2022) describes Basic Channel's 1994 album *Quadrant Dub I* as an album that can be listened to with headphones. For him, the album is appropriate for headphone listening "maybe at your desk or while lounging or going for kind of a calm slow walk" (Dub Monitor, 2022). Spruill puts emphasis on the above-mentioned distinction made by another critic in different words. From his point of view, there are two different experiences: 'active listening' and 'passive listening' (2022):

> "Although indeed techno, this variant is not exactly music meant for dancing. You would be hard-pressed to find a warehouse party going hard until sunrise blasting these soothing sounds. Rather, dub techno is music meant for the car ride home after the party; satisfying for both active and passive listening."

Oswald also appears to make a similar distinction, as there is a significant difference in terms of the story and attraction created by two experiences of listening to the same recording with headphones or personal sound systems and listening to the same recording in the 'right room', perhaps with a different and larger system (Red Bull Music Academy, 2018). On the other hand, the functional aspects of techno music on the dancefloor were discussed in the previous sections. These discussions carried clues to understand how the aesthetics adopted in the production process of techno music were affected by consumption on the dancefloor. Similarly, it can be argued that dub music has an aesthetic, social, and cultural characteristic that is shaped by the technological equipment, social and psychological conditioning, and environmental arrangements used in sound-system events where it is listened to.

The responses gathered from the 19 anonymous participants, consisting of electronic music producers, performers, and listeners, shed light on the nuanced differences and similarities between listening to EDM in a nightclub versus with headphones. The participants' insights reveal multifaceted perspectives on how the listening experience differs based on the listening environment, sound system, physical sensations, and social aspects.

One recurring theme in the responses is the immersive and physical nature of the nightclub experience. Several participants noted that the volume, vibrations, and bass frequencies in a nightclub create a unique atmosphere that cannot be replicated with headphones. As one participant aptly stated, *"When listening to music at a loud volume, the low frequencies (bass) physically cause objects and even people in the room to feel the vibrations. This makes it a very physical experience. This effect does not happen in headphones"* (Appendix A.1). The club environment, including lighting shows, acoustics, and the social aspect of experiencing music with others, was also highlighted as significant in shaping the overall impact of the music. This is reflected in the comment of one participant who stated, *"Nightclubs are a social activity where experiencing music with others is an essential part of the atmosphere, and individual listening experiences may not be as enjoyable"* (Appendix A.1).

On the other hand, listening to EDM with headphones was noted to offer a more introspective and focused listening experience. Participants highlighted that headphones provide better stereo perspective and allow for adjustments in sound and bass preferences, resulting in a more personalized experience. As one participant mentioned, *"In headphones, I can adjust the sound and bass according to my preference"* (Appendix A.1). The absence of external factors such as room acoustics interfering with the audio reproduction was also pointed out by some participants, who highlighted that headphones offer a more controlled listening environment.

Furthermore, the responses reflected the impact of the sound system in the nightclub setting. Club sound systems are often designed to prioritize sub and bass-heavy sounds for danceability, creating a visceral and energetic experience. As one participant noted, *"I enjoy listening to techno in a nightclub more because the vibrations from the sound system create a unique dancing experience and allow for better immersion in the music"* (Appendix 1). In contrast, headphones provide a more detailed stereo perspective, allowing listeners to appreciate the nuances of music production.

In conclusion, the following key ideas can be extracted from the responses of 19 anonymous participants on the nuanced differences and similarities between listening to Electronic Dance Music (EDM) in a nightclub versus with headphones.

Participants noted that the nightclub experience is immersive and physical, with unique atmospheric elements such as volume, vibrations, and bass frequencies that cannot be replicated with headphones.

- The club environment, including lighting shows, acoustics, and social aspects, was highlighted as significant in shaping the overall impact of the music in a nightclub setting.

- On the other hand, listening to EDM with headphones was noted to offer a more introspective and focused listening experience, with better stereo perspective and personalized sound and bass preferences.
- Headphones provide a more controlled listening environment, free from external factors such as room acoustics.
- The impact of the sound system in a nightclub setting, prioritizing sub and bass-heavy sounds for danceability, was also mentioned
- Overall, participants appreciated the visceral and energetic experience of nightclub listening, while also valuing the detailed stereo perspective and nuances of music production with headphones.

In summary, techno and dub, as inclusive super-genres, have been consumed communally in open or closed spaces created for playing music, with powerful systems, and this practice continues today. Therefore, it can easily be argued that the aesthetic paradigm adopted in the production stages of both music genres is created with the precedent of playing on the dancefloor. Due to the reasons mentioned and emphasized throughout the study, assuming the dancefloor as the 'default' consumption space for techno or dub music, dub techno seems to have aspects that disrupt this old precedent.

Considering the discussions made above, the right room issue in dub techno music refers to the specific acoustic and spatial qualities of an environment in which the music is intended to be experienced. The right room issue highlights the significance of the listening environment in shaping the listener's experience and perception of the music. Dub techno music is known for its spatial qualities, which are achieved through a combination of production techniques such as reverb, echo, and spatial panning (Spruill, 2022). The spatial characteristics of the music are intended to create a sense of immersion and depth, which can be enhanced or compromised by the listening environment.

From a philosophical perspective, the right room issue raises questions about the relationship between the listener, the music, and the environment. The right room issue suggests that the listening experience is not solely determined by the music itself but also by the context in which it is heard. This raises questions about the nature of musical meaning and the role of the listener in creating and interpreting that meaning. It also highlights the interdependence of music and the environment and the potential for environmental factors to shape and influence musical experiences. It is currently widely accepted that the environment in which music is experienced can significantly influence its perception (Yost, 2015, p. 46). However, when considering the impact of headphones on this relationship, the issue becomes more complex, requiring the establishment of new boundaries. Headphones, for instance, allow access to virtual spaces created in binaural or stereo mixes, effectively marking a transition from real to virtual environments. This transition has evident effects on various aspects of music, such as experience, aesthetics, and perception, highlighting the relevance of the right room issue to psychoacoustics. Without specifically referring to binaural or stereo mixes, it is possible to assert that headphones represent a shift from one sonic space to another. In exploring the aesthetics of dub techno, several authors have proposed ideas related to dub techno's association with headphones and which listening environment is most appropriate (Spruill, 2022) (Dub Monitor, 2022) (Schmidt, 2008).

The circumstances mentioned above possess certain characteristics that provide indications of the spatiality involved in the experience and portrayal of the aesthetic features of dub techno. Furthermore, this issue concerning dub techno's suitability for a particular medium has triggered a hypothesis that emerged from the concept of orphic experience discussed in this thesis. The right room issue in dub techno music is a complex and multifaceted phenomenon that reflects the interplay between music, the listener, and the environment. It is a topic that touches on musicology, psychoacoustics, and philosophy, and highlights the significance of the listening environment in shaping the perception and 'meaning' of music. So, in the following section of the study, the phenomenon of the right room issue in the context of dub techno is examined through a systematic analysis of six distinct musical compositions. These compositions are then subjected to auditory evaluation by a sample of 41 participants, comprising electronic music producers, performers, and listeners. The participants are tasked with discerning the appropriateness of the analyzed tracks for either headphone listening or dancefloor settings, with the option to abstain from responding. Through this rigorous evaluation, the intricate interplay between individual and collective listening practices and their connection to sonic aesthetics is illuminated from a multifaceted perspective. Notably, the tracks chosen for analysis, namely *Aerial* by Rhythm & Sound, *Phylyps Trak* by Basic Channel, *The Salt On Her Cheeks* by Yagya, *Listing, Sinking* by Overcast Sound, and *Resonance* by Substance and Vainqueur, along with *B4* by Topdown Dialectic, are carefully selected as exemplars for this examination. Furthermore, participants are probed to explicate the specific criteria they employ in assessing the suitability of a track for a given medium. The criteria used by the anonymous participants, consisting of electronic music producers, performers, and listeners, in making their decisions about whether a track is suitable for listening with headphones or on the dancefloor can be categorized into several key themes. These themes include the physical and sensory experience of the music, the context in which the music is being listened to, the rhythm and energy of the track, the technical aspects of the music, and the personal impression and emotional response evoked by the music.

1. Physical and Sensory Experience:

Many participants mentioned the physical and sensory aspects of listening to music in a nightclub, such as feeling the kicks and bass in their bodies or experiencing the music at high volume with a powerful sound system. They described how the physicality of the music, including the rhythm, energy, and stereo movement, influenced their decision. For example, one participant stated, "For me, listening to tracks with high volume in a nightclub, feeling the kicks hitting my body and the bass area, is always more enjoyable than listening with headphones" (Appendix A.1).

2. Context:

The context in which the music is being listened to was also an important consideration for many participants. They mentioned the nightclub atmosphere, with its enclosed environment, social interaction, and dancing, as a key factor in their decision-making process. Some participants mentioned that they considered whether a track would work well as an intro, outro, or break during a DJ set. They also mentioned the importance of the acoustics and technical equipment of the venue in their decision. One participant stated, "I believe that every song deserves to be listened to in venues with good acoustics and technical equipment" (Appendix A.1).

3. Rhythm and Energy:

The rhythm and energy of the music were significant criteria for many participants. They mentioned the presence of a steady rhythm, prominent kick drums, and the overall energy level of the track as factors influencing their decision. Some participants stated that they preferred tracks with a more danceable rhythm for listening in a nightclub, while others mentioned that they chose tracks with calmer or more ambient sounds for headphone listening or moments when they need to focus.

4. Technical Aspects:

Some participants mentioned technical aspects of the music, such as the use of BPM, melody, and drums, as criteria for their decision. They considered the complexity and depth of the tracks, as well as the stereo movement and three-dimensional thinking in the music. They mentioned that headphones may be preferred for tracks with intricate details that require more focused listening.

5. Personal Impression and Emotional Response:

The personal impression and emotional response evoked by the music were also important criteria for many participants. They mentioned that they made their decision based on how the tracks made them feel, and how the music created an impression or atmosphere for them. Some participants mentioned that their decision was influenced by their own aesthetic codes, habits, and experience as performers or DJs.

Overall, the criteria used by the anonymous participants in making their decisions about whether a track is suitable for listening with headphones or on the dancefloor are multifaceted and include physical and sensory experience, context, rhythm and energy, technical aspects, and personal impression and emotional response. These criteria highlight the subjective nature of music appreciation and the importance of individual preferences, context, and sensory perception in determining the suitability of music for different listening environments.

During the analysis process, sections of each track were highlighted, taking into consideration linear occurrences. Occurrences that were deemed significant in terms of altering the structure and sound, such as the addition or removal of elements, usage of LPF and HPF, amplitude changes, and harmonic modifications, were treated as the end of one section and the beginning of a new section. Mono spectrum images were generated for each track, and sections were marked on these images. This allowed for discussions on the reasons behind noticeable changes in the spectrum images, providing direct insights into the perceptual aspects of the track's sonic palette. Additionally, structure diagrams were created for each track, with short sentences describing the characteristics of each section. Furthermore, notations were made for distinct layers such as main melodic and harmonic sequences, bass riffs, and drum patterns, and sequencer images were generated. The use of notation in the analysis process revealed the nature of sound design for each track, as seemingly simple elements on paper revealed their complexity when listened to, highlighting the unique aspects and importance of sound processing and sound designing in dub techno. The notation and sequencer images were also helpful in discussing specific elements and their relationships with each other in order to understand the overall composition.

At the end of these processes, the participants' evaluations for each track were summarized in a chart and discussed briefly in text form.

Rhythm & Sound's *Aerial*

Rhythm & Sound's *Aerial* is a seminal piece in the history of dub techno, a genre that emerged in Berlin during the early 1990s by blending the dub production techniques of Jamaican sound system culture with the rhythms and textures of techno music. Aerial[81] represents a quintessential example of the genre's signature sound, characterized by a deep, driving bassline, shimmering percussion, and enveloping layers of reverb and echo. The track's minimalist, hypnotic groove is fashioned through a sparse arrangement of dub chords and stabs, punctuated by sporadic bursts of static and noise.

Aerial is a good example that deserves to be examined closely in this section, with its sound design and harmonic progression influenced by dub music production techniques that manifest simplicity and reduction Its relentlessness is reflected in a stable tempo and sound palette that hangs without sudden drops or rises. The primary focus in analyzing this track is to reveal how Moritz von Oswald and Mark Ernestus adapted the inspiration of dub music to the realm of techno music by following several pioneering principles. In light of the characteristics revealed in the analysis, the data obtained from the question posed to the participants during the survey, 'In which medium is this track suitable to experience?', has also been evaluated and briefly interpreted.

Aerial

The piece's structure has been identified as having 8 sections as its core blocks (Image 7.1) (Chart 7.2).

---

[81] In this section, the B track of the *Aground/Aerial* album, which consists of two pieces released in 2002 and produced by Moritz von Oswald and Mark Ernestus, has been subjected to track analysis. For further information, see https://www.discogs.com/release/55405-Rhythm-Sound-Aground-Aerial.

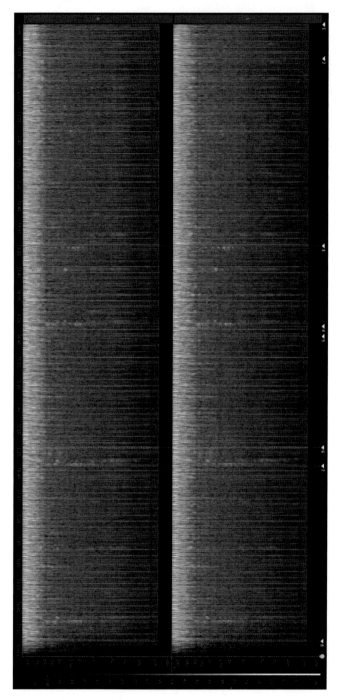

Image 7.1 : Spectrum image of 8 core blocks of *Aerial*

Section	1	2	3	4	5	6	7	8
Time	00:00	00:31	03:20	04:12	04:41	06:21	06:40	09:15
Occurence	The piece starts with noise and drum pattern, with dub stabs softened by low-pass filter and reverb. Vocal melody serves as 'glue' between bars and adds dynamism to the steady pulse.	Vocal melodies gain a progressively richer and more expressive character. Vocals serve as the most dynamic element in supporting the transition between bars.	A vocal melody of high amplitude is accompanied by pronounced echo feedback applied to the drum pattern and vocals.	The most distinct application of echo articulation is heard in this section, exemplifying dub qualities.	Ethnic percussion instruments support the drum pattern with a syncopated rhythm, subjected to wet reverb effect for a large space perception.	Ethnic percussion instrument's decay of reverb and an increase in the feedback knob of the echo effect give it a highly characteristic quality.	Small changes in echo feedback and reverb decay were applied to the stabs, with similar processes dominant in the percussion	The track fades out.

Chart 7.2 : The structure scheme of Aerial

Section 1 - The piece starts with a distinct layer of noise, accompanied by a drum pattern (Figures 7.3 and 7.4) brought into the dub context with the help of spring reverb.

Figure 7.3 : The notation of the main drum pattern of *Aerial*[82]

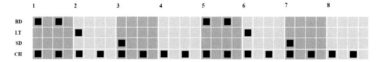

Figure 7.4 : The main drum pattern of *Aerial* on the sequencer

The dub stabs (Figures 7.5 and 7.6) heard on the off-beats are softened with a low-pass filter and reverberated in a wet manner, using a relatively high pre-delay ratio.

Figure 7.5 : The notation of the harmonic sequence of the stab track of *Aerial*

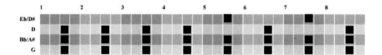

Figure 7.6 : Folded view of the harmonic sequence of the stab track of *Aerial* on the sequencer (G4-D#5)

This section can be considered as an introduction. On the other hand, not many changes, apart from various echo and reverb articulations and changing vocal melodies throughout the track. The vocal melody functions like 'glue' that connects the bars. It is clear that the vocals add dynamism to the track and give an alteration feeling to the stagnation of the steady pulse. Section 2 - can be considered as a continuation of the first section[83]. However, in this section, the vocal melodies gain a progressively richer and more expressive character in some parts. It would not be wrong to argue that the most dynamic element in this

---

[82] This line, due to its accentuation, reverberant structure, and texture, embodies dub characteristics. For further information, see the section discussing dub percussion in the fifth heading.

[83] So, this section is not highlighted because a sharp change has been detected.

track is the vocals that support the transition between bars. The first section carries an exposition. In this section, it can be hypothetically suggested that the listener has already become accustomed to the track's mood. Section 3 - begins with a vocal melody of high amplitude, as can be seen in the spectrum (see Image 7.1). What makes this section noteworthy is the application of echo feedback articulation to the drum pattern, perhaps for the first time in a pronounced manner. Especially between 3:20 and 3:40, it is evident that the techniques presented in the relevant section of this study on the utilization of the echo feedback knob in dub music are applied to both the vocals and the drum pattern. Section 4 - It is noteworthy that the most distinct application of echo articulation in stabs is heard for the first time in this brief section, clearly exemplifying dub qualities. Section 5 - ethnic percussion instruments start to accompany the drum pattern with a syncopated rhythm that supports the groove. The percussion channel has been subjected to a wet reverb effect, which indicates that a large space has been deemed suitable for the percussion in the mixing stage. Section 6 - the ethnic percussion instrument has a highly characteristic quality due to both the decay of reverb and an increase in the feedback knob of the echo effect, as shown in Figure 7.7.

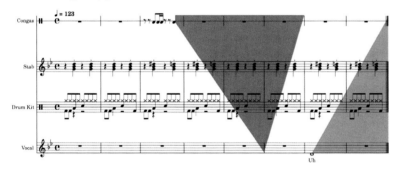

Figure 7.7 : The echo feedback movements in the sixth section

These sudden changes in reverb and echo parameters applied to the percussion elements reveal that all elements in *Aerial* that do not undergo significant changes in amplitude are transformed and altered in their spatial perception through knob movements. Section 7 - is characterized by small changes in echo feedback and reverb decay applied to the stabs. In addition to the variations in spatial effects applied to the percussion, similar processes are dominant in the stabs in this section. The frequency of these changes seems to have progressively increased from the first section to this one. Section 8 - The track fades out.

The main reason why *Aerial* stands out as a characteristic track is its stable and relentless nature. However, when compared to the *Minus* track, which has been analyzed under the reduced sides title of this study, the factor that makes this track dynamic and transforms the sound into a spur-of-the-moment dynamism is nothing but the dominant use of echo and reverb. Additionally, it is possible to indicate the integration of noise very clearly in the track. Also, considering the absence of a distinct bass instrument in the track, it should be noted that the low frequencies are emphasized through kick and tom. The most important aspect of this track is that it is a good example of the active use of dub production and performance techniques, which were examined under the fifth title of the research. While adhering to the traditional dub arrangement style, it seems more appropriate to label *Aerial* as 'reduced dub' or 'minimal dub', considering both its sound and sonic palette. On the other hand, it is possible to think of this track as a gateway to the dub techno examples that Oswald and Ernestus began to provide.

Aerial was presented to 41 different participants including electronic music producers, electronic music performers, and electronic music listeners to test its dominance in communal and individual listening. The participants were asked to indicate whether they found the track closer to headphone listening or dancefloor medium. Additionally, the participants were given the option to leave the question unanswered and to consider both mediums appropriate. The results revealed that a vast majority of participants (n = 32; 78%) believed that *Aerial* was more suitable for listening on headphones, while a minority of participants (n = 9; 22%) believed that the track was better suited for the dancefloor (see Chart 7.3).

Chart 7.3 : The preferences made by 41 participants for *Aerial*

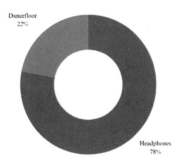

This suggests that the characteristics of the track, such as its simplicity, harmonic structure, and relentlessness, may make it more conducive to private listening and personal reflection than to communal dancing and socializing[84].

---

[84] It is important to restate, however, that these findings are based on a relatively small sample of participants and may not generalize to larger populations or other contexts. Further research is needed to replicate these findings and to explore the subjective

Basic Channel's *Phylyps Trak*

Phylyps Trak by Basic Channel is another seminal track in the history of dub techno. Released in 1993[85] on the Basic Channel label, *Phylyps Trak* is a minimalist and hypnotic composition that features a steady 4/4 beat, a deep bassline, and sparse but intricate layers of atmospheric sound. One of the distinctive characteristics of *Phylyps Trak* is its use of space and texture to create a sense of depth and movement. The track's soundscape is built on the interplay of reverberation and echo effects, which give the sounds a sense of spatial expansion and contraction. The result is a sonic environment that seems to envelop the listener and evoke a feeling of immersion.

The previous track, *Aerial* shares some similarities with *Phylyps Trak* in terms of its use of dub sound processing techniques and its emphasis on space and texture. However, *Aerial* also incorporates elements of dub reggae, with its prominent use of dub sirens and echoes, and features a more pronounced bassline than *Phylyps Trak*. The aesthetic elements of *Phylyps Trak* are deemed to provide a favorable opportunity to comprehend how spatial effects unique to dub music are harnessed within the boundaries of techno music, given its closer proximity to the techno music paradigm. The primary focus in analyzing this track is to reveal how Moritz von Oswald and Mark Ernestus adapted the inspiration of dub music to the realm of techno music by following several pioneering principles. In light of the characteristics revealed in the analysis, the data obtained from the question posed to the participants during the survey, 'In which medium is this track suitable to experience?', has also been evaluated and briefly interpreted.

Phylyps Trak

The piece's structure has been identified as having 8 sections as its core blocks (Image 7.2) (Chart 7.4).

---

experiences and preferences of individuals who listen to electronic music in different contexts.

[85] In this section, the A track of the *Phylyps Trak* album, which consists of three pieces released in 1993 and produced by Moritz von Oswald and Mark Ernestus, has been subjected to track analysis. For further information, see https://www.discogs.com/release/2163-Basic-Channel-Phylyps-Trak.

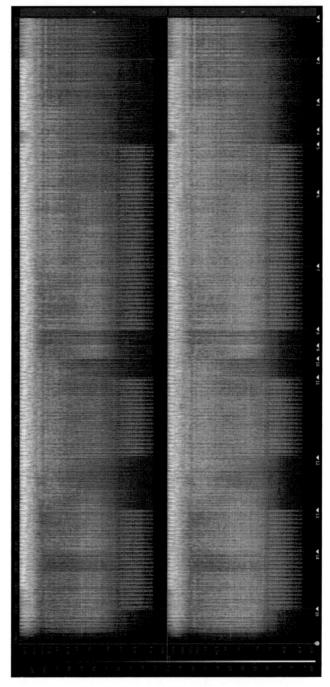

Image 7.2 : Spectrum image of 15 core blocks of *Phylyps Trak*

Section	1	2	3	4	5	6	7
Time	00:00	00:38	01:20	01:47	02:01	02:47	03:58
Occurence	The piece begins with a Gm/B stab and 1/16 echo, creating the primary spatial perception and a significant groove element.	The four-on-the-floor kick drum serves as the foundation and essential anchor for the techno-style rhythm of the piece.	Second stabs fill in the gaps of the first stabs' harmonic sequence, creating a progressive increase in traffic.	A brief break before the first climax, achieved by muting the kick drum, creates a suspenseful effect.	The drum pattern in Figures 7.11 and 7.12, along with the stabs, creates the formula for the climax and a hypnotic sensation due to the dominant echo effect.	Another stab layer marks the progression and ultimate climax of the piece, as delicately balanced elements, become audible.	The arrangement is relaxed by muting the first stabs to emphasize the dynamic range and rises and falls.

Section	8	9	10	11	12	13	14	15
Time	05:00	05:17	05:26	05:42	06:57	07:50	08:30	09:24
Occurence	The reduction continues, leaving only the kick drum and highest-pitched stab layers, creating a lull after the climax.	A new stab layer signals the approach of a new climax.	The arrangement returns to its original form with only the kick, clap, and first stab layer.	The previous climax is recreated using the same elements.	A sudden drop in intensity is created by muting all elements except for the kick and stab layers, followed by a new rise.	Hi-hats return but with reductions, indicating the piece is coming to an end.	Stab layers and kick drum are muted, preparing for the outro.	The piece ends with a fade-out lasting approximately 32 seconds.

Chart 7.4 : The structure scheme of *Phylyps Trak*

Section 1 - The piece commences with Gm/B stabs (Figures 7.8 and 7.9) that have a relatively high feedback ratio, processed by a 1/16 echo.

Figure 7.8 : The notation of the harmonic sequence of the first stabs of *Phylyps Trak*[86]

Figure 7.9 : Folded view of the harmonic sequence of the first stabs of *Phylyps Trak* on the sequencer (Bb2-G3)

This passage serves as an introduction, exposing the rhythmic structure that forms the bedrock of the entire arrangement to be heard later. The sound heard in this section is clearly the result of passing through various linear and non-linear processors, such as phasers, distortions, and similar texture-creating tools. The echo effect is applied in a way that triggers the groove between stabs, taking advantage of the high feedback amount in the gaps.

Considering the echo practices in dub music discussed in the fifth section, it is apparent that the spatial perception of the piece is primarily created by the echo. This constitutes one of the most vital applications that reveal the dub effect. It is undeniable that if the echo were not applied in this line, the piece would lose a significant groove element. To illustrate this point, a comparison is made between the sound of the harmonic sequence in Figure 7.8 with and without the echo effect applied in the piece.

Section 2 - The four-on-the-floor kick drums are heard, representing the initial manifestation of the groove that has taken shape around the kick drum axis in the piece. The 'rumble' heard in association with the kick drum is just one

---

[86] Whilst transcribing the stab tracks within the composition, the attainment of an exact correspondence with the original piece was not deemed to be the principal objective. The primary purpose of noting down the first and second stab lines was to highlight the manner in which harmonic sequences, endowed with specific rhythmic information, undergo metamorphosis as a result of the echo effect. Moreover, the intention was to underscore the significance of sound processing techniques in achieving the ultimate sensory perception during the production phase of dub techno.

of the conventional techno characteristics that the piece embodies. Furthermore, the fact that all the dynamics are shaped around the kick drum, or in other words, the kick drum's shaping effect gives rise to a particular rhythmic pattern, can be considered an essential element in most techno tracks. This kick drum-centric approach is crucial for the piece's overall sound and serves as a significant anchor for the rhythm. Section 3 - The second stabs (Figure 7.10) can be perceived as an additional layer that serves to bolster the first stab, possessing a quality of support that is almost equal to that of the initial layer, which has undergone a similar echo process. Consequently, the gaps present in the harmonic sequence of the first stabs are filled by G minor inversions, while the traffic of the piece steadily grows more intense in a progressive fashion.

Figure 7.10 : The notation of the harmonic sequence of the second stabs of *Phylyps Trak*

Section 4 - Prior to the first climax, a brief break is implemented by muting the kick drum, which can be considered an effective practice of placing the listener in a state of anticipation, as it creates a suspenseful effect. Section 5 - The audible presence of the drum pattern shown in Figures 7.11 and 7.12 causes the higher frequencies of the hi-hats and claps to fill in (see Image 7.2), thereby creating the formula for the climax of the track.

Figure 7.11 : The notation of the main drum pattern of *Phylyps Trak*

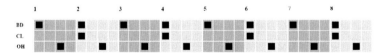

Figure 7.12 : The main drumline of *Phylyps Trak* on the sequencer

In this section, the harmonic sequence of the first and second stabs, along with the drum pattern, can be heard prominently. Notably, the dominant echo effect heard in this section has a structure that allows the elements to blend together, dissolve, and form a kind of 'harmonized layer'. One of the reasons behind the hypnotic sensation of the piece is that the echo effect alters the harmonic context in a progressive manner through the interactive intermingling of all the layers. Section 6 - Another stab layer is added to the arrangement. This section is marked to draw attention to the progression of the piece, and it cannot be considered separately from the previous section. The climax that began in

Section 5 reaches its ultimate form in this section, as all of the various stab layers that have been delicately balanced with echo and other effects become audible. Section 7 - The arrangement is somewhat relaxed by muting the first stabs. This practice illustrates how the high dynamic range and progressive nature expressed through rises and falls are embraced. Section 8 - The reduction that began in the previous section reaches its final form in this part, where only the kick drum and its rumble and the highest-pitched stab layers can be heard. The muted channels in this section serve to bring the arrangement to a lull after the climax and create a sense of alternating intensity. Section 9 - This section is a continuation of the previous one. The only difference is the addition of a stab layer filling the 2.5 - 6 kHz range (see Image 7.2), which seems to signal the approach of a new climax. Section 10 - The arrangement loses the information dominant in high frequencies and returns to its original form with only the kick, clap, and first stab layer left alone. Section 11 - This section is a continuation of the previous one. The climax heard for the first time in sections 5 and 6 is recreated using the same elements without any modifications. Section 12 - By muting all elements except for the kick drum, first and second stab layers, the piece is taken to a sudden drop in intensity. Towards the end of the section, the dominant high frequencies return, giving way to a new rise. Section 13 - Although it may sound like a new climax due to the reappearance of hi-hats, it is clear that there are some reductions indicating that the piece is coming to an end. As seen in Image 7.2, the stab layer that was dominant in the 400 Hz - 1.2 kHz range in the previous section has been lost, giving the piece a sense of reduced intensity due to the weakening in the mid-range. Section 14 - Reductions in the stab layers continue. In addition to the stab layers that are faded out and occasionally suddenly muted, the kick drum is also muted towards the end of the section. The piece is ready for the outro. Section 15 - The piece ends with a fade-out lasting approximately 32 seconds.

Phylyps Trak was presented to 41 different participants including electronic music producers, electronic music performers, and electronic music listeners to test its dominance in communal and individual listening. The participants were asked to indicate whether they found the track closer to headphone listening or dancefloor medium. Additionally, the participants were given the option to leave the question unanswered and to consider both mediums appropriate. The results revealed that a vast majority of participants (n = 35; 85.4%) believed that *Phylyps Trak* was more suitable for listening on the dancefloor, while a minority of participants (n = 6; 14.6%) believed that the track was better suited for headphones (see Chart 7.5).

Chart 7.5 : The preferences made by 41 participants for *Phylyps Trak*

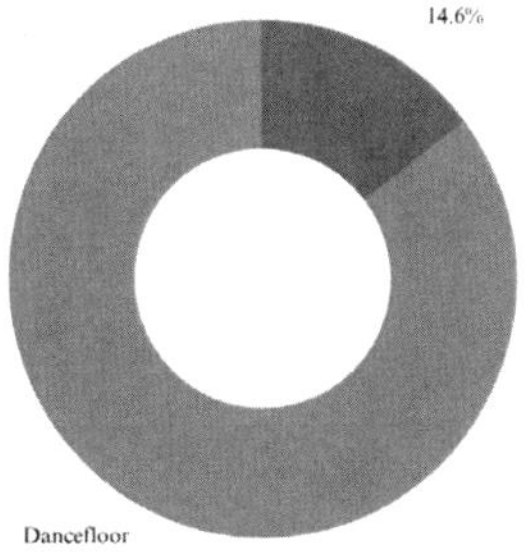

Headphones
14.6%

Dancefloor
85.4%

Phylyps Trak's suitability for being experienced through dancing on the dancefloor by most participants, as opposed to being listened to through headphones, may be attributed to various reasons, which have been discussed under the 'discussions' section of this study. However, it is crucial to consider the techno attributes that the track possesses, including its drum pattern, structural elements functioning on the dancefloor such as breaks and drops, and its affinity with techno aesthetics, as well as its relatively high tempo of 144 BPM. Hence, it would not be entirely erroneous to assume that it is well-suited for the dancefloor. As a dub techno track, *Phylyps Trak* serves as a remarkable example of the amalgamation of techno and dub music aesthetics, achieved through the inspiration drawn from dub music's echo processing practices, while incorporating conventional techno elements[87].

Yagya's *The Salt On Her Cheeks*

Aðalsteinn 'Yagya' Guðmundsson's *The Salt On Her Cheeks*, released in 2012[88], is considered exemplary for several reasons. Firstly, its relatively recent production date highlights the stylistic adaptation of dub music's echo and reverberation techniques to the techno paradigm with an original and distinctive style. Moreover, it demonstrates how dub techno aesthetics can generate specific results in an arrangement that revolves around a particular chord progression

---

[87] It is important to restate, however, that these findings are based on a relatively small sample of participants and may not generalize to larger populations or other contexts. Further research is needed to replicate these findings and to explore the subjective experiences and preferences of individuals who listen to electronic music in different contexts.

[88] In this section, the ninth track of the *The Inescapable Decay of My Heart* album, which consists of ten pieces released in 2012 and produced by Yagya, has been subjected to track analysis. For further information, see https://www.discogs.com/master/461430-Yagya-The-Inescapable-Decay-Of-My-Heart

and carries functional harmony. Secondly, the piece embodies a techno sensibility that carries the signals of the minimal continuum (Nye, 2013, p. 165) and therefore, represents an exemplar of this genre. Lastly, the piece references the ambient aesthetic, providing a multi-faceted listening experience that engages listeners in a variety of ways. The piece's engaging and multifaceted qualities make it a remarkable musical work, highlighting the creative and expressive possibilities of contemporary electronic dance music production.

The spectrum image in Figure 7.3 conveys that the sound design of the track has a dominant nature below 2 kHz, especially in sub-frequencies. Furthermore, the peaks and troughs visible in the same image provide insights into the structure of the piece. What makes the analysis of this piece compelling is the consistent data it provides about the reduced, relentless, unsharp, and unpretentious structure and sound design, as well as its relatively rich harmonic structure, and how these elements relate to the dub techno framework. In light of the characteristics revealed in the analysis, the data obtained from the question posed to the participants during the survey, 'In which medium is this track suitable to experience?', has also been evaluated and briefly interpreted.

The Salt On Her Cheeks

The piece's structure has been identified as having 7 sections as its core blocks (Image 7.3) (Chart 7.6).

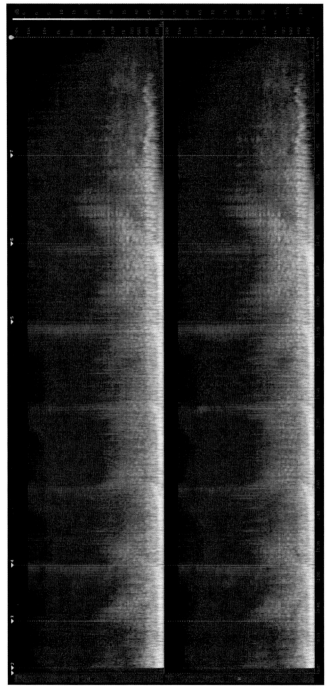

Image 7.3 : Spectrum image of 7 core blocks of *The Salt On Her Cheeks*

Section	1	2	3	4
Time	00:00	00:03	00:35	01:11
Occurrence	The seaside soundscape sets the mood for the piece.	Introduction of kick, shaker, bass, stabs, and pad with LPF effects.	The addition of rimshot sounds and completion of the drum pattern, deepening of the pad with LPF, and use of echo feedback create a wide space and soft dynamic.	Variations in LPF and echo feedback in stabs.

Section	5	6	7
Time	03:49	04:40	05:38
Occurrence	The climax with elements freed from LPF, richer melodic information, and expansion of space, including a sine-like soft key melody as a narrative element.	Relaxation of low frequencies and fading out of bassline, and use of LPF to bring back elements to their starting position.	The key melody changes and all instruments except the key accompany the rising soundscape and disappear, ending with a seaside soundscape.

Chart 7.6 : The structure scheme of *The Salt On Her Cheeks*

Section 1 - This brief section imbues the piece with a spatial mood through a seaside soundscape. While the soundscape may not serve a specific musical function, it is 'symbolic' in the sense that it positions the piece on a particular axis, prepares the listener, and enables the track to create a reflection in the imagination. Section 2 - The section begins with a four-on-the-floor kick, shaker (Figure 7.13), bass (Figures 7.14 and 7.15), stabs (Figures 7.16 and 7.17), and pad (Figure 7.18) with applied echo effects, providing initial ideas about the piece's sound palette in the first few seconds. Considering these aspects, this section can be regarded as an introduction.

Figure 7.13 : The notation of the shaker pattern of *The Salt On Her Cheeks*

Figure 7.14 : The notation of the bass riff of *The Salt On Her Cheeks*

Figure 7.15 : Folded view of the bass riff of the stab track of *The Salt On Her Cheeks* on the sequencer (F2-D3)

Figure 7.16 : The notation of the harmonic sequence of the stabs of *The Salt On Her Cheeks*[89]

Figure 7.17 : Folded view of the harmonic sequence of the stabs The Salt On Her Cheeks on the sequencer (D3-C4)

In this section, elements other than kick and bass are subjected to a low-pass filter, imparting a mellow character to their sound. As the LPF effect is gradually eased, the textures of high-frequency elements, such as the shaker, gradually come into sharper focus, culminating in the next section. It is evident that the

---

[89] The stabs heard on off-beats and the aesthetic paradigm adopted in the sound design of the stab track constitute a significant example of the dub influence.

main harmonic sequence, furnished by the pad, revolves around the Dm/F-Am-G chord progression, as illustrated in Figure 7.18.

Figure 7.18 : The notation of the main harmonic sequence of *The Salt On Her Cheeks*

Section 3 - Rimshot sounds begin to be heard on the third beat of each bar, and the drum pattern is completed (Figures 7.19 and 7.20).

Figure 7.19 : The notation of the main drum pattern of *The Salt On Her Cheeks*

Figure 7.20 : The main drum pattern of *The Salt On Her Cheeks* on the sequencer

In addition, the 'deepening' of the pad with the LPF and the prominent use of echo feedback articulation on the stabs causes the track to be heard in a wide space. The relatively slow and unhurried nature of the peaks and troughs has given the track a soft dynamic. Section 4 - The section showcases variations of LPF usage, both increasing and decreasing in intensity, accompanied by changes in the amount of echo feedback, especially in the stabs (Figure 7.21). Even though no major alterations took place in this section, it still stands out from the preceding ones.

Figure 7.21 : An example representation of the echo feedback movements

While highlighting different sections, the hypothetical perception that the track will create in the listener has been taken into consideration. The second and third sections are particularly effective in introducing the elements in the sound palette and the dynamics of the piece, and all elements are fixed in this section. This section has been approached as a long section that gives the track a kind of 'suspended' or 'anchored to a certain mode' quality. At the points where LPF is applied to pads, the piece attains a kind of 'isolation' feeling, and the space constructed in the mix is shrinking. In this case, the expansion-contraction movement of the space in the piece is a quality that is felt. Section 5 - This section can be considered as a climax where the elements that have been freed from the LPF effect become more distinct, the track becomes richer in terms of melodic information, the groove settles, and the space created in the mix grows thanks to the effects used. The sine-like soft key melody (Figure 7.22) adds a narrative quality to the track as a harmonic context-carrying melody line that complements the pad chords heard from the beginning as a complete fade-in in this section.

Figure 7.22 : The notation of the melodic sequence of *The Salt On Her Cheeks*

It could be readily argued that musical narratives with such 'stretched' or 'extended' repetitions are not very common within the framework of dub techno. Section 6 - As can be seen on the spectrum (see Image 7.3), the amplitude decrease that starts below 400 Hz gives clues that the piece is relaxing for the first time in terms of low frequencies, the bassline is fading out, and the outroduction is approaching. Similarly, as can be seen in the upper frequencies, elements such as shaker, stab, and pad are being brought back to their starting position with the use of LPF. Section 7 - The key melody that has been heard since the fifth section changes. All instruments except for the key gradually accompany the rising soundscape and disappear. At the end of this section, all elements are silenced, and a soundscape related to the seaside soundscape heard in the first section is heard. Thus, the track starts and ends with the soundscape, as if the track has been merged with a seaside memory.

The Salt On Her Cheek was presented to 41 different participants including electronic music producers, electronic music performers, and electronic music listeners to test its dominance in communal and individual listening. The participants were asked to indicate whether they found the track closer to headphone listening or dancefloor medium. Additionally, the participants were given the option to leave the question unanswered and to consider both mediums appropriate. The results revealed that a vast majority of participants (n = 30; 73.2%) believed that *The Salt On Her Cheeks* was more suitable for listening on headphones, while a minority of participants (n = 11; 26.8%) believed that the track was better suited for the dancefloor (see Chart 7.7).

Chart 7.7 : The preferences made by 41 participants for *The Salt On Her Cheeks*

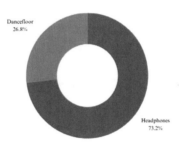

Dancefloor
26.8%

Headphones
73.2%

The track's use of dub techno elements, slow buildups, and stretched-out repetitions create a complex musical narrative that may be better appreciated in a more focused and isolated listening environment. Furthermore, the track's emphasis on atmospheric sounds and textures, as well as its use of space and reverb, may create a more immersive experience when listened to through headphones. Overall, while the track certainly has the potential to be enjoyed in a club setting, its intricate and introspective qualities suggest that it may be better suited for a more personal and introspective listening experience[90].

Overcast Sound's *Listing, Sinking*

With its deep, pulsing bassline, haunting synths, and dub-inspired echo effects, Overcast Sound's *Listing, Sinking*, released in 2016[91], exemplifies the genre's characteristic fusion of techno and dub reggae influences. Beyond its musical qualities, the track also embodies the aesthetic paradigm of dub techno, which emphasizes atmospheric, immersive soundscapes and a focus on the sonic details of each element in the mix. As such, *Listing, Sinking* is not only a standout

---

[90] It is important to restate, however, that these findings are based on a relatively small sample of participants and may not generalize to larger populations or other contexts. Further research is needed to replicate these findings and to explore the subjective experiences and preferences of individuals who listen to electronic music in different contexts.

[91] In this section, the first track of the *Water Lines EP* album, which consists of five pieces released in 2016 and produced by Overcast Sound, has been subjected to track analysis. For further information, see https://www.discogs.com/release/11710703-Overcast-Sound-Water-Lines-EP

example of dub techno music, but also a touchstone for the broader creative ethos of the genre.

Following the analysis of Overcast Sound's *Listing, Sinking*, there are two primary reasons why it is deemed worthy of hypothesis for yielding productive results in the discussion of this thesis. The first reason is attributable to the piece's aesthetic qualities, which are characterized by the absence of complex harmonies and a sound design method that follows the minimal continuum paradigm. Composed of only four elements - drums, pad, stabs, and bass - the piece is imbued with an aesthetic sensibility that is marked by understated simplicity and restraint. The second crucial detail lies in the textural and spatial perception of the piece as an exemplar of dub techno[92]. Considering that this perception largely adapted to the techno realm, inspired by the aesthetics of dub music, despite the small number of elements and harmonic simplicity in the sound palette of *Listing, Sinking*, it is an exceptional analysis subject that elevates immersion to a high level. In light of the characteristics revealed in the analysis, the data obtained from the question posed to the participants during the survey, 'In which medium is this track suitable to experience?', has also been evaluated and briefly interpreted.

Listing, Sinking

The piece's structure has been identified as having 7 sections as its core blocks (Image 7.4) (Chart 7.8).

---

[92] Despite appearing primitive on paper when only considering the notes displayed below, the piece reveals a high level of dexterity in the sound processing and design process, as well as in the mixing stage.

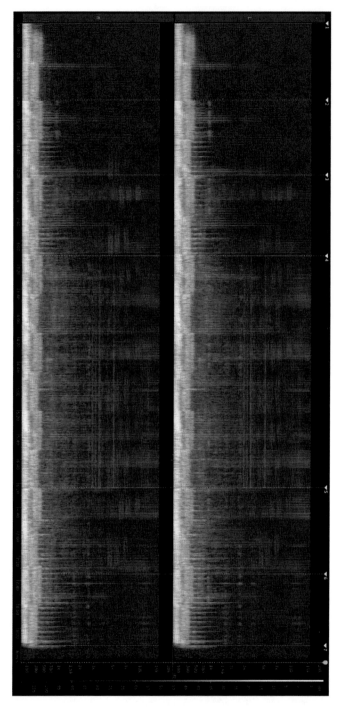

Image 7.4 : Spectrum image of 7 core blocks of *Listing, Sinking*

Section	1	2	3	4	5	6	7
Time	00:00	01:03	02:07	03:12	06:23	07:35	08:33
Occurrence	Introduction of four-on-the-floor kick pattern and pad layers, with pronounced sub-frequencies and echoing reverberation signifying dub effect.	Pad track layered with stab track using echo effect, with specific parameters contributing to the backbone of the piece.	The sound gets balanced and present thanks to hi-hats, echo effect altering perceived rhythm, no new occurrences.	Ride cymbal added, creating balance in the spectrum and contributing to climax, wooden percussive instrument and harmonic stab also present.	Ride cymbal muted, classic dub effects exhibited in stab, signifying decrease.	Gradual reduction and cessation of hi-hats, track sinking and muting high frequencies, kick and bass are still heard predominantly.	The track ends with an echo applied to the stab layer.

Chart 7.8 : The structure scheme of *Listing, Sinking*

Section 1 - The piece commences with the introduction of a four-on-the-floor kick pattern and pad layers, which serves as an initial exposition, providing the listener with preliminary insights into the track's rhythm, sound palette, mode, and the spatial environment created by the mixing process. As can be observed in Image 7.4, the track exhibits a preponderance of sub-400 Hz frequencies, with a marked attenuation above that threshold. The pronounced sub-frequencies perceptible in the kick and bass layers (Figure 7.23), evince a profound, echoing reverberation, signifying the dub effect, which is a salient aspect of this music genre. This feature serves as an indicative cue for the dub influences inherent in this track, which is similarly manifest in many other examples of this sonic style[93].

Figure 7.23 : The notation of the bass riff of *Listing, Sinking*

Section 2 - The pad track (Figure 7.24), featuring a 32-bar harmonic sequence of Bm-F#m, is layered with the stab track (Figure 7.25), which spans the same 32 bars and is articulated with approximately 237 milliseconds of dotted time, 50% feedback, and 70% wet signal amount using the echo effect.

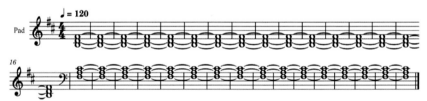

Figure 7.24 : The notation of the harmonic sequence of the pads of *Listing, Sinking*

---

[93] Conversely, it should be emphasized that in the following sections, the gradual intensification of frequencies above 3 kHz not only restores equilibrium in the mix but also reinforces the spatial intricacies of the sound design.

Figure 7.25 : The notation of the stabs of *Listing, Sinking*

Given the pivotal role of the echo effect in shaping the groove of the track, it is worth illustrating the specific parameters of the echo effect applied to the stab layer. As demonstrated in the example below, the chosen echo effect, with a dotted time of approximately 237 milliseconds, 50% feedback, and 70% wet signal amount, articulates the stab layer and contributes to the backbone of the piece.

An Example of the Applied Echo Effect

The realization of how extensively the elements are distributed within the soundscape becomes more apparent in this section, particularly after the stabs become audible. Section 3 - can be considered the section right before the climax. The mix is balanced and audible thanks to the information above 4 kHz provided by the hi-hats. The echo-applied stab and pad layers are shaped around a particular groove axis due to sharp elements such as the kick and hi-hats. The echo effect applied to the stabs audibly alters the perceived rhythm by placing them on a specific click axis. Apart from the hi-hats, which are heard for the first time in the track, there are no new occurrences in this section. Section 4 - the drum pattern is completed with the addition of the ride cymbal (Figures 7.26 and 7.27). As seen in Image 7.4, the ride cymbal creates a clear balance in the spectrum as the section begins. As a result, the track seems to gain a bit more volume and richness.

Figure 7.26 : The notation of the main drum pattern of *Listing, Sinking*

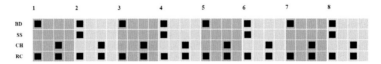

Figure 7.27 : The main drum pattern of *Listing, Sinking* on the sequencer

In this section, the climax of the track can be thought of as reached. The spatial aspect of the piece is 'fixed' or 'completed' in this section. All elements heard reverberate throughout a wide space. Another stab, which contributes to the harmonic context with its tuned structure and alternates between rhythm and dominant frequency, clearly heard between 05:25-05:40, also supports the creation of a climax in this section. The wooden percussive instrument heard more distinctly in the right stereo channel from beginning to end also contributes to the groove created in this section. Section 5 - The ride cymbal is muted, and the drum pattern continues to be heard without it. The echo and reverb characteristics of the stab exhibit classic dub effects (for example, at 06:48). This section signifies a decrease. Section 6 - The fall that began in the previous section continues with the gradual reduction and cessation of the hi-hats in this section. The overall sound of the track begins to 'sink' by gradually muting all elements that fill the high frequencies, brightness, and sharpness one by one. Although the number of audible elements decreases, the kick and bass are still heard predominantly, as seen in Image 7.4. Section 7 - The track ends with the articulation of the echo applied to the stab layer heard once solo.

Listing, Sinking was presented to 41 different participants including electronic music producers, electronic music performers, and electronic music listeners to test its dominance in communal and individual listening. The participants were asked to indicate whether they found the track closer to headphone listening or dancefloor medium. Additionally, the participants were given the option to leave the question unanswered and to consider both mediums appropriate. The results revealed that a vast majority of participants (n = 24; 58.5%) believed that *Listing, Sinking* was more suitable for listening on the dancefloor, while a minority of participants (n = 17; 41.5%) believed that the track was better suited for headphones (see Chart 7.9).

Chart 7.9 : The preferences made by 41 participants for *Listing, Sinking*

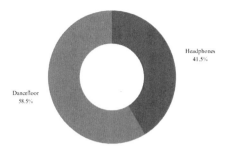

Dancefloor
58.5%

Headphones
41.5%

Listing, Sinking is a good demonstration of how minimal aesthetics influenced by dub music can generate a distinct texture, structure, and sound in electronic dance music. With only two chords heard steadily for 32 bars, a conventional techno drum pattern, a slow progression, a limited number of elements in the sound palette, rolled-off highs, and a 'deep feeling', *Listing, Sinking* shares structural similarities with *The Salt On Her Cheeks*, except for its harmonic structure. This piece, although leaning towards the dancefloor direction in the 'dancefloor vs. headphones' debate, should also be noted to have received a considerable number of headphone-oriented votes from participants. On the other hand, the analysis conducted confirms the hypothesis that the distinctiveness and 'hardness' of the kick drum, the richness of transient, sharp percussive elements, and the relatively high tempo are fundamental values that serve the dancefloor function in techno music. Indeed, while the drum pattern is nearly identical to that of *The Salt On Her Cheeks*, and the slow-burning narrative and minimal sound palette are similarly present, the voting results suggest that the kick drum and tempo are the determining factors[94].

7.3.5 Substance & Vainqueur's *Resonance*

Substance & Vainqueur's *Resonance* can be considered another seminal track in the history of dub techno for several reasons. The track, released in 2007[95],

_____

[94] It is important to restate, however, that these findings are based on a relatively small sample of participants and may not generalize to larger populations or other contexts. Further research is needed to replicate these findings and to explore the subjective experiences and preferences of individuals who listen to electronic music in different contexts.

[95] In this section, the B track of the *Libration/Resonance* album, which consists of two pieces released in 2007 and produced by Substance & Vainqueur, has been subjected to track analysis. For further information, see https://www.discogs.com/master/256093-Substance-Vainqueur-Libration-Resonance

embodies the minimal, atmospheric, and dub-influenced sound that characterizes the genre, with its deep, resonant basslines, echo articulations, spacious reverb, 'haunting' textures, and intricate percussive characteristics.

The reason why *Resonance* is of particular interest for analysis in this thesis can be attributed to several factors. First and foremost, the piece places echo feedback articulation at the core of its aesthetic framework. The three stab layers that have been subjected to echo articulation possess a rhythmic call-response effect, which demonstrates why the design process for echo effects is an iconic feature of dub techno. As noted in previous examples, these layers, represented on paper with notes and sequencer images, do not convey much meaning in themselves. This is because the elements that shape the overall feel of the piece are largely produced through texture, sound processing, spatial design, and other production concepts. The second reason is that the repetitive and slow-burning structure of the piece highlights its dub techno characteristics. In the example of *Resonance*, despite the presence of repetitive structures, a limited sonic palette, minimal changes throughout the track, and extended sections, it is evident that certain sonic qualities directly linked to the use of effects keep the listener attentive. This situation provides a good example of the fundamental characteristics of dub techno. In light of the characteristics revealed in the analysis, the data obtained from the question posed to the participants during the survey, 'In which medium is this track suitable to experience?', has also been evaluated and briefly interpreted.

Resonance

The piece's structure has been identified as having 9 sections as its core blocks (Image 7.5) (Chart 7.10).

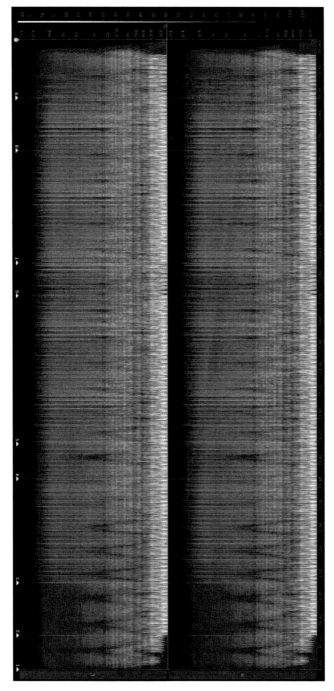

Image 7.5 : Spectrum image of 9 core blocks of *Resonance*

Section	1	2	3	4	5
Time	00:00	00:30	01:16	02:46	03:17
Occurence	A large space is created through shimmer reverb and noise effects with the phaser adding texture. It introduces the space for upcoming layers but doesn't expose the sound palette fully.	The first stab layer is introduced with a chord progression, kick pattern, and bassline, with a conventional ambient music form. The echo articulation is not exaggerated.	The shaker pattern completes the drum layer, and the second stab layer matches the shaker rhythm, contributing to the piece's sense of motion.	A brief dip in the piece's presence occurs when the shakers are united, leading to a temporary weakening in the high frequencies, and contributing to the piece's motion.	All sound palette elements, including the third stab layer with heavy echo articulation, enter a four-bar call-response relationship with intersections and motion created by the echo effect.

Section	6	7	8	9
Time	05:26	05:54	07:34	08:20
Occurence	Similar to section four, a brief drop is created by muting only the kicks.	No new elements are introduced beyond those demonstrated in the fifth section.	The echo feedback amount of the third stab layer is increased, and the shaker is faded out, marking the outroduction.	The second stab layer and kick are subjected to a long fade-out, pushing all elements except for the bassline into a huge space with shimmer reverb and ending the piece with a different setup than it started with.

Chart 7.10 : The structure scheme of *Resonance*

Section 1 - features a prominent introduction, characterized by a large space created through the use of shimmer reverb and noise effects. Another defining effect of this introduction is the phaser, which adds to the overall texture of the piece. Although this section primarily serves to introduce the massive space that the subsequent stab layers will occupy, it does not fully expose the sound palette of the track. Section 2 - the first stab layer (Figure 7.28) is introduced with a Cm/G - Gm (iv-i) chord progression, accompanied by a four-on-the-floor kick pattern and the bassline (Figures 7.29 and 7.30). The exposition can be considered to have taken place to some extent in this section. The echo articulation in the first stab layer is not exaggerated. Additionally, a noisy Cm drone accompanies the elements as a 'backcloth' heard in this section. These characteristics have aspects that evoke the conventional form of ambient music.

Figure 7.28 : The notation of the harmonic sequence of the first stabs of *Resonance*

Figure 7.29 : The notation of the bass riff of *Resonance*

Figure 7.30 : Folded view of the bass riff of *Resonance* on the sequencer (Bb1-C2)

Section 3 - The drum layer (Figures 7.31 and 7.32) is completed with the introduction of the shaker pattern.

Figure 7.31 : The notation of the main drum pattern of *Resonance*

Figure 7.32 : The main drum pattern of *Resonance* on the sequencer

In this section, the second stab layer (Figure 7.33) also becomes audible.

Figure 7.33 : The notation of the second stab layer of *Resonance*

The second stab layer has undergone sudden increases in feedback amount, following the spur-of-the-moment approach, such as around 01:42. Additionally, it is important to note that the second stab layer matches the rhythm of the shaker at high frequencies, as observed at 01:16, and manipulates the perception of the shaker. These minor alterations in sound design exemplify how they can transform the groove. It would be accurate to state that the echo articulation in this layer contributes to the piece's sense of motion. Section 4 - features a brief dip in the presence of the piece when the shakers are muted. As demonstrated in Image 7.5, this dip causes a temporary weakening in the high frequencies. It is noteworthy that this reduction, leading to a slight decline in the presence of the piece, is another aspect contributing to the piece's motion. Muting the shakers in this section serves as a preparation for the climax of the piece in the following section. Section 5 - marks the climax section, where all the elements in the sound palette are audible, and the percussive tails enter into a four-bar call-response relationship with each other. Along with the elements heard since the first section, the third stab layer (Figure 7.34) is also included in this section.

Figure 7.34 : The notation of the third stab layer of *Resonance*

It would not be inaccurate to suggest that the third stab layer is the layer in which echo articulation is heavily applied. The simplicity in this layer strongly supports the four-bar rhythmic narrative of the piece through the echo effect. The representation of the intersections created by the decay of the echo effect between 05:56-06:03 in this climax section is illustrated in Figure 7.35 below.

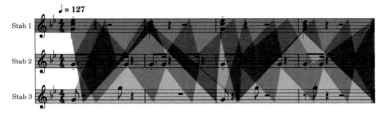

Figure 7.35 : The intersections created by the decay of the echo effect between 05:56-06:03[96]

Additionally, the layering of the motion created by the echo effect between 05:56-06:03 is illustrated in Figure 7.36 below.

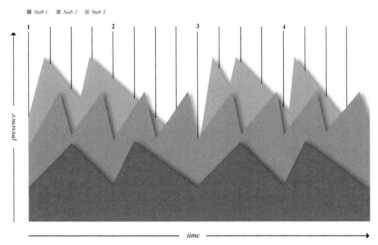

Figure 7.36 : The layering of the motion created by the echo effect between 05:56-06:03[97]

---

[96] A high amount of feedback allows for the intersection of echo decays from different layers of stabs, ultimately leading to altered spatial and musical perception. The areas where the main colors intersect and transform into other colors represent this alteration in simple terms.

[97] This figure is designed to illustrate the layered perception created by the echo effect applied to three stab layers in the 7th section (05:56-06:03) without considering the intersection points. The presence of the stab tracks dynamically rises and falls thanks to the echo effect applied to each layer, which not only confirms a rhythmic call-response relationship but also creates a sonic character in which the layers are in a kind of harmony with each other. *Resonance* is a good example of how layers are created and intertwined through echo effects, so this illustration is believed to be useful. While the figure's horizontal axis 'time' has fixed values, the vertical axis 'presence' does not have any predetermined values and has not been subjected to any specific scale in the Y-plane. Thus, the Y-axis of the figure is relative. In this context, 'presence' refers to the distinctness that occurs in the listener's perception rather than sharp transients or dominance in high

Section 6 - A brief drop is created similar to the fourth section by only muting the kicks. Section 7 - Nothing is shown beyond the sound palette and design structure demonstrated in the fifth section. Section 8 - can be considered as part of the outroduction in which the echo feedback amount of the third stab layer is increased and the shaker is faded out. Section 9 - The second stab layer and kick are subjected to a long fade out. This fade-out seems to be effective in ending the piece with a different setup than it started with. All elements except for the bassline are pushed into a huge space with shimmer reverb, bringing the piece to an end.

Resonance was presented to 41 different participants including electronic music producers, electronic music performers, and electronic music listeners to test its dominance in communal and individual listening. The participants were asked to indicate whether they found the track closer to headphone listening or dancefloor medium. Additionally, the participants were given the option to leave the question unanswered and to consider both mediums appropriate. The results revealed that a vast majority of participants (n = 30; 73.2%) believed that *Resonance* was more suitable for listening on the dancefloor, while a minority of participants (n = 11; 26.8%) believed that the track was better suited for headphones (see Chart 7.11).

Chart 7.11 : The preferences made by 41 participants for *Resonance*

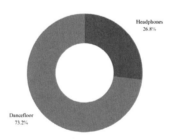

Headphones
26.8%

Dancefloor
73.2%

When considering the qualities of *Resonance*, it is possible to make multiple inferences for the purpose of interpreting the result. First, it is important to note that the dominance below 350 Hz in the track from Section 2 to the outro did not disappear (see Image 7.5). The emphasis on repetitive low frequencies, as

frequency. Additionally, it is possible to include other elements such as drums, bass, and drones in this layered illustration. Essentially, with this visualization created through the figure, it is possible to approach the 'three-dimensional' perceptual experience created in the sound design of dub techno in a concrete manner. For more details, refer to the part that analyzes the fundamental features of echo articulation in dub music, which discusses how these points of intersection change the perception and can even alter the harmony.

discussed at length in the topic of sound system culture, represents a powerful aesthetic element that embodies the influence of dub music. This quality appears to be significant. In addition, considering the information gathered from the entirety of tracks presented and scrutinized in this thesis, the existence of low frequencies harmonized with high frequencies (through the use of percussion components such as hi-hat, ride, shaker, or stabs), the pronounced or unyielding consistency of the kick drum[98], and the tempo all seem to play a crucial role in determining the track's compatibility with the dancefloor as perceived by the participants[99].

Topdown Dialectic's *B4*

B4 by Topdown Dialectic, released in 2018[100], provides an example of a different aspect of dub techno. It should be considered that experimental productions, such as *B4*, expand the sonic range of dub techno's discography. *B4* provides a solid domain for understanding how this range can be extended through aesthetic elements and how the intersectional nature of dub techno (see Figure 7.2) can be concretized. The track's primary characteristic is the use of noises like vinyl crackles and pops at a radical level[101] to create texture. Furthermore, it seems that the diverse melodic and harmonic sequences and the percussive components were produced by manipulating the same elements[102]. Hence, it is crucial to acknowledge that all the layers perceived in *B4* essentially originate from sonic artifacts.

The sonic aesthetic of *B4* has multiple aspects that must be discussed from different perspectives. However, this section will focus on how the individual

---

[98] In jargon terms, the discussion pertains to a 'thumpy' and 'stiff' kick drum sound.

[99] It is important to restate, however, that these findings are based on a relatively small sample of participants and may not generalize to larger populations or other contexts. Further research is needed to replicate these findings and to explore the subjective experiences and preferences of individuals who listen to electronic music in different contexts.

[100] In this section, the B4 track of the *Topdown Dialectic* album, which consists of eight pieces released in 2018 and produced by Topdown Dialectic, has been subjected to track analysis. For further information, see https://www.discogs.com/release/12133432-Topdown-Dialectic-Topdown-Dialectic.

[101] Considering the previously mentioned Clicks & Cuts phenomenon, the use of elements such as vinyl noise, crackle, or pop to create musical compositions is not a particularly new method.

[102] Another album that utilized the microsampling technique and was constructed on top of noise, clicks, and pops is Jan Jelinek's *Loop-Finding-Jazz-Records* album. For further information, see https://www.discogs.com/master/11367-Jan-Jelinek-Loop-Finding-Jazz-Records.

and communal listening experiences are triggered by the sonic characteristics that are immediately noticeable in the track. In this section, *B4* has been analyzed to reveal its sonic and structural characteristics. In light of the characteristics revealed in the analysis, the data obtained from the question posed to the participants during the survey, 'In which medium is this track suitable to experience?', has also been evaluated and briefly interpreted.

B4

The piece's structure has been identified as having 9 sections as its core blocks (Image 7.6) (Chart 7.12).

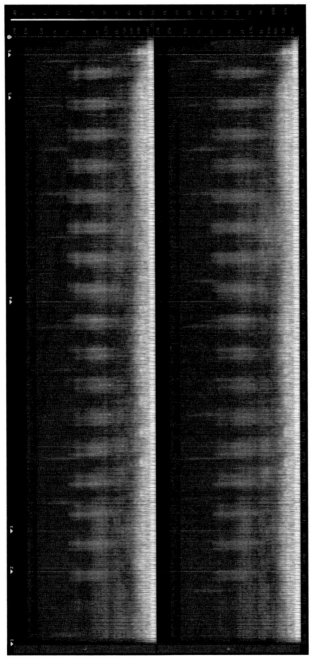

Image 7.6 : Spectrum image of 6 core blocks of B_4

Section	1	2	3	4	5	6
Time	00:00	00:36	00:56	02:49	04:30	04:52
Occurence	Fast fade-in introduces movement with pulsating bass layer. Noise heard at the end connects blocks until the end.	The drop between 3 kHz and 6 kHz marks a dynamic change. Triplet hits resembling rim shots were heard.	Drop and rise movements deepen, and a sine tone rings. Db every drop. Compatible 8-bar narrative present.	Prominent groove in low frequencies. Metallic impact sound creates variation. Ends with the noise effect leading to the outro.	A Low-pass filter was used, resulting in decreased presence. Focus shifts to elements dominant below 300 Hz, preparing for the outro.	The piece ends with a short fade-out.

Chart 7.12 : The structure scheme of $B4$

B4 is not as suitable as the previous five pieces to separate and discuss the tonal elements that make up its structure. This is because the sound created by combining the elements in the sound palette is more focused on textural richness rather than tonal richness. Dub techno is already a genre that presents challenges in the analysis process due to its aesthetics. The experimental sound of B4 has made this analytical observation task even more difficult. However, in this section, the structure of the piece is discussed, and the key characteristics that are important in the context are revealed. For instance, when taking notation, it is considered more reasonable to highlight the most distinct elements that determine the rhythm and tonal axis, instead of analyzing each element separately. Likewise, the structure of B4 is not conventionally linear. Therefore, when determining the section in Image 7.6, only the patterns formed by the occurrences and repeating motifs were considered.

Section 1 - opens with a fast fade-in. A distinct movement is heard in the piece from this section until the end (Figure 7.37).

Figure 7.37 : The notation of the distinct movement of B4

The movement is heard along with a pulsating bass layer, which functions as the kick (Figure 7.38). This layer constitutes the dominant element that brings out frequencies below 300 Hz, as can be seen in Image 7.6.

Figure 7.38 : The notation of the pulsating bass of B4

The two layers shown in Figure 7.37 and Figure 7.38, which are heard together throughout the piece, provide multiple ideas about qualities such as rhythm, texture, and the Fm sounding key. The noise heard at the end of the section, which is also clearly visible in Image 7.6, can be considered a transition embellishment that connects the 8-bar blocks until the end of the piece. Section 2 - as seen in Image 7.6, there is a 'drop' between 3 kHz and 6 kHz after the noise transition. The reason for marking this section is due to this drop, which is both an element that dynamically affects the overall perception of the piece and a harbinger of the drops and rises that will begin in the next section. The drops seen in the spectrum were most likely obtained through LPF. The triplet hits resembling rim shots heard around 00:51 can be considered one of the characteristics of this section. Section 3 - begins with the 'deepening' of the drop movement at 01:12. The drop and rise movements introduced in the previous section occur more prominently in this section. The movements are also visible in the spectrum image (Image 7.6) and contain long rhythmic phrases within themselves. In this section, every drop is filled with a sine character sound that rings Db. Therefore, a compatible 8-bar narrative of the pulsating bass, distinct movement, and sine tone is present in this section (Figures 7.39 and 7.40). Since this narrative continues until the end of the piece, it is possible to consider the harmony of these three fundamental elements (or movements) among the characteristics of the piece.

Figure 7.39 : The notation of the narration between 01:12-01:27

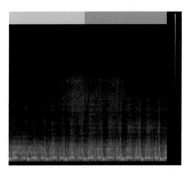

Figure 7.40 : Spectrum image of the narration between 01:12-01:27[103]

Section 4 - begins with a prominent groove in the low frequencies. A metallic impact sound heard around 03:03 creates a variation in the percussive narrative of the piece. These variations fill the gaps in the fourth section with frequencies ranging from 700 Hz to 3 kHz, which are fuller than the previous section (Image 7.6). The section ends with a noise effect leading to the outro. Section 5 - all elements are 'deepened' using a low-pass filter, resulting in a decrease in presence. The decrease in presence shifts the focus on the elements dominant below 300 Hz preparing the piece for the outro. Section 6 - The piece ends with a short fade-out.

---

[103] The spectrum presented in Figure 7.39 illustrates the narrative between 01:12-01:27, as indicated by the corresponding notation in the figure. The two colored bands on the spectrum can be associated with the notation in Figure 7.39. Additionally, this figure exemplifies the concept of the 'rise and fall' mentioned in the main text.

B4 was presented to 41 different participants including electronic music producers, electronic music performers, and electronic music listeners to test its dominance in communal and individual listening. The participants were asked to indicate whether they found the track closer to headphone listening or dancefloor medium. Additionally, the participants were given the option to leave the question unanswered and to consider both mediums appropriate. The results revealed that a vast majority of participants (n = 29; 70.7%) believed that *B4* was more suitable for listening on headphones, while a minority of participants (n = 12; 29.3%) believed that the track was better suited for the dancefloor (see Chart 7.13).

Chart 7.13 : The preferences made by 41 participants for *B4*

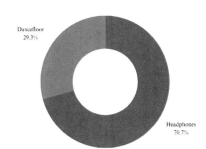

Dancefloor
29.3%

Headphones
70.7%

The fact that a vast majority of participants found *B4* more suitable for headphone listening suggests that the track may be more complex and intricate in terms of its sonic elements and production techniques. Listening to music through headphones may enhance the perception of subtle nuances in the music compared to listening in a communal dancefloor setting, due to the reduced environmental distractions and the closer proximity of the sound source to the ears. This could suggest that the track may contain more subtle elements, such as intricate sound design, complex rhythms, or detailed textures[104], that require a more attentive and focused listening approach.

On the other hand, the minority of participants who found *B4* more suitable for the dancefloor may have been drawn to the track's more visceral and physical qualities, such as its driving rhythm or powerful bassline. These elements may have been more effective in creating a communal, immersive experience on the dancefloor, where the music is often felt as much as it is heard[105].

_____

[104] Moreover, the results of the analysis seem to confirm this.

[105] It is important to restate, however, that these findings are based on a relatively small sample of participants and may not generalize to larger populations or other contexts. Further research is needed to replicate these findings and to explore the subjective

Below, a discussion was conducted using six different graphics to determine the tonal balance of the six previously analyzed pieces, *Aerial, Phylyps Trak, The Salt On Her Cheeks, Listing, Sinking, B4,* and *Resonance.* Tonal balance may be a factor that distinguishes the headphone and dancefloor experience for listeners. Testing this hypothesis and including tonal balance values in the analysis may provide further insight. The tonal balance graphics were obtained by representing the climax sections of the six analyzed pieces using the iZotope's Tonal Balance Control software[106].

Figure 7.41 : A representation of the tonal balance of *Aerial*

Considering the position of the horizontal line (Figure 7.41), which represents the information of the piece and is depicted in white, with respect to the guide range shown in blue, it can be observed that *Aerial* is highly dominant in the 20-200Hz range. On the other hand, by examining the position of the line and the guide range in the frequency ranges of 800Hz-3kHz and 4kHz-7kHz, it can be said that the piece is relatively weak in mid and high-mid regions. The region above 8kHz falls within the guide range, nearly providing optimal information.

---

experiences and preferences of individuals who listen to electronic music in different contexts.

[106] iZotope's Tonal Balance Control software's UI is designed to provide a visual representation of the tonal balance of a piece of music. The UI allows users to compare the frequency balance of their own music against a reference target curve, which is based on a statistical analysis of thousands of professionally mixed and mastered tracks (iZotope, 2020). Additionally, to give insights about the bass heavy music's typical curve, a guide curve has been added to the UI. By utilizing the software for the analysis, it is possible to discuss and analyze the curves that deviate from the established limits.

Figure 7.42 : A representation of the tonal balance of *Phylyps Trak*

When observing the guide range shown in blue (Figure 7.42), it can be seen that the dominance is quite consistent up to 300Hz. On the other hand, it can be observed that the piece is weak in the mid-range. While the *Phylyps Trak* is dominant in the high-mid and presence ranges, above 8kHz in the brilliance range, it is within the guide range, albeit not providing optimum information.

Figure 7.43 : A representation of the tonal balance of *The Salt On Her Cheeks*

Considering the reference curve (Figure 7.43), it is evident that *The Salt On Her Cheeks* has a prominent low-frequency dominance in the range of 20Hz-300Hz. While the graph indicates a balanced mid-range, it also highlights the weakness in the high-mid frequencies. Given that the transients are present in these frequency bands, the graph also reflects the 'smooth' sound palette of the piece. On the other hand, the high-end band of the piece is quite balanced. In summary, it is important to take into account the low-frequency dominance of the piece.

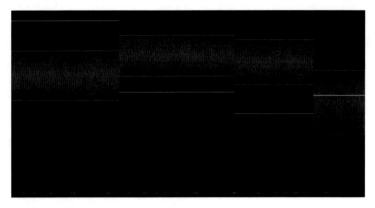

Figure 7.44 : A representation of the tonal balance of *Listing, Sinking*

Listing, Sinking has a prominent low-frequency dominance (Figure 7.44). In addition, the weakness in the mid-range and high-mid bands suggests that the focus of the piece is on the low-frequencies. The balanced position in the high-end region may indicate the texture produced by snappy percussions. In summary, in terms of the balance of the mid-range, this piece is similar to *B4*. It is evident that this piece is heavily dominated by low frequencies.

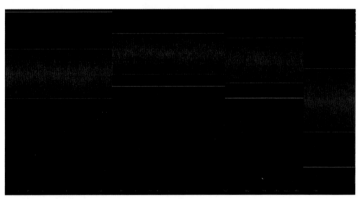

Figure 7.45 : A representation of the tonal balance of *B4*

When considering Figure 7.45, it is evident that the analyzed track has extreme dominance in the low-frequency ranges. The piece falls below the guide range in all areas except for the low-frequencies. This situation is particularly extreme above 8kHz. This extreme dominance places this track in a special position among the analyzed ones[107]. In summary, the graph demonstrates that

---

[107] *B4*, on the other hand, is an example that stands out from conventional sound due to its focus on low frequencies and its overall sound, which is not rich in transients.

the track is focused on low frequencies and has a relatively 'smooth' sound in terms of transients.

Figure 7.46 : A representation of the tonal balance of *Resonance*

When considering Figure 7.46, it is clear that the track has dominance in the low end. On the other hand, the piece appears weak in terms of mid-range. The position of the high-mid and high-end curves in relation to the guide ranges indicates a balance. The high-mid and high-end information of the track is complementary to the dominance in the low frequencies, resulting in a balanced overall sound.

8

Discussion

Since its inception in cities like Detroit, Berlin, and London, techno music has undergone constant changes[108] in different dimensions due to its distinct aesthetic paradigm and functional centrality to dance. This transformation, however, extends beyond the aesthetic considerations involved in music production to the process of music consumption. Initially, techno music was a catalyst for communal dance experiences, but it has now become an individualized experience consumed through headphones, leading to a shift from communal to individual experiences of music consumption. This shift is closely related to the use of headphones, which not only transformed the aesthetics of the music but also led to an introspective experience associated with renewed aestheticization.

Similarly, dub music also emerged from dance and communal listening, with the sound system culture eventually spreading to various countries. Dub techno, one of the current links in the minimal continuum chain, emerged through the fusion of Jamaican dub music and the relentless nature of techno music by German music producers in Berlin. Dub techno is considered by many individuals as more appropriate for headphone listening than other techno sub-genres, likely due to its distinctive sound and aesthetic. This emergence of dub

---

[108] When considering the current state of the production and consumption processes of techno music, it seems possible to conclude that this transformation is still ongoing. It is important to note the nature of concepts such as metaverse or AI that have caused a sensation in the years this thesis was written (2022-2023), as they infiltrate various aspects of our lives. Even simply contemplating how these concepts will impact the entertainment industry, artistic productions, and the realm of music is sufficient to predict that this transformative process will continue.

techno and the shift from communal to individual musical experiences raises questions about the social and cultural implications of this transformation. Is listening to music through headphones an individualistic act that isolates the listener from the communal experience of live music events? Does the shift from nightclubs to headphones reflect broader societal trends toward individualism and the privatization of cultural experiences? These questions highlight the need for further research into the cultural and social implications of music consumption and the role of technology in shaping the way we experience and interact with music.

By investigating the unique qualities of dub techno and its relationship to the rise of individualism in music consumption, this research sheds light on the ways in which music consumption and cultural experiences are changing in the digital age. The issue at hand is not just the transformation of music consumption, but also the impact of technology on the aesthetics and function of techno music, dub techno in particular.

The concept of orphic media, closely related to individualism and sonic politics, was explored by media researcher Mack Hagood, who considered how experiences are changing in this context. Orphic media can be seen as a new type of media that creates sonic self-control. However, it is important to consider that active noise-canceling headphones were a driving force behind the creation and discussion of concepts such as orphic media and sonic self-control. This illustrates how recently developed technological devices have affected the field of media, as well as sound and music. Active noise-canceling headphones can be perceived as a modern solution to the challenge of encountering sound with sound, which can be compared to the myth of Orpheus' encounter with the captivating melodies of the Sirens. The opportunity for individuals to block out external noise and alter any sound they desire, such as a music track, clearly suggests the notion of individual emancipation.

The encounter that individuals undergo to counter environmental noise may be considered a *casus belli* due to the inconvenience, disturbance, public nature, or lack of privacy in crowded public spaces that noise creates. This challenge, coupled with the solution provided by headphone technology, leads to the individual's attainment of freedom, which holds significant political, social, and cultural implications.

Through the suppression of environmental sound, individuals gain emancipation from it. While the extent, nature, and relationship with politics of this liberation are debatable, it is evident that headphones are a means of individual music consumption, whether or not they are noise-canceling. As a result, this notion discussed in the context of orphic media allows for the concept of orphic experience to be considered: music can be experienced in an orphic way. With headphones, listeners can create not only a filtered bubble by blocking out external sounds but also a sonic inner space that is customized and altered for their own preferences. The idea of an inner space that individuals create and personalize for themselves is crucial to this research. Furthermore, examining the connection between headphones and spatial politics in the media field and subjecting the status quo to consistent examination are also important for further research.

The concept of orphic experience refers to a new medium in which individuals can consume music in an extremely personalized manner, completely isolated from their sonic environment. This medium is made possible through the use of headphones, which allow individuals to enjoy music that was previously only accessible through communal listening on large sound systems. Dub music, for example, is a genre that traditionally requires the use of such systems to fully appreciate the low-frequency vibrations and amplification that create a visceral impact on the body, making it an almost sacred experience. Techno, on the other hand, is typically associated with large crowds and the use of light shows and visual effects to enhance the overall aesthetic of the experience.

However, the fusion of these two genres has resulted in the emergence of a new subgenre known as dub techno, which offers a sound and culture that takes the act of listening from communal to individual. This transformation is significant because it has been brought about by a simple technological device that individuals have attached to their ears. Understanding how the rise of individual listening has affected niche genres like dub techno provides insight into how other phenomena have been and will be affected by this shift.

Headphones have provided a new context for dub techno, making it a highly suitable genre for orphic experience, while also seeming to have been designed for this aesthetic paradigm. This could be a coincidence, but the fact that headphones have become a popular medium for music consumption and that the rise of individual listening has freed producers from various constraints suggests otherwise. Dub techno producers have seemingly taken advantage of the rise of headphones as a preferred listening medium, with their musical style being inherently conducive to the personal and private nature of headphone listening. In addition to the soft kick drums, complex midrange sounds, and low-frequency prominence, reduced transient ratios and other production elements suggest that dub techno may not be well-suited for traditional dancefloor settings, but instead offer a more comfortable and intimate listening experience through headphones.

In this context, it is crucial to acknowledge the role of techno music on the dancefloor. Techno music has strict rules for its auditory aesthetics, as it is intended to facilitate dance. These rules were discovered through interviews conducted for this research. Therefore, it can be argued that using headphones separates techno music from its intended function on the dancefloor, which diminishes the significance of the aesthetic elements associated with that function. The liberation of music from its practical function is transforming the overall aesthetic of music, as seen in the contrast between conventional sub-genres of techno music consumed on the dancefloor and dub techno music, which is often associated with headphone listening. The production of music intended for headphone listening versus large sound systems has significant differences, such as atmospheric elements, textual elements, subtle movements, details added to the arrangement, and the enrichment of stereo images. Dub techno music has been referred to as 'headphone music' by dub techno-oriented community members, critics, or researchers, and the piece titled *B4* analyzed in this study is a good example of this phenomenon. Structural elements, such as drops, rises, suspenses, and climaxes, reinforce the function of techno music on the dancefloor, and the linear narrative that manipulates, anticipates, satisfies, arouses curiosity, or surprises the listener is crucial for the design process of a techno piece intended for the dancefloor. The absence of these structural elements in techno music calls for compatibility with the headphone experience. The analysis of *Phylyps Trak* and the 'dancefloor' reaction of the participants confirms this conclusion.

It could be argued that the centrality of communal listening, particularly within rave culture, during highly specific techno dance sessions that adhere to certain capitalist codes, measures, and boundaries, has caused the genre to deviate from its original anti-mainstream essence. As a result, techno has restructured itself to comply with the commercial norms of aboveground music. Therefore, the entertainment concept that techno music ignites represents a controlled raving taking place in a modern context. When approached from this perspective, the orphic experience and sonic self-control allow the individual to detach themselves from the capitalist sonic environment while also personalizing the consumption of music produced for communal listening on similar grounds. In this way, the listener can free themselves from being one of Pierre Bourdieu's plebs in the techno music arena by experiencing the music in an orphic manner and through sonic self-control. On the other hand, it is also important to note the existence of new consumption methods involving headphones. The transformation of techno music into dub techno represents the conversion of communal consumption into individual consumption. So, the phenomenon of consumption, while persistently present, often camouflages itself under the guise of individualism.

Dub techno is characterized by various unique features in terms of aesthetics, the first of which is the utilization of echo and reverberation

206

techniques that have been inherited from dub music. These techniques result in 'vast virtual spaces'. Stylistically, the echo and reverberation techniques generate an expansive acoustic field that envelops the entire mix. From a technical standpoint, it would not be inaccurate to state that the stereophonic spatiality is more discernible via headphones. In an unchanging and unyielding arrangement, the dynamism, spontaneity, and the sensation of a vast and extensive perception captured by the echo and reverb effects serve to describe a stylistic aspect of dub techno. Conversely, repetition serves as a framing characteristic that encompasses all of these elements.

Dub techno has a unique perception, which is often created through the use of effects. Through dub techno, it is possible to draw attention to the interconnected nature of 'inner' and 'outer' spatiality. The echo and reverberation techniques create an aesthetic definition and position the music itself in space. When considering virtual spaces created by various sound effects during the mixing process, dub techno, in general, typically has a sound positioned in a large and wide virtual space. While this is the inner space of dub techno, the actual acoustic space where the music is listened to can be considered outer space. In this case, it would not be wrong to say that the music has a dual spatiality. The large stereo images created during the mixing process will directly affect the perception of the inner space when the music is listened to in outer space, for example, when listened to in a car or a mono club system. The change effect that applies in this direction is also valid in the opposite direction. Indeed, the perception of the inner space of the music designed by the producer during the mixing process can determine which medium would create a more effective experience: pieces that are mono-compatible or do not contain harsh and erratic stereo modulation can create a better experience in a nightclub, or the inner space perception of a piece can be designed directly to create a good experience in a nightclub. In this case, simply put, the perception of the inner space created in the music production process can shape the medium in which the music is consumed-vice versa.

Dub techno is characterized by its unique aesthetic feature of noise presence in its sound palette. Whether it is a natural soundscape or an artifact originating from hardware, noise has a place in the musical arrangement of dub techno. This study examines the hardware-generated noises heard in the first examples created by Oswald and Ernestus, and how the idea of noise reduction, which is one of the benefits of modern mixing technology, was not adopted by Oswald and Ernestus. Considering that various producers who have produced within the dub techno form shaped by Oswald's personal views and sonic aesthetic thoughts also used noise as a layer in their music (Redbull Music Academy, 2008), it is clear that resorting to the use of a noise layer, created either through equipment used in the production process or artificially attached to the arrangement, is a kind of dub techno 'tradition'. Oswald's concept of noise being beautified, not seeing noise as an element that needs to be purified or eliminated, has given noise an aesthetic nature in dub techno productions that have been and are being presented. The way in which this phenomenon evokes Jacques Derrida's concept of hauntology has been brought to light in this study, where the specters of the past begin to appear in contemporary cultural productions and occupy the aesthetics of these products to varying degrees.

Considering retro trends such as Vaporwave, Synthwave, and Lo-Fi, which embrace noise, distorted sound, glitch effects, low resolution, and various artifacts arising from the impossibilities and inadequacies of the past as a stylistic element, it can be observed how hauntology manifests itself in music. Noise in dub techno is used as a musical layer by utilizing the feeling produced by analog equipment on the one hand and by incorporating soundscapes or found sounds into the arrangement using the same method on the other hand. This prompts us to think about how the aesthetics of the 'specters' of the past have shaped and formatted dub techno.

Dub music, which was born earlier than techno music (in the early 60s), may be a source that called the concept of noise into the field. Indeed, it can be seen that noise is quite prominent and dominant in some archetype dub recordings. Dub techno shows how noise has become a characteristic element of the aesthetic of a music genre. This interesting issue deserves further research. On the other hand, when noise is viewed from a hauntological perspective, the question of whether dub techno music can free itself from its hauntological aesthetics by shaking off this dust in the future is noteworthy. For dub techno, the debate of whether the references and glorifications made to noise and analog perception will continue to exist in the future and whether its aesthetics will be reshaped by the transformative power of new technology is a matter for discussion.

It is noteworthy to mention that dub techno has already undergone a period of stylistic consolidation within the broader history of electronic music, with contemporary works often mimicking past productions. As such, it begs the question of whether dub techno has reached its full potential as a musical genre or if there remains untapped potential for innovative reinterpretations and revitalization.

The examination of dub techno's sound characteristics necessitates speculation on the process of minimalism within techno. The emergence of dub techno coincided with the influence of the minimalism movement on techno music and marked the birth of its first fruits. It is arguable that the sound characteristics of dub techno were directly or indirectly impacted by the minimalism process in techno. Some researchers have even considered dub techno as one of the last fruits of the minimal continuum (see Nye, 2013, p. 165) which refers to the minimalism process in techno. Considering these viewpoints and how dub techno was stylistically influenced by ambient music, it is reasonable to conclude that dub techno's sound is shaped by a paradigm of minimalism.

The process of minimalism in techno involves reducing details, utilizing fewer and less abrupt movements in the structure, reducing the number of sections, and simplifying the elements in the sound palette. In some cases, this process has led to a relinquishing of the dancefloor function of techno music. Therefore, the shift from communal to individual listening experiences in niche subgenres such as dub techno can be attributed to the minimalist trend in music. The process of minimalism also includes the evolution of complex drum patterns into simpler ones, reshaping drum sounds from high-transient to low-transient, and transforming stiff and thumpy kick sounds into less stiff and deeper ones. These transformations in percussive and melodic elements can be observed in dub techno sound.

The rise of individual listening experiences, which occurred under the shadow of isolated listening made possible by headphones, seems to be related to the minimalism trend in techno. Headphones can create a new dominant medium, encourage current producers involved in the minimalism process in techno music, and allow for a greater perception of smaller details. In turn, this takes techno music from the default medium of the dancefloor to a more introspective and individualized listening experience.

Dub music, in its pure form unadulterated by techno, is a music genre that has evolved through performance practices. Dub engineers use consoles and effects processors to transform sounds into artistry. During a live performance, sound system operators turn knobs, press buttons, and move faders to manipulate basic parameters. The buttons, knobs, and faders, which were essentially integrated into the devices by manufacturers for technical reasons, are used like instruments in dub music production and performance. These tools are constantly customized to adjust parameters frequently changed during production and performance.

Analysis conducted through the echo feedback parameter, which directly influenced the aesthetic of dub techno music, reveals that the echo feedback knob has been used to facilitate transitions between sections, articulate and enrich the overall ambiance. The ability to improvise by manually altering parameters such as echo feedback, reverb size, and decay amount during performance and recording creates a spur-of-the-moment atmosphere that defines the natural and qualitative aspects of the final sound. Although these parameters can be automated through DAWs today, the spur-of-the-moment approach values human naturalness and spontaneity, thereby excluding automation. From a purist perspective, dub music's essence lies in the instant and improvised manipulation of various parameters on the console. Therefore, the echo and reverberation techniques used in dub techno music, which are adapted from dub music's production and performance practices, also adhere to the same principles. The improvisational rules born out of the concept of live improvisation in dub music, are applicable in dub techno music. This practice leads to the deviant aesthetics of dub techno music being under the influence of dub music.

This study is based on two fundamental pillars: musical analysis and surveys/interviews. In the musical analysis process, six different dub techno tracks[109], two dub[110], two Detroit techno[111], two acid techno[112], and two minimal techno[113] pieces were analyzed. When analyzing dub music pieces, the focus was on understanding how the echo effect functions as a stylistic element in dub music. The initial hypothesis was that the echo practices in dub music were one of the most prominent inspirations in the creation of the sound of dub techno music. Indeed, the analysis has confirmed that the use of echo practices in dub music, especially the echo feedback amount parameter, is a dominant and spontaneous feature of dub techno music. Thus, the echo feedback amount in dub music has been adapted as an articulation in the sound of dub techno music. Of course, the influence of dub music on dub techno is not limited to this feature, but it is one of the most prominent ones.

The analysis of the echo feedback amount in dub music has revealed that it is both an articulation used in different instrument tracks to connect two different sections and make the transition seamless and also a characteristic feature of the general sound when used constantly. In dub techno music, the echo feedback amount is primarily used not to connect sections or make structural transitions smoother, but rather to provide a relatively high and constant echo feedback amount. Therefore, when echo feedback amount is considered as an adapted console articulation in dub techno, it can be said that this articulation is a default element that supports the relatively stable and circular structure of dub techno. This study has shown that the use of echo

---

[109] Rhythm & Sound's *Aerial*, Basic Channel's *Phylyps Trak*, Yagya's *The Salt On Her Cheeks*, Overcast Sound's *Listing*, *Sinking*, Topdown Dialectic's *B4*, Substance & Vainqueur's *Resonance*

[110] King Tubby and Augustus Pablo's *King Tubby Meets Rockers Uptown*, Linton Kwesi Johnson's *Reality Dub*

[111] Model 500's *No UFOs*, Derrick May's *Strings of Life*

[112] Plastik Man's *Plasticine*, Emmanuel Top's *Acid Phase*

[113] Robert Hood's *Minus*, Daniel Bell's *Baby Judy*

feedback amount in dub music is an essential inspiration for the sound of dub techno music. The adaptation of this articulation in dub techno has made it a default and dominant feature of the sound, contributing to the stable and circular structure of the genre.

Through analyses conducted under the techno umbrella, it has become possible to infer why and how stylistic differences arise between its three distinct subgenres. Dub techno is one such subgenre of techno music. By analyzing Detroit, acid, and minimal techno, this study offers a wider perspective on the changes and transformations that have affected dub techno over time, while also examining the chronological evolution of techno as a whole. The assumption that all these genres were initially produced for the dancefloor during techno's early days has provided insight into which elements of the music undergo change when it is restyled through headphones. When examining the six different tracks analyzed under the techno umbrella, the first issue to be discussed is the difference between how the layers of notation appear 'on paper' and how the final product sounds. This difference is even more apparent in dub techno analyses. This highlights the need to develop new methods and approaches to analyze the various aspects of techno music to yield productive results. Approaching techno music aesthetically through notation or spectrum images and descriptions is often insufficient, especially when it comes to sound synthesis and design. To overcome these shortcomings in this research, QR codes, surveys, and interviews were used[114]. However, it is important to remember that the issue of visualizing music has long been an area of concern, and deeper visualization and analysis methods are necessary for techno music. Despite this gap, this research has yielded various conclusions and possibilities for inference. At the forefront of these results, when examining the six techno tracks, there is a sharp, stable, 'chopped-up', and 'stiff' sensation in both notation and the perceived final product, compared to dub techno. It could be argued that these qualities were not as prominent in the examined Detroit, acid, and minimal techno samples. Several fundamental reasons can be discussed for this situation. Firstly, the structural features of dub techno, such as generally not being harsh or punchy in low frequencies, having less distinct transient aspects, or lower drum track amplitude compared to the other three genres, can lead to a softer and more atmospheric feeling. Secondly, in dub techno music, as discussed above, the incorporation of noise and the sonic qualities of the output of analog equipment (or digital emulations) can be argued to be more 'analog-organic'. Furthermore, this analog-organic sonic quality can be considered a distinctive feature and aesthetic criterion in the production process of dub

---

[114] In this study, visualization and analysis methods have been employed in addition to notation. The rationale behind this decision is that the study aimed to explore not only the musical aspect of dub techno but also its spatial aspect in relation to its musical dimension.

techno. Additionally, this phenomenon is also evident in the sound design and synthesis process of percussion elements. Thirdly, dub techno may not have focused on the dancefloor experience as much as Detroit, acid, or minimal techno, which may have directly or indirectly influenced the sound created during its origin and development. Therefore, it seems reasonable to attribute the absence of a precursor that produces sharp, stable, 'chopped-up', and 'stiff' sensations in dub techno's nature after production to this reason.

In this study, the data provided by examples of Detroit, acid, and minimal techno indicate that techno music has never had a precursor with rich and developed harmonic and melodic functions that could be considered from a classical perspective. Therefore, the issue of how to analyze techno music is a problem that needs to be solved. Upon examining the notated sections, it is clear that sequencers, drum machines, mixing consoles, or samplers are the main instruments of techno music. Therefore, the fact that techno music generally has a repetitive, loop-based, and circular form can be related to the technological equipment used in its genesis and development. In particular, sequencers appear to have created the aesthetic paradigms of all sub-genres of techno music.

At this point, it is vital to distinguish the linear composition in which repetition is used as a narrative element and the circular composition in which repetition is a foundation, a default setting, or a template upon which all other elements of the music are built. This distinction is crucial because techno music production is shaped around the dance medium and emerged within aesthetic templates that suggested repetition due to the limited technology of the time, without taking this into consideration, approaching this issue can be misleading.

The backbone of this research is the analysis of six different dub techno tracks, in addition to examining various examples within the aesthetic boundaries of dub and techno genres. Along with the analysis process, obtaining insider knowledge through surveys and interviews with producers, performers, and listeners has provided a multitude of discussion topics for this research, which will be explored below.

The analysis of the six different tracks within the framework of dub techno, comparing the results of these analyses, and using survey and interview results to make more consistent conclusions, has ultimately been useful in understanding the qualitative, affective, spatial, sonic, and political differences between communal dancefloor listening and individual headphone listening.

Dub music serves as the primary foundation for dub techno. Stylistically, it can be easily said that dub techno inherited the inner-spatiality of dub music. The inner-spatiality of dub music is shaped by spatial illusions created through effects such as echo and reverb, which have been used since its early beginnings.

In simpler terms, these effects create large spaces in a typical dub music mix, and all the musical elements in a dub track are placed within these large spaces by the mixing engineer. Reverberation should be considered one of the main characteristics of dub music. Dub techno also involves a similar perception of a large space with comparable characteristics. Therefore, the spatiality of dub music has significantly influenced dub techno. The spatial inspiration of dub music is the most cohesive aspect of the stylistic relationship between dub and dub techno. Similarly, guitar chops or staccato harmonica sounds, commonly used in dub music, serve similar functions in dub techno: the spaces between sharp and short sounds are filled by increasing the feedback ratio of the echo effect, creating the groove, adding rhythmic sensation to harmonic sequences, and increasing the overall volume of the sound. The characteristic harmonic progressions in dub music, such as i-iv-i, I-IV-V, I-vi-IV-V, ii-V-I or vi-IV-I are frequently observed in dub techno. Thus, the fact that the characteristic harmonic walks encountered in dub music are also present in dub techno clearly indicates the musical inspiration that dub techno derives from dub music. Although dub techno is rooted in dub music in terms of mixing and harmonic ideas, it can be said that classic drumming in dub music has less influence on dub techno than the four-on-the-floor pattern, except for various examples produced by different producers such as Oswald and Ernestus through Maurizio and Basic Channel. On the other hand, it seems reasonable to suggest that one of the fundamental criteria that enables a piece to be labeled as dub techno is the four-on-the-floor pattern, which is a hallmark of techno music. When examining a piece with typical dub drum patterns, such as steppers or one-drop, from a purist perspective, it would be more accurate to label it as an electronic dub version rather than dub techno. This raises a few questions: is it possible to still call a piece dub techno if it heavily utilizes dub music mixing techniques, carries harmonic qualities characteristic of dub music, and has a groovy drum pattern associated with dub music, such as the one-drop? If so, what elements must be considered in addition to mixing techniques, harmonic structure, and drum pattern to classify a piece as dub techno? Perhaps the only answer to this question is where the music is being listened to or for which listening medium it is suitable. Both dub and techno music are produced to be listened to communally and at high volume, but when examining extreme examples of dub techno, it is not necessarily intended to be played at techno events. This is evident because we know that at least one piece can still be labeled as dub techno without necessarily carrying the premise of delivering good results both technically and setting-wise when played on the dance floor. Nonetheless, it seems useful to flag this issue as a problem.

Additionally, techno music is the second pillar upon which dub techno builds. So, techno music has had a significant influence on the development of dub techno music in several ways, both technically and philosophically. Technically, the influence of techno on dub techno can be seen in the use of similar production techniques and equipment. Both genres often use drum machines, synthesizers, and effects processors to create their soundscapes. Dub techno, however, typically features more ambient and atmospheric textures, with a focus on reverb and delay effects. This can be traced back to the influence of dub music, which also emphasizes these effects to create a spacious and immersive listening experience. In terms of listening mediums, both techno and dub techno are typically experienced in club environments with high-quality sound systems. This creates a communal experience that is highly valued in both genres. However, dub techno has also been influenced by the rise of headphone listening culture, which allows for a more personal and introspective experience of the music.

Philosophically, techno and dub techno share a focus on futurism, technology, and the possibilities of human creativity. Both genres emerged in the context of post-industrial cities where technological advancements were rapidly transforming society. This context gave rise to a sense of optimism and a belief in the transformative power of technology that is reflected in music. Additionally, both genres have been influenced by political and socio-cultural factors, such as the rise of neoliberalism and globalization in the late 20th century. This has led to a focus on issues such as individualism, social alienation, and the need for community and connection in a rapidly changing world. In summary, techno has influenced dub techno both technically and philosophically. The use of similar production techniques and equipment, communal listening environments, and a focus on futurism and technology are all shared characteristics of the two genres. However, dub techno also draws on the influence of dub music and has been shaped by the rise of headphone listening culture and changing socio-political contexts.

This study was reinforced with a survey and interview process involving 41 participants consisting of producers, performers, and listeners. The data obtained from the surveys and interviews have been useful in many ways. Most importantly, thanks to the interviews, dub techno has been defined from an insider's perspective. There is an extreme lack of sources regarding the technical qualities, political, philosophical, and cultural dimensions of the genre in the literature. Therefore, in this study, at least the first steps have been taken to fill this gap, and a ground has been established for further research. Similarly, the survey method was used to analyze whether the medium of dub techno is communal or individual in a more analytical way. At this point, it was considered important to discuss the issues emphasized in the interview process and the insights generated by the interview process. Five different topics that made notable contributions to this research can be mentioned, which were identified based on the answers of the 41 participants consisting of music producers, performers, and listeners, and analyzed in this study due to their absence in the literature:

1. The communal experience shapes the sound of techno music and thus the sensation on the dancefloor through mixing:

Considering the answers provided by the participants (Appendix A.1), the guidelines for mixing techno music in a club environment can be broadly categorized into technical and aesthetic aspects. Technical guidelines include ensuring the music sounds good and adhering to the genre's production techniques and rhythm structures. The music should have enough bass, loudness, mono compatibility, and DJ-friendly arrangement. It is also recommended to mix in mono, ensure beat matching and phrasing, and keep the transitions smooth to help the set's flow. Live effects should also be used to keep the music entertaining for the audience.

In terms of aesthetics, the music should capture the sounds that the general audience of the club prefers. It should have a well-arranged composition with clear high-end, punchy low-end, and powerful mids. The music should have high energy, suitable for dancing, and be captivating. Rhythmic elements should be added and subtracted to build the dance and allow the listener/dancer to rest and experience the climax more distinctly. Finally, the mastering should be done to industry standards, and mono compatibility should be ensured to avoid phase issues that may arise due to technical differences between venues.

Based on the responses provided, it can be hypothesized that the guidelines for mixing techno music for clubs aim to create an immersive communal experience where the music becomes the central focus for a group of people. The technical aspects of the guidelines are necessary to ensure the music sounds 'good' and is suitable for the club environment. The aesthetic aspects aim to create a sense of energy, captivation, and immersion that enhances the communal experience. The communal experience is central to techno music and its club culture, as it creates a shared experience that goes beyond individual enjoyment.

2. An understanding of the precise meaning of the term 'atmosphere', frequently used in the genres of techno and dub techno among insiders, and what it can signify for communal and individual listening experiences:

The data collected on the meaning of 'atmosphere' in techno music (Appendix A.1) provides insights into how the music creates an immersive environment that enhances this communal experience. The respondents describe the atmosphere as a key element that draws the listener into the story of the track and sets the beginning of a story. It adds depth and ambiance to the track with subtle sounds that float in the background, giving the music a sense of mystery and emotion. Moreover, the description of different atmospheres for different techno genres, such as dark, happy, sad, intense, or uplifting, highlights how techno music can evoke a range of emotions and moods that are essential to the communal experience on the dancefloor. The fast-paced and energetic nature of techno music creates a rhythm that functions on the dancefloor, bringing people together to move to the beat. The respondents also note that using ambient sounds and atmospheric elements, such as pads and drones, contributes to the immersive environment that enhances the communal experience.

Overall, the data suggest that the atmosphere in techno music is an essential aspect of the communal experience on the dancefloor. It creates a sense of depth and immersion that draws the listener into the story of the music and enhances the emotional and sensory experience of the music. Understanding the role of the atmosphere in techno music can provide insights into how the music creates a communal experience that is unique to the genre and why it has become such an important part of dance culture.

3. *Defining, describing, and identifying the distinctive qualities of dub techno sound by insiders for the purpose of contributing to the literature:*

The responses collected from techno music insiders (Appendix A.1) provide a diverse range of descriptions for the sound of dub techno. However, what stands out is the emphasis on the atmospheric quality of the genre. The use of reverb, delay effects, and ambient sounds creates a sense of spaciousness and ethereal qualities that can transport listeners to another world.

One interesting aspect to consider is the orphic or individual experience of listening to dub techno through headphones. Headphones provide a more intimate and personal listening experience, as opposed to the communal experience of listening to music on a dancefloor. Dub techno's use of atmospheric sounds can create a sense of immersion and transport the listener to a different mental space. The slow, hypnotic rhythms can also induce a meditative state, allowing listeners to disconnect from their surroundings and focus on the music. Additionally, the use of headphones allows for a more nuanced and detailed appreciation of the music. Listeners can pick up on the subtle grooves, repetitive chords, and ambient atmospheres that characterize dub techno. They can also discern the interplay between different elements of the music, such as the role of delay effects in creating a sense of space and the use of echoes to add depth to the sound.

In conclusion, the responses collected on the sound of dub techno highlight its unique combination of elements from techno and dub, creating a style characterized by a slow tempo, deep rhythms, and atmospheric sounds. The use of headphones can provide a more intimate and personal listening experience that allows for a nuanced and detailed appreciation of the music's various elements. Overall, the sound of dub techno has the potential to transport listeners to a different mental space and induce a sense of immersion and meditative reflection.

4. *The examination and description of the differentiation between communal and individual listening experiences through the distinction between dancefloor listening and headphone listening:*

The data (Appendix A.1) suggests that there are notable differences between communal and individual listening experiences in the context of techno music. One of the most significant differences between listening with headphones and on the dancefloor is the physicality of the experience. Listening in a club with a powerful sound system creates a physical experience with the sound waves and vibrations felt throughout the body. In contrast, headphones provide a more isolated and introspective listening experience, where the listener can focus on the stereo perspective and the acoustics of the recording[115].

Moreover, the atmosphere in a nightclub, created by lighting shows, ambiance, and sound, contributes significantly to the overall impact of the music. This ambiance is not easily replicated when listening to music on headphones, as the communal experience is a significant part of the nightclub atmosphere. The social aspect of clubbing and experiencing music with others is also crucial in creating an immersive and engaging experience that cannot be replicated through individual listening. However, listening with headphones

---

[115] The stereophonic experience of dub techno, with its heavy use of echo and reverb effects, can make it an ideal genre for headphones. With headphones, the listener can fully immerse themselves in the music, experiencing the spatial and auditory dimensions of the recording in a way that may not be possible in a communal listening environment such as a club. The intricate details of the sound design, such as the panning of individual sounds across the stereo field, can be appreciated to a greater degree when listening through headphones. Additionally, the isolating effect of headphones allows for a more introspective listening experience, where the listener can focus on the subtleties and nuances of the music, as well as their emotional response to it. Furthermore, the use of stereo effects in dub techno is not only an aesthetic choice but also an integral part of the genre's sound. These effects create a sense of space and depth in the music, making it feel expansive and immersive. When listening through headphones, the listener can fully appreciate the intricate use of stereo effects, allowing them to experience the music in a more profound and meaningful way. Therefore, it's not surprising that many fans of dub techno prefer listening to the genre through headphones, where they can fully immerse themselves in the music and experience its rich stereophonic qualities.

also has its benefits, as the listener can adjust the sound and bass according to their preferences, and the acoustics of the environment do not interfere with the reproduction of the audio. Headphones also allow the listener to focus on the details of the recording, such as mash-ups, mixes, and effects, that might be lost in the loud and dynamic atmosphere of a nightclub.

Therefore, it can be concluded that both communal and individual listening experiences have their advantages and limitations in the context of techno music. While listening in a nightclub creates a unique and physical experience, headphones provide an isolated and introspective experience that allows the listener to focus on the details of the music. However, the communal aspect of clubbing and experiencing music with others is an essential part of the atmosphere and cannot be replicated through individual listening.

The difference between individual and communal listening experiences is not only a matter of technical aspects such as sound quality, but it also involves social and cultural factors. The nightclub culture and the communal listening experience have a long and complex history that is intertwined with politics, power dynamics, and social hierarchies. To fully understand the implications of individual and communal listening experiences, it is important to examine the political background of the dancefloor and the idea of hierarchy in communal experience.

5. Evaluation of the politics within the communal listening of techno music on the dancefloor through the concept of hierarchy:

The responses to the question of whether there is a perceived hierarchical relationship between the DJ and the listener in a club setting are diverse (Appendix A.1). Some respondents assert that the DJ is the king, and all listeners are slaves, while others view the DJ and the listener as being in the club for fun and, therefore, in equal standing. However, a majority of respondents agree that there is some form of hierarchy between the DJ and the audience. Some feel that the DJ is the conductor, and the listeners are the orchestra, while others believe that the DJ is the person who creates the atmosphere and determines whether the audience is having fun or not.

The elevated physical position of the DJ plays a significant role in creating this hierarchy, with some respondents noting that the DJ performs in an elevated or designated area, and people usually face the DJ while dancing. Furthermore, the DJ often assumes the role of a leader managing the crowd, which further reinforces this hierarchy. The physical distance between the DJ and the audience is also evident in the VIP or backstage area, where the DJ is the only one allowed to smoke in a non-smoking area, creating a sense of exclusivity and elitism. However, some respondents feel that the idea of hierarchy goes against the spirit of the communal listening experience in a nightclub and creates uncomfortable symptoms. They emphasize that the interaction between the DJ and the audience is more of a collaboration than a hierarchy, with the DJ being in the club to entertain the audience and the audience going to the club to have fun and listen to their favorite DJ.

Overall, while some respondents view the relationship between the DJ and the listener as hierarchical, the majority agree that it is a collaboration between the two. The physical distance between the DJ and the audience and the DJ's role as a leader managing the crowd play a significant role in creating this hierarchy, but it does not necessarily mean that the relationship is strictly hierarchical in nature.

In this study, 6 different dub techno tracks[116] were played to 41 participants, who were asked which experience, headphone or dancefloor, was more appropriate for each track. Participants were also given the option to indicate their indecision. The survey process enabled the discussion of communal and individual orphic listening through the lens of dub techno aesthetics, and the data obtained made this possible.

The analysis of the survey data and interviews conducted with participants offers insights into the relationship between musical features, communal and individual listening experiences, orphic experience, politics, technical qualifications, aesthetics, spatiality, and sound. When considering all these factors, the results reveal that individual and communal preferences for musical features are affected by a variety of social, cultural, and political factors.

The analysis of the data reveals that tracks with a higher dynamic range and brilliance, such as *Phylyps Trak* by Basic Channel and *Listing, Sinking* by Overcast Sound, tend to be preferred by participants in a communal dancefloor setting. This is consistent with previous research on the topic, which suggests that communal listening experiences are characterized by a preference for music with a strong beat and high energy. In addition, the arrangement of the music on the dancefloor plays a significant role in shaping communal preferences. The placement of speakers, the size and shape of the dancefloor, and the lighting all contribute to the overall experience of the music. The data collected from interviews suggest that participants often choose tracks that are in line with the genre and culture of the specific event they are attending, which can be seen as a reflection of the politics of the space and the wider cultural context.

---

[116] Rhythm & Sound's *Aerial*, Basic Channel's *Phylyps Trak*, Yagya's *The Salt On Her Cheeks*, Overcast Sound's *Listing, Sinking*, Topdown Dialectic's *B4*, Substance & Vainqueur's *Resonance*

On the other hand, when listening individually with headphones, participants tend to prefer tracks with a smoother sound palette and lower dynamic range, such as Aerial by Rhythm & Sound, *The Salt On Her Cheeks* by Yagya, and *B4* by Topdown Dialectic. This preference for a more subdued sound can be attributed to the orphic experience of listening in isolation, where participants seek to immerse themselves in the music and explore its nuances and textures. This is consistent with previous research on the topic, which suggests that individual listening experiences are characterized by a preference for music that is emotionally and intellectually engaging.

The analysis also reveals that the dominance of frequencies between 20-250Hz and higher kick stiffness ratings appear to be preferred by participants in both communal and individual settings. This preference can be attributed to the technical qualifications of the music, which emphasizes the physicality of sound and the bodily experience of listening. The spatiality of the music also plays a significant role in shaping preferences. Participants tend to prefer music that has a well-defined spatial image, with a clear separation between the different elements of the music.

When considering the aesthetic dimension, the survey data reveals that participants tend to prefer music that is characterized by simplicity, repetition, and minimalism. This preference can be attributed to the influence of minimal techno, a genre that has become increasingly popular in recent years. However, the interviews also suggest that participants value music that is innovative, experimental, and challenging. This tension between tradition and innovation is a hallmark of contemporary electronic music culture.

The analysis of the data also reveals several areas that warrant further research. For example, the relationship between technical qualifications and communal listening experiences requires further investigation. Additionally, the politics of space and the wider cultural context in which electronic music is produced and consumed require further exploration. Finally, the orphic experience of listening in isolation requires further investigation, particularly in relation to the role of technology in shaping individual listening experiences.

In conclusion, the analysis of the survey data and interviews conducted with participants reveals that individual and communal preferences for musical features are shaped by a variety of social, cultural, and political factors. The data suggest that communal preferences are characterized by a preference for music with a strong beat and high energy, while individual preferences are characterized by a preference for music that is emotionally and intellectually engaging. Technical qualifications, aesthetics, spatiality, and sound all play a significant role in shaping preferences.

Although it may seem peripheral to the focus of this study, it is worth noting that dub techno production is mainly dominated by European and American labels and producers. Production in Eastern and Middle Eastern countries is almost non-existent, and there is a significant lack of non-male producers in the genre[117]. Considering the contributions of individuals in the areas of artistic attitude, creative sound design, and performance to the aesthetic universe of this genre, it can be argued that dub techno's widespread production among other regions and genders could broaden the aesthetic understanding discussed in this research, leading to enrichment in this direction.

After all these debates, there is a valid question that can be asked with considerable justification but without a single answer: Does dub techno have a future that will bring noticeable changes to its sound and perception, or will it remain a niche music genre that has opened up in a specific period of techno history, reached its aesthetic maturity, and will not undergo any significant changes? On the one hand, it is possible to answer this question with 'yes, it is possible to predict a future that will bring change to dub techno'. This response is based on the reasons that dub techno has not yet reached a wide range of producers and enthusiasts who can bring creativity to the genre, and that the changing world can provide an environment for the stylistic evolution of dub techno to continue through new music listening media. On the other hand, it is also possible to answer this question with 'no, the stylistic evolution of dub techno has been completed, and the production and performance paradigms have been established. Dub techno was a genre that caused a certain sensation for a period, but that sensation has ended for various reasons'. This response can be seen as logical when one considers the idea that various producers, including Maurizio, Rhythm & Sound, Oswald, Ernestus, and other significant producers, have brought dub techno's sound to its final form through various experiments, and that most of the concepts produced after this period are imitations of sounds produced during that time. Indeed, off-the-record interviews with members of various dub techno communities conducted during this research process suggested that this view is widespread. Nevertheless, it seems more reasonable to assume that dub techno will continue to evolve in the future or inspire new ideas due to the individualization of music production and consumption, the development of new technologies, media, and marketing systems, and the changing nature of niche art. At the very least, it is a more optimistic and colorful assumption to think that the future will restructure dub techno.

---

[117] To observe this phenomenon, it is sufficient to examine the results of a search on the Discogs database using the 'dub techno' tag. To have an impression, see https://www.discogs.com/search/?style_exact=Dub+Techno&country=US.

9

Conclusion

This study examines the transformative force of the orphic experience on dub techno, offering new insights into the role of orphic media, technology, and individualization of music consumption. It uses quantitative analysis to identify common characteristics associated with the orphic experience, providing a novel approach to studying this phenomenon. The research sheds light on the impact of orphic media on music consumption and inspires further exploration in this field.

The analysis of dub techno tracks revealed that those associated with the orphic experience tended to have slower tempos, sparse arrangements with emphasis on rhythmic textures, prominent use of reverb and delay effects to create a sense of space and immersion, and a subdued but distinct timbral palette featuring low-frequency sounds and subtle variations in tonality. These characteristics suggest that the orphic experience in dub techno is often facilitated by a distinct sonic atmosphere that encourages individual contemplation and introspection.

Alongside the musical analysis, we conducted a survey and interviews with electronic music producers, performers, listeners and dub techno enthusiasts to gain insight into their producing listening habits and experiences. The findings of this study indicate that while dub techno is frequently associated with communal listening in club settings, it can also be enjoyed as an individual, personal experience. The transformative power of the orphic experience can change the aesthetic paradigm and sound of a genre, as evidenced by dub techno.

Our research also delved into the relationship between dub techno and spatiality, both inner and outer. The expansive, ambient qualities of dub techno give rise to a unique sense of inner spatiality, transporting the listener to a new sonic environment. Outer spatiality, on the other hand, refers to the physical environment in which the music is heard. Although dub techno is often associated with club environments, our findings suggest that the orphic experience can be achieved through personal listening with headphones or speakers in various settings.

The findings of this study have significant implications for our understanding of the individualization of music consumption and the role of technology and media in this process. As we analyzed the characteristics of music pieces associated with the orphic experience, we found that the communal and individual listening experiences are quite distinct. Communal listening is characterized by a shared experience where the music is enjoyed in a group setting, such as at a concert or club. In contrast, individual listening is more solitary, where the listener can fully immerse themselves in the music without the distractions or influence of others. These distinct listening experiences are particularly relevant in today's digital age, where technology has made it easier than ever to access and consume music. With the rise of streaming services, individualized playlists, and personalized recommendations, the individual listening experience has become the norm. However, our research highlights the significance of communal listening experiences in the orphic transformation of dub techno and the techno music landscape as a whole. Therefore, it is essential to recognize the value of both individual and communal listening experiences and to understand their unique roles in shaping music consumption.

As this study focuses specifically on the relationship between the orphic experience and dub techno, future research could explore other sub-genres of techno music and their relationship with the orphic experience. For instance, it would be interesting to investigate whether the orphic experience is also present in sub-genres like acid techno, trance, or ambient techno. Moreover, it could be beneficial to examine the role of other technological devices and media contexts in the individualization of music consumption. For example, future studies could explore how the orphic experience is influenced by virtual reality, augmented reality, or other immersive technologies. In addition, it would be valuable to examine the role of communal versus individual listening practices in the orphic experience. While our study primarily focused on individual listening experiences, it would be worthwhile to explore whether communal listening experiences, such as club or festival environments, also foster the orphic experience. This line of research could offer insight into how music listening practices shape social interactions and group identities, as well as individual experiences of transcendence. Overall, there are many exciting avenues for future research to further explore the orphic experience in techno music and its implications for music consumption and production.

In conclusion, this study emphasizes the importance of comprehending the orphic experience in the context of music consumption and genre transformation. Understanding the transformative power of this experience and its ability to create personalized musical experiences is critical in grasping the role of technology and media in music consumption. Further research into the orphic experience in other subgenres of techno music and in other technological and media contexts is necessary to fully comprehend the implications of this phenomenon.

References

Albiez, S. (2005). Post Soul Futurama: African American cultural politics and early Detroit Techno. *European Journal of American Culture*, *2*(24), 131-152. 10.1386/ejac.24.2.131/1

Allen, R. (2021, August 27). *Techno Drums | Mixing Techno | How To Make Tehcno*. Touch Loops. Retrieved October 16, 2022, from https://touchloops.com/blogs/news/techno-101-drums

Anderson, R. (2004). Reggae Music: A History and Selective Discography. *Notes*, *61*(1), 206-214. 10.1353/not.2004.0085

Andrews, H., & Roberts, L. (2015). Liminality. In J. D. Wright (Ed.), *International Encyclopedia of the Social & Behavioral Sciences* (pp. 131-137). Elsevier Science. https://doi.org/10.1016/B978-0-08-097086-8.12102-6

The Associated Press. (2003, 02 13). Techno Music Pulses In Detroit. *The Associated Press*. https://web.archive.org/web/20071012184221/http://cnn.com/2003/TRAVEL/02/10/techno.exhibit.ap/

Baines, J. (2015, October 15). *A Bullshitter's Guide to Dub Techno*. VICE. Retrieved December 5, 2022, from https://www.vice.com/en/article/pg8gg9/a-bullshitters-guide-to-dub-techno

Barrow, S., & Dalton, P. (2004). *The rough guide to reggae*. London: Rough Guides.

Becker, T., Woebs, R., & Fujie, L. (1999). "Back to the Future": Hearing, Rituality and Techno. *The World of Music*, *1*(42), 59-71. http://www.jstor.org/stable/41700113

Bein, K. (2020, October 30). *Sound Behind the Song: "Strings of Life" by Derrick May*. Roland Articles. Retrieved January 31, 2023, from https://articles.roland.com/strings-of-life-derrick-may/

Beklenoglu, B. (1997). *A Brief History of Drug Taking in Popular Music and the Influence of Drugs on the Creation of Music*. [Master's Thesis, City University of London]. https://www.academia.edu/42057492/A_Brief_History_of_Drug_Taking_in_Popular_Music_and_the_Influence_of_Drugs_on_the_Creation_of_Music

Bourdieu, P. (1998). *Acts of Resistance*. Polity Press.

Boyle, D. (2020, September 3). *6 Tips for Dub-Style Mixing In the Box with Daniel Boyle | Waves*. Waves Audio. Retrieved October 24, 2022, from https://www.waves.com/dub-mixing-tips-daniel-boyle

Bradley, L. (2001). *Bass Culture: When Reggae Was King*. Penguin Adult.

Burns, T. L. (2015, May 23). *Robert Hood*. Red Bull Music Academy. Retrieved February 5, 2023, from https://www.redbullmusicacademy.com/lectures/robert-hood

Chen, W., & Chang, K. O. (1998). *Reggae Routes: The Story of Jamaican Music*. Philadelphia, PA: Temple University Press.

Ching, K. (2022, March 29). *A Beginner's Techno Music Guide: Brief History, Artists & Clubs - 6AM*. 6AM Group. Retrieved 10 12, 2022, from https://www.6amgroup.com/a-beginners-techno-music-guide-brief-history-artists-clubs/

Ching, K. (2022, April 6). *Minimal Techno Music Guide: History, Artists, & Tracks - 6AM*. 6AM Group. Retrieved January 26, 2023, from https://www.6amgroup.com/minimal-techno-music-guide-history-artists-tracks/

Computer Music. (2020, March 2). *Keep it simple, stupid: 7 stripped-back minimal house and techno production tips*. MusicRadar. Retrieved January 26, 2023, from https://www.musicradar.com/how-to/keep-it-simple-stupid-7-stripped-back-minimal-house-and-techno-production-tips

Çoruh, D. O. (2019). Bir Manipülasyon ve Motivasyon Alanı Olarak Kentsel Ortam [Milieu]. *İdealkent Kent Araştırmaları Dergisi*, *10*(28), 1097-1129. https://doi.org/10.31198/idealkent.574540

Coverley, M. (2021). *Hauntology*. Oldcastle Books.

D'Aquino, B. (2008). Rewinding the Tape of History: King Tubby and the Audiopolitics of Echo. *Riffs Journal*, *2*(2), 66-72. https://riffsjournal.org/2018/12/17/volume-2-issue-2-brian-daquino-rewinding-the-tape-of-history-king-tubby-and-the-audiopolitics-of-echo/

Deleuze, G., & Guattari, F. (1987). *A thousand plateaus : capitalism and schizophrenia* (B. Massumi, Trans.). University of Minnesota Press.

Discogs. (n.d.). *Rhythim Is Rhythim - Strings Of Life | Releases*. Discogs. Retrieved February 2, 2023, from https://www.discogs.com/master/695-Rhythim-Is-Rhythim-Strings-Of-Life

Dönmez, B. M., & Kılınçer, Z. (2011). Müziğin Yunan Mitolojisi ve Batı Kültürü İçindeki Algılanışı. *İnönü Üniversitesi Sanat ve Tasarım Dergisi*, *1*(1), 101-113. https://dergipark.org.tr/tr/pub/iujad/issue/8720/614857

Dub Monitor. (2020, October 30). *The History of Dub Techno (in 17 Minutes)*. YouTube. Retrieved October 23, 2022, from https://www.youtube.com/watch?v=utRndKWR93Q&t=40s

Dub Monitor. (2021, December 5). *A Beginner's Guide to Deep Techno Styles*. YouTube. Retrieved October 23, 2022, from https://www.youtube.com/watch?v=EqaZTgsVYfA

Dub Monitor. (2021, September 19). *Before Basic Channel, There Was....* YouTube. Retrieved December 3, 2022, from https://www.youtube.com/watch?v=SoWltdoq6-g

Dub Monitor. (2022, January 9). *A Brief Tour of "Fast" Dub Techno*. YouTube. Retrieved October 23, 2022, from https://www.youtube.com/watch?v=qwFhm_HTw3U

Dub Monitor. (2022, February 13). *A Brief Tour of Ambient Dub Techno*. YouTube. Retrieved October 23, 2022, from https://www.youtube.com/watch?v=oWydDG7JBgs&t=299s

Eaton, R. M. D. (2014). Marking Minimalism: Minimal Music as a Sign of Machines and Mathematics in Multimedia. *Music and the Moving Image*, 7(1), 3-23. http://www.jstor.org/stable/10.5406/musimoviimag.7.1.0003

Esen, A. (2021, March 29). *Basic Channel-Style Dub Techno*. Attack Magazine. Retrieved December 8, 2022, from https://www.attackmagazine.com/technique/beat-dissected/basic-channel-style-dub-techno/

FabFilter. (2022, July 13). *The Philosophy of Bass*. YouTube. Retrieved October 26, 2022, from https://www.youtube.com/watch?v=1xPO2Q2QHXk

Fabric London. (n.d.). *Introducing...Daniel Bell*. fabric London. Retrieved February 14, 2023, from https://www.fabriclondon.com/posts/introducing-daniel-bell

Fintoni, A. (2014). *The reggae sound system: sound, space and politics* [Bachelor Thesis, University of Strathclyde]. Semantic Scholar. https://www.semanticscholar.org/paper/The-Reggae-Sound-System%3A-Sound%2C-Space-and-Politics-Fintoni/301c97208200e608d2ddeffa49fc503a95acc4f6

Fintoni, A., & McLauchlan, A. (2018). Assembling the dance: reggae sound system practices in the United Kingdom and France. *Scenes and Society*, 13(2), 163-178. 10.1080/17458927.2018.1483655

Fisher, M. (2012). What Is Hauntology? *Film Quarterly*, 66(1), 16-24. http://www.jstor.org/stable/10.1525/fq.2012.66.1.16

Future Music. (2021, February 11). *The beginner's guide to: dub*. MusicRadar. Retrieved October 22, 2022, from https://www.musicradar.com/news/the-beginners-guide-to-dub

Gaillot, M. (1998). *Multiple Meaning Techno: An Artistic and Political Laboratory of the Present*. Editions Dis Voir.

Gamberini, A. (2019). *The History of Detroit Techno and its growing influence on American and European culture and philosophy*. Unpublished. Gamberini, A.

(2019). The History of Detroit Techno and its growing influence on American and European culture and philosophy. Unpublished. https://doi.org/10.13140/RG.2.2.14429.15848

Glasspiegel, W., & Bishop, M. (2011, May 27). *Get Familiar With Detroit Techno: 10 Essential Songs*. NPR. Retrieved October 13, 2022, from https://www.npr.org/2011/05/27/136655438/get-familiar-with-detroit-techno-10-essential-songs

Grimal. (1986). *A Concise Dictionary of Classical Mythology*. Oxford: Basil Blackwell.

Haddon, M. (2017). Dub is the new black: modes of identification and tendencies of appropriation in late 1970s postpunk. *Popular Music, 36*(2), 283-301. 10.12801/1947-5403.2015.07.02.01

Hagood, M. (2011). Quiet Comfort: Noise, Otherness, and the Mobile Production of Personal Space. *American Quarterly, 63*(3), 573-589. https://www.jstor.org/stable/41237567

Hagood, M. (2019). *Hush: Media and Sonic Self Control*. London: Duke University Press.

Hanf, M. K. (2010). *Detroit Techno: Transfer of the Soul through the Machine*. VDM Verlag Dr. Müller.

Henriques, J. (2003). Sonic Dominance and the Reggae Sound System Session. In M. Bull & L. Back (Eds.), *The Auditory Culture Reader* (pp. 451-80). Bloomsbury Academic.

Henriques, J. (2010). The Vibrations of Affect and their Propagation on a Night Out on Kingston's Dancehall Scene. *Body & Society, 16*(1), 57-89. 10.1177/1357034X09354768

Henriques, J. (2011). *Sonic Bodies: Reggae Sound Systems, Performance Techniques, and Ways of Knowing*. Bloomsbury Academic.

Hiphop Electronic. (2022, June 18). *Juan Atkins, Detroit Techno Pioneer — Hip Hop Electronic*. Hip Hop Electronic. Retrieved January 31, 2023, from https://www.hiphopelectronic.com/detroit-techno-artists/juan-atkins

Hitchins, R. (2014). *Vibe Merchants: The Sound Creators of Jamaican Popular Music*. Ashgate.

Howard, D. N. (2004). *Sonic Alchemy: Visionary Music Producers and Their Maverick Recordings*. Milwaukee, WI: Hal Leonard Corporation.

Hyperbits. (2022, June 21). *The Ultimate Guide to Using Reverb for Music Producers*. Hyperbits. Retrieved October 16, 2022, from https://hyperbits.com/how-to-use-reverb/

iZotope. (2020, June 8). *Tonal Balance Control—A Plug-in to Balance Your Mix*. iZotope. Retrieved April 27, 2023, from https://www.izotope.com/en/products/tonal-balance-control-2.html

Jerrentrup, A. (2000). Techno Music: Its Special Characteristics and Didactic Perspectives. *1*(42), 65-82. http://www.jstor.org/stable/41699314

Johannesen, R. L. (2009). The ethics of plagiarism reconsidered: The oratory of Martin Luther King, Jr. *Southern Communication Journal, 60*(3), 185-194. 10.1080/10417949509372978

John, G. S. (2017). Electronic Dance Music: Trance and Techno-Shamanism. In C. Partridge & M. Moberg (Eds.), *The Bloomsbury Handbook of Religion and Popular Music* (pp. 278-285). Bloomsbury Academic.

Kolioulis, A. (2015). Dub Techno's Hauntological Politics of Acoustic Ecology. *Dancecult: Journal of Electronic Dance Music Culture, 7*(2), 64-85. http://dx.doi.org/10.12801/1947-5403.2015.07.02.04

Köse, H., & Bingöl, T. (2021). Neoliberal Düzende Panoptik Denetim Tahayyülü: The Platform Filmi ve Düşündürdükleri. *Galatasaray Üniversitesi İletişim Dergisi*, (35), 5-31. https://doi.org/10.16878/gsuilet.957719

Lang, J. (2016). *A Book of Myths*. North Charleston, SC: Independent Publishing Platform.

Lee, M. O. (2010). *The Myth of Orpheus and Eurydice in Western Literature* [Doctoral Dissertation, British Columbia University]. https://open.library.ubc.ca/media/stream/pdf/831/1.0105982/1

Lefebvre, H. (1991). *A Production of Space*. Conwall: Blackwell.

Loopmasters. (2020, September 26). *16 Techno Tips: The Essential Guide for Music Producers*. Loopmasters. Retrieved October 16, 2022, from https://www.loopmasters.com/articles/4328-16-Techno-Tips-The-Essential-Guide-for-Music-Producers

Macdonald, R. (2021, January 23). *6 Dub Production Tips To Get Your Speaker Cones Rattling | Production Expert*. Pro Tools Expert. Retrieved October 24, 2022, from https://www.pro-tools-expert.com/production-expert-1/6-dub-production-tips

Malitoris, J. (2019, March 22). *Q&A with Mack Hagood, Author of Hush | Duke University Press News*. Duke University Press Blog. Retrieved December 25, 2022, from https://dukeupress.wordpress.com/2019/03/22/qa-with-mack-hagood-author-of-hush/

Marazi, K. (2020). Mack Hagood, Hush: Media and Sonic Self-Control. *European Journal of American Studies*. https://journals.openedition.org/ejas/15991

Masterclass. (2021, June 7). *Detroit Techno Music Guide: A Brief History of Detroit Techno - 2022*. MasterClass. Retrieved October 13, 2022, from https://www.masterclass.com/articles/detroit-techno-music-guide

Masterclass. (2021, June 7). *Detroit Techno Music Guide: A Brief History of Detroit Techno - 2023 - MasterClass*. Masterclass. Retrieved January 31, 2023, from https://www.masterclass.com/articles/detroit-techno-music-guide

Masterclass. (2021, June 11). *Dub Music Guide: 4 Characteristics of Dub Music - 2022*. MasterClass. Retrieved October 22, 2022, from https://www.masterclass.com/articles/dub-music-guide

Matheos, C. (1998). *Reggae Grooves for Electric Bass*. Mel Bay Publications.

May, B. (2015). Techno. In P. K. Maultsby & M. V. Burnim (Eds.), *African American Music: An Introduction*. Routledge.

Miller, N. (2015, April 21). *History and Hauntology in Jacques Derrida's Spectres of Marx*. Nodo50. Retrieved January 3, 2023, from https://www.nodo50.org/cubasigloXXI/taller/miller_100304.pdf

Mixmag. (2017, July 20). *Supernatural creature: Robert Hood is the techno pioneer who refuses to slow down*. Mixmag. Retrieved February 5, 2023, from https://mixmag.net/feature/pioneers-robert-hood

Mixmag Carribean. (2023, January 18). *Richie Hawtin, aka Plastikman - News*. Mixmag Caribbean. Retrieved February 8, 2023, from https://mixmagcaribbean.com/read/richie-hawtin-aka-plastikman-news

Miyer, T., Holodiuk, L., Omelchuk, S., Savosh, V., Bondarenko, H., Romanenko, L., & Romanenko, K. (2021). An Overview Of The Continuous Education System Components In Dimensions «Umwelt», «Mitwelt» And «Eigenwelt». *Journal of Interdisciplinary Research*, *11*(1), 52-56. http://www.magnanimitas.cz/ADALTA/110117/papers/A_10.pdf

Moayeri, L. (2022, April 1). *Richie Hawtin Interview: 20 Questions*. Billboard. Retrieved February 8, 2023, from https://www.billboard.com/music/music-news/richie-hawtin-plastikman-interview-20-questions-1235053211/

909 Originals. (2019, June 6). *THROWBACK THURSDAY: Plastikman – Helikopter [1993] – 909originals*. 909originals. Retrieved February 7, 2023, from https://909originals.com/2019/06/06/throwback-thursday-plastikman-helikopter-1993/

Nicolas, B. (2013). *An Approach to Composition Based on a Minimal Techno Case Study* [Doctoral Dissertation, University of Huddersfield]. http://eprints.hud.ac.uk/id/eprint/18067/

NTS Radio. (2020, December 5). *Emmanuel Top | Discover music on NTS*. NTS Radio. Retrieved February 11, 2023, from https://www.nts.live/artists/24935-emmanuel-top

Nye, S. (2013). Minimal Understandings: The Berlin Decade, The Minimal Continuum, and Debates on the Legacy of German Techno. *Journal of Popular Music Studies*, *25*(2), 155-184. 10.1111/jpms.12032

Olivas, D. (2018, April 27). *Foundational Beats: Reggae Drums*. zZounds Music Blog. Retrieved November 7, 2022, from https://blog.zzounds.com/2018/04/27/foundational-beats-reggae-drums/

Ott, B. L. (2017). Affect. *Oxford Research Encyclopedia of Communication*, 1-26. 10.1093/acrefore/9780190228613.013.56

Point Blank Music School. (2016, October 11). *Style Guide: Techno – Part 1: History and Sound Design*. YouTube. Retrieved October 18, 2022, from https://www.youtube.com/watch?v=kXwA-BRoYQs

Red Bull Music Academy. (2018, March 23). *Moritz von Oswald talks Dub, Remixing and being inspired / Red Bull Music Academy*. YouTube. Retrieved December 2, 2022, from https://www.youtube.com/watch?v=C7cEb-fbHOE

Reis, S. (2022, April 28). *Tech-house overtakes techno as the most popular electronic music genre*. We Rave You. Retrieved October 14, 2022, from https://weraveyou.com/2022/04/https-weraveyou-com-ims-business-report-2022/

Resident Advisor. (2021a, January 12). *Richie Hawtin · Artist Profile*. Resident Advisor. Retrieved February 8, 2023, from https://ra.co/dj/richiehawtin

Resident Advisor. (2021b, April 21). *Derrick May · Biography*. Resident Advisor. Retrieved February 2, 2023, from https://ra.co/dj/derrickmay/biography

Resident Advisor. (2021c, July 3). *Mix Of The Day: Juan Atkins · News RA*. Resident Advisor. Retrieved January 31, 2023, from https://ra.co/news/75615

Reynolds, S. (1998). *Energy Flash: A Journey Through Rave Music and Dance Culture*. Picador.

Reynolds, S. (1999). *Generation Ecstasy: Into the World of Techno and Rave Culture*. Routledge.

Rietveld, H. C. (2018). Dancing in the Technoculture. In S. Emmerson (Ed.), *The Routledge Research Companion to Electronic Music: Reaching Out with Technology* (pp. 113-134). Routledge. https://openresearch.lsbu.ac.uk/item/86qxq

Robb, D. (2002). Techno in Germany. Musical Origins and Cultural Relevance. *German as a Foreign Language*, (2), 130-149.

Rodgers, T. (2003). On the Process and Aesthetics of Sampling in Electronic Music Production. *Organised Sound*, 8(3), 313-320. 10.1017/S1355771803000293

Roholt, T. C. (2014). *Groove: A Phenomenology of Rhythmic Nuance*. Bloomsbury Academic.

Roser, M., Ritchie, H., & Ortiz, E. (2015). *Internet*. Our World in Data. Retrieved October 16, 2022, from https://ourworldindata.org/internet

Russell, A. (2022, September 13). *How To Make Techno: 11 Need-To-Know Techniques*. EDMProd. Retrieved October 16, 2022, from https://www.edmprod.com/how-to-make-techno/

Sadoux, S. (2021). London's Underground Acid Techno Scene: Resistance and Resilience in the Global City (1993–2020). In D. Charrieras, J. Willsteed, & S. Darchen (Eds.), *Electronic Cities: Music, Policies and Space in the 21st Century* (pp. 59-77). Springer Singapore.

Scaruffi, P. (2010, February 5). *The History of Rock Music. Robert Hood: biography, discography, review, best albums, ratings.* Piero Scaruffi. Retrieved February 5, 2023, from https://www.scaruffi.com/vol5/hood.html

Schaub, C. (2011). Beyond the Hood? Detroit Techno, Underground Resistance, and African-American Metropolitan Identity Politics. In W. Raussert & M. Habell-Pallán (Eds.), *Cornbread and Cuchifritos: Ethnic Identity Politics, Transnationalization, and Transculturation in American Urban Popular Music* (pp. 185-202). Bilingual Press.

Schlein, Z. (2020, March 4). *Interview With Techno Pioneer Derrick May.* Miami New Times. Retrieved January 31, 2023, from https://www.miaminewtimes.com/music/interview-with-techno-pioneer-derrick-may-11580235

Schmidt, T. (2006). *Derrick May.* Red Bull Music Academy. Retrieved February 2, 2023, from https://www.redbullmusicacademy.com/lectures/derrick-may-it-is-what-it-isnt

Schmidt, T. (2008). *Moritz von Oswald.* Red Bull Music Academy. Retrieved December 2, 2022, from https://www.redbullmusicacademy.com/lectures/moritz-von-oswald-early-morning-freestyles

Self, H. (2002). Digital Sampling: A Cultural Perspective. *UCLA Entertainment Law Review, 9*(2), 347-359. 10.5070/LR892027036

Sennett, R. (2015). *Yeni Kapitalizmin Kültürü.* İstanbul: Ayrıntı Yayınları.

Sherburne, P. (2017). Digital Discipline: Minimalism in House and Techno. In D. Warner & C. Cox (Eds.), *Audio Culture, Revised Edition: Readings in Modern Music* (pp. 319-326). Bloomsbury Academic.

Sicko, D. (1999). *Techno Rebels: The Renegades of Electronic Funk.* Billboard Books.

Sioros, G. (2015). *Syncopation as Transformation.* [Doctoral Dissertation, University of Porto]. https://repositorio-aberto.up.pt/bitstream/10216/96185/2/123703.pdf

Sotirios, S. (2021). Orpheus' Argonautica: The Voyage of the Argonauts. *Annals of Archeology, 4*(1), 1-7. 10.22259/2639-3662.0401001

Spruill, M. (2022, April 21). *Techno History Guide: A Deep Dive Into Dub - 6AM.* 6AM Group. Retrieved December 18, 2022, from https://www.6amgroup.com/techno-history-guide-a-deep-dive-into-dub/

Spruill, M. (2022, May 5). *Acid Techno Guide: History, Artists & Classics - 6AM.* 6AM Group. Retrieved October 13, 2022, from https://www.6amgroup.com/acid-techno-guide-history-artists-classics/

Statista. (2022, September 20). *Internet and social media users in the world 2022.* Statista. Retrieved October 16, 2022, from https://www.statista.com/statistics/617136/digital-population-worldwide/

Studio Slave. (2020, July 10). *Classic Techno Production Tips*. Studio Slave. Retrieved October 16, 2022, from https://studioslave.com/studio-slaves-classic-techno-production-tips/

Sullivan, P. (2014). *Remixology: Tracing the Dub Diaspora*. London: Reaktion Books.

Sweetwater. (1997, May 5). *What is "Flat Response"?* Sweetwater. Retrieved October 23, 2022, from https://www.sweetwater.com/insync/flat-response/

Sweetwater. (2022, June 30). *9 Best Tape Emulation Plug-ins*. Sweetwater. Retrieved January 8, 2023, from https://www.sweetwater.com/insync/best-tape-emulation-plug-ins/

Sword, H. (2016, June 3). *London Acid Techno*. Red Bull Music Academy Daily. Retrieved October 13, 2022, from https://daily.redbullmusicacademy.com/2016/06/london-acid-techno-feature

Techno Station. (2017, January 22). *Top Tracks & Mixes of Emmanuel Top The Return of the Acid Phase*. Techno Station. Retrieved February 11, 2023, from https://www.technostation.tv/return-acid-phase/

Tool Room Academy. (2021, December 3). *10 Techno Production Tips You Must Know*. Toolroom Academy. Retrieved October 16, 2022, from https://toolroomacademy.com/features/10-techno-production-tips-you-must-know

Turner, V. (1982). *From Ritual to Theatre: The Human Seriousness of Play*. Performing Arts Journal Publications.

Turner, V. W. (1977). *The Ritual Process: Structure and Anti-structure*. Cornell University Press.

Veal, M. (2007). *Dub: Soundscapes and Shattered Songs in Jamaican Reggae*. Wesleyan University Press.

Vendryes, T. (2015). Versions, Dubs and Riddims: Dub and the Transient Dynamics of Jamaican Music. *Dancecult*, 7(2), 5-24. 10.12801/1947-5403.2015.07.02.01

Vitos, B. (2014). *Experiencing Electronic Dance Floors A Comparative Research of Techno and Psytrance in Melbourne*. Monash University. Retrieved 10 10, 2022, from https://bridges.monash.edu/articles/thesis/Experiencing_electronic_dance_floors_a_comparative_research_of_techno_and_psytrance_in_Melbourne/4683736

Wilson, J. (2013). The Concept of Abstract Space in the Work of Henri Lefebvre. *Space and Culture*, 16(3), 364-380. 10.1177/1206331213487064

Yost, W. A. (2015). Psychoacoustics: A Brief Historical Overview. *Acoustics Today*, 11(3), 46-53.

Zahner, K. (2022, February 6). *3 Reggae Drum Beats Drummers Should Know*. Rhythm Notes. Retrieved November 7, 2022, from https://rhythmnotes.net/reggae-drum-beats/

Abbreviations

BD	: Bass drum
BPM	: Beats per minute
CB	: Cowbell
CH	: Closed hi-hat
CL	: Clap
CR	: Crash cymbal
EDM	: Electronic Dance Music
FX	: Effects
HPF	: High-pass filter
HT	: High tom
Hz	: Hertz
IDM	: Intelligent Dance Music
KHz	: Kilohertz
LFO	: Low-frequency oscillator
LPF	: Low-pass filter
MT	: Middle tom
OH	: Open hi-hat
Q	: Quality factor
RB	: Ride bell
RC	: Ride cymbal
R&B	: Rhythm and blues
SD	: Snare drum
SH	: Shaker
SFX	: Sound effects
SS	: Sidestick
UK	: United Kingdom
USA	: United States of America
W	: Watt

List of Charts

List of Figures

List of Images

Appendices

Appendix 1: Responses of anonymous participants

Appendix 1

What are the vital rules for mixing techno music for clubs? Why?

1. The music needs to sound good. People need to be able to dance to the music.
2. The music should adhere to the genre. Dub techno is generally inspired by dub reggae, techno, and house music. It draws the production techniques from old dub reggae in its use of feedback delays, reverbs, and unusual EQing often done on-the-fly using old analog gear which adds both noise and distortion to the sound. The rhythm structure mostly comes from house music and techno, often having a four-to-the-floor kick drum and hi-hats on the odd 8th notes, even though there are variations on this. Dub techno ranges from almost entirely ambient music - with little or no sense of rhythm - to almost danceable techno, albeit usually much slower than typical dance music, as dub techno is listening to music more than dance music.
3. Enough bass, general loudness, mono compatibility, and DJ-friendly arrangement. This is due to the design of sound systems, except obviously the last one.
4. Mix in mono.
5. Beat matching and phrasing, transitions should be smooth to help the flow of a set.
6. Keep it entertaining with live effects so it's not boring for the crowd.
7. Stereo width has to be controlled otherwise sounds will not be played as most club systems are in mono. Other than that as long as the track sounds good, there are no rules.
8. It should have DJ-friendly tracks, suitable for intro and outro mixing. Tracks should be at least 320 kbps or WAV.
9. Having a good mono perception of your work is the most important rule in my opinion.
10. It's crucial to capture the sounds that the general audience of that day's club prefers.
11. A well-arranged composition with clear high-end, punchy low-end, and powerful mids.

12. It should have high energy. Although we may think in detail, sometimes we shouldn't get too caught up in the details because the listener simply surrenders to the energy of the music at that moment. Also, the build-up and pre-drop sections are important because they prepare for the drop. Therefore, the listener's expectation is shaped accordingly. Of course, if you want to surprise, that's a different story!

13. I believe it makes sense to produce high-quality content that appeals to the sound system of the nightclub. Besides that, I think the nightclub's sound should generally be dance-inducing, enchanting, and captivating.

14. Having mastering done to industry standards will minimize the imbalance between tracks and paying attention to mono compatibility will eliminate phase issues that may arise due to technical differences between venues.

15. Not straying too far from the usual tones in productions that gave birth to EDM. The tones of this music genre that has been built for years should not confuse the listeners with different infrastructure, regardless of whether they are music producers or DJs.

16. Dance should be built by adding and subtracting rhythmic elements. Sometimes rhythmic elements should be completely diminished so that the listener/dancer can rest and then experience the climax more distinctly.

17. I think the sound should be ready before going into the mix. A good mix with mastering and balance will sound as it should in the club. Of course, in my opinion, what's important is to go through the "creative mix" phase before going into the mix. After all, the best perception is in the hands of the creator of the piece. This way, the friend who does the mix and mastering won't have to struggle with their own ideas.

How do you describe the "atmosphere" in techno music?

1. Different atmospheres for different techno genres. Can be dark, happy, sad, intense, or uplifting.

2. Usually, techno is fast-paced and energetic and meant for people to dance to. The atmosphere is dominated by clean or distorted electronic sounds. There's usually very little use of reverb. However, the subgenre "dub techno" is slower, more mellow, and has a sense of "dust" to it as a result of the very prominent use of reverb and delay. It also usually has a sense of melancholy to it resulting from the frequent use of minor third chords.

3. It can be anything, from melodic to percussive to industrial to ambient. What ties the genre together is a kick drum in a pattern that typically functions on the dancefloor.

4. Building context within a song.

5. The atmosphere in techno music can be described as a combination of lead, pad, and FX elements shaped by a 4/4 rhythm.

6. It is a sound that exists in the background of the track for extended periods of time, but subtly makes its presence felt.
7. Ambient sounds, typically with generous reverb on pads, etc.
8. It sets the beginning of a story.
9. It adds depth and ambiance to the track with subtle sounds that float in the background.
10. Atmosphere is the element that gives techno its mysterious sounds and adds emotion to the track.
11. I use sounds like pads with heavy reverb in the background.
12. As a producer, I would define atmosphere as the key element that draws the listener into the story of the track. It should be more than just filling the background.
13. Atmosphere fills in the gaps in the arrangement.
14. Sounds that are outside the rhythmic and melodic elements of the music, which can be categorized as pads and drones, create the atmosphere.
15. Atmospheric sound can be achieved with a reasonable level of reverb and depth and can be complemented with atmospheric pad chords. The advantage of atmospheric sound is that it can disconnect you from the earthly realm. You feel like it's playing all over the planet. This takes you on a deeper and more introspective journey. In fact, we can say that atmosphere is the sensation of depth.

How do you describe the dub techno sound?

1. Originating from Jamaica, dub techno builds upon this foundation by adding elements of techno, such as a driving beat and synthesizers, to create a unique sound that combines the driving energy of techno with the spacious, ethereal qualities of dub.
2. Science fiction, ambiance.
3. Uses a lot of delay effects.
4. Slower than normal techno, with effects playing a larger role than the instruments themselves.
5. Incorporates dub effects like echoes very obviously.
6. Repetitive chords, ambient atmospheres, small and subtle grooves.
7. Chilled progressive.
8. Deep, rhythmic, hypnotic.
9. It's a style that can fit any mood, sometimes I can listen to it comfortably, sometimes I can dance to it, and sometimes I can play it on stage.
10. Mystic and atmospheric.
11. It's a music genre with low BPM and generally heavy on atmospheric sounds.
12. It's a type of techno characterized by repetitive kick and melody sequences.

13. It's a sound that allows you to feel your heartbeat and sense the flow of seconds.
14. Dark, atmospheric, and slow.
15. It has a lower BPM and a more minimal sound compared to the general techno genre.
16. It's sharp and edgy music. I don't prefer it much, but I can say it's a genre that draws you in completely when the time comes.
17. Minimal techno.
18. Calming.

What is the difference between listening to EDM in the club and listening to EDM with headphones?

1. Headphones make you feel the music better, on the other hand, listening in the club just makes you dance and trip.
2. When you use headphones, you feel the rhythm and flow with it much better.
3. In the club, I will go deaf and the heartbeat syncs with the base. with headphones, I can adjust the volume and it plays like it's inside my head.
4. In the club, I will dance, but not so much at home with headphones. The bass frequencies in the club will be felt through my body.
5. When listening to music at a loud volume, the low frequencies (bass) physically cause objects and even people in the room to feel the vibrations. This makes it a very physical experience. This effect does not happen in headphones. However, in headphones, you tend to hear the stereo perspective better, and the acoustics of the room do not interfere with the reproduction of the audio.
6. Volume mainly, causes a massive psychological reaction, regardless of the music. The acoustics of the room are also a factor in clubs.
7. Listening in a club is a physical experience with the sound system, listening on headphones is boring in comparison.
8. The biggest difference is that club sound systems are usually in mono, while headphones provide a stereo experience, which creates a distinct contrast.
9. Lighting shows in nightclubs can enhance the impact of music, making it a unique aspect of the atmosphere.
10. The environment and sound are crucial in shaping the atmosphere in techno music production.
11. Mash-ups, mixes, and effects in nightclubs can create a different perception of tracks, and the overall atmosphere has a significant influence.
12. High volume and vibrations are integral to the nightclub experience and contribute to the atmosphere.
13. It is impossible to capture the grandeur of the nightclub experience through headphones, which is the biggest difference.

14. I can adjust the sound and bass according to my preference with headphones.
15. There are notable differences between listening to EDM in a nightclub and with headphones. In a nightclub, the physical sensation of sub-frequencies and the ambiance of the venue are significant factors in creating the overall impact.
16. Nightclubs are a social activity where experiencing music with others is an essential part of the atmosphere, and individual listening experiences may not be as enjoyable.
17. The energy felt in a nightclub cannot be replicated through headphones.
18. I enjoy listening to techno in a nightclub more because the vibrations from the sound system create a unique dancing experience and allow for better immersion in the music. When listening with headphones, I focus more on how the music is produced.
19. Club sound systems usually prioritize sub and bass-heavy sounds for danceability, while headphones can provide a more introspective listening experience. However, the strong impact of high volume in a club setting cannot be ignored, while headphone listening can be more thought-provoking.

Is the presence of the kick drum considered a critical component in EDM? If so, what is the rationale behind its significance?

1. Yes, I think the kick drum is setting the rhythm for the music.
2. The kick drum plays a central role in the beat of a techno track, providing the foundation for the rest of the music. It is typically the most prominent element in the mix, driving the track forward and helping to create a sense of momentum.
3. I think so yeah. it's hard to tell the rhythm without it.
4. It's both the rhythm and has bass frequencies which can be felt through your body if listening to the music on a large sound system. The kick mimics the rhythm of walking.
5. The kick drum is like the spine that connects the body parts of the techno beast. It's the fundamental pulse that everything else in the music is based on. Without the kick drum, techno music would not gain the forward momentum necessary to make people dance. However, in dub techno - which is not necessarily meant as dance music - it might be possible to leave it out, even though it would perhaps no longer be considered to be dub techno at all, but rather ambient or chill-out music.
6. Drums obviously contribute to a rhythm more than anything else. I am not aware of a single genre of dance music that does not contain a lot of bass. When you combine those 2 points, you realize the importance of a bass drum.
7. It is the main element, the driving force.

8. All elements are equal, if you make the kick the most crucial element as a producer, the other elements won't be as good and the track will suffer.
9. No.
10. The kick drum may not be essential, as music can still exist without it or with other elements. It depends on the day, let's say.
11. In the techno genre, we often come across songs without a kick drum, and it is usually referred to as experimental. It may not be essential in subgenres or new styles of techno.
12. I think the kick drum is the foundation of EDM music, although it may not be used in certain genres depending on taste or style (e.g. ambient music).
13. Kick/Rumble and Hat/Ride are essential in techno music for me. Kick/Rumble creates a unique feeling, and Hat/Ride makes me dance until I sweat.
14. It is definitely indispensable. Kick is the heart of techno music.
15. I think it is crucial because it's like the feet of a song. Without it, a track may feel incomplete.
16. Of course.
17. Well, obviously. There must be a kick, it must hit. Without a kick, there's no "drop" in a drop. Please, at least let there be a kick in the drop.
18. It's enjoyable to keep the tempo with it.
19. I define it as indispensable in dance music, but the sky is the limit, so I can't say it's indispensable in general.
20. Since techno music was born with analog drum machines, kick drums and techno are inseparable.
21. Generally, yes, but I guess their significance varies as subgenres.
22. As a listener who values melody more than kick and drums, I still believe that tempo is essential to keep the rhythm intact.
23. It's indispensable because the kick drum is the element that makes techno.
24. Yes. It is one of the things that reflects energy in the highest way.
25. Yes, because the rhythm of the kick drum generally determines the groove.
26. The kick drum is always one of the most important elements that moves people.
27. I like the effect of the kick drum, but there are DJs who think that a techno track consists only of the kick drum. They believe that by adding a kick drum to a plain track, they make it techno, but they actually ruin the music.
28. No, it's not essential. We can achieve the groove effect created by the kick drum with various synths and percussive sounds by manipulating them.
29. I don't think it's essential, as you can fill its place with other elements or sounds, but kick usage is prevalent in a significant portion of techno music.
30. No, it's not. Techno can be made with other drum elements as well.

31. Because the kick drum is the instrument that makes the head nod in rhythm. It's essential. Maybe it can be softened in the side EQ, but the rhythm should always be evident in tech sound, just like the groove in funk music, I guess.
32. Yes, because for music to sound pleasant, harmony and richness of all elements are necessary.
33. I believe that good music can still be created even without it.
34. It's important for uplifting the listener's mood.
35. No, it's not. Because nothing is indispensable.

Is there a perceived hierarchical relationship between the DJ and the listener in a club setting? If so, in what manner does it manifest?

1. Yes. The DJ is the king. And all of the listeners are slaves of him. So, if you don't submit to the DJ, he will torture you by tickling your ears. Where obviously there is a hierarchy, the listeners kneel down and swear their loyalty to the DJ. Even where there is the opposite of that, this will happen sneakingly. Swear your loyalty to the DJ!
2. Yes, but in a different way. DJ makes the crowd hyped and everybody thinks that it's the DJ's job to entertain people but I think both DJ and the listener are in the club just for fun. so basically clubs make the hierarchy.
3. No.
4. At large events, the DJ is usually someone you cannot talk to, being placed above the dancefloor at some distance. At very small parties where the DJ is simply standing on the dancefloor, I don't think there's the same sense of a hierarchy, and the whole thing feels more intimate and personal.
5. A lot of DJs like to see themselves as someone manipulating a crowd, leading it. In a sense they're right.
6. Yes everyone points toward the DJ.
7. Yes, the DJ is the conductor and the listeners are the orchestra.
8. Yes, we are connected.
9. Nightclubs are places where loud music plays and people dance. Having hierarchy in a nightclub goes against the spirit of the environment and creates uncomfortable symptoms.
10. There is no specific hierarchy, but interaction is high. Especially in clubs where there are no VIP or backstage concepts, interaction is even higher.
11. No, I don't think so.
12. The DJ is the person who creates the atmosphere and determines whether the audience is having fun or not.
13. The crowd is completely under the control of the DJ. It's not just about the songs played, but also the DJ's stage presence, movements, and energy that influence the crowd.
14. Yes, through their reactions to the music.

15. Yes, there is a hierarchy, and it's all about the audience. The atmosphere of the club and the speed of the night are determined by their energy. The DJ feeds off their energy.

16. There is a hierarchy related to the positioning of DJs, especially in Turkey.

17. Not to a great extent, but the DJ is the person who determines the flow of the night and the show. The listeners just let themselves go and have fun with the DJ's music. So, there is a little bit of hierarchy, but it's more like a collaboration.

18. In some cases, there might be a hierarchy due to tight security or a celebrity-like demeanor. Some DJs focus on their music and do their job professionally, while others make the audience feel like they are partying together.

19. Yes, there is a hierarchy, but I also believe there shouldn't be one, because we are there to entertain the audience.

20. Yes, I believe there is a relationship similar to that of a seller and a customer.

21. I don't think there is a hierarchy. The interaction between the performance artist and the audience is always shaped by the physical conditions provided by the venue and the architecture.

22. I believe there is more of a collaboration between the DJ and the audience rather than a hierarchy. The DJ is in the club to entertain the audience, and the audience goes to the club to have fun and listen to their favorite DJ.

23. Yes.

24. Yes, indeed. I think the DJ plays a role similar to that of an orchestra conductor, directing the audience to enjoy themselves fully.

25. I don't prefer going to nightclubs very often, but when I do, I sometimes have thoughts like "I wish they played this song," which creates a sense of hierarchy.

26. Definitely yes. The DJ performs in a physically elevated or designated area, and people usually face the DJ while dancing. Moreover, the DJ assumes the role of a leader managing the crowd. This inevitably changes their position.

27. I feel it in most nightclubs. The fact that higher-priced tickets are sold for the backstage area behind the DJ, and that the DJ is the only one allowed to smoke in a non-smoking area, makes me feel the presence of a hierarchy.

28. I feel it less in smaller nightclubs because people and the DJ are usually in the same area. But in larger stages, I feel this hierarchy more. Especially the backstage area makes it very noticeable.

29. Yes, DJs are often idolized more because they are highly focused on music. I think the elevated stage also plays a role here.

30. I haven't noticed.

31. There is no need to feel it, it is quite obvious that it exists. Even if we look beyond nightclubs and VIP events, DJs clearly isolate themselves despite being among people. They don't look at us the way we look at each other, they look down from a few steps higher and make it known.

32. Yes, the DJ becomes a master figure. After all, they are the ones who choose the music and therefore determine the atmosphere and mood of the environment.

33. Yes. While the DJ can make decisions about many factors, such as how the listeners dance and their moods, the opinions of the listeners as individuals are not always important.

What were your criteria for making decisions between headphones and dancefloor?

1. I looked for background sounds that can be understood better with headphones, and for the others, I looked for a rhythm that I can dance to when I am in the club.

2. My mind, my heart, my soul.

3. The pieces with mostly ambient sounds and kicks suits being played as background music people would talk over and nod to if they're alone - in the club. Ones with more audible chords I like to listen to while doing stuff or work.

4. If I would enjoy listening to the track in a club or not.

5. I think all the tracks can work on both headphones and in the club. In fact, I've heard some of them in both situations already. I would have chosen both if I could. I also could not leave these fields empty. So I've chosen "headphones", but my actual answer is "both" for all the tracks.

6. The steady rhythm and amount of energy.

7. Rhythm and context.

8. Listening to music in a club is the ultimate musical experience.

9. What I'd play as intros outros breaks, etc.

10. The sound.

11. I considered whether the track had a percussive quality that would be suitable for the dancefloor, or if it would be better enjoyed with headphones.

12. As a DJ, I created a criterion by asking myself if I would play this track in a club setting.

13. I would personally like to listen to all the tracks with headphones and on the dancefloor, but I believe that tracks with prominent kick drums are more ideal for nightclubs.

14. I focused on how prominent the kick drums were in the tracks. For me, the kick and drums are what make the crowd dance on the dancefloor.

15. I considered how well the track's tension would fit with the nightclub atmosphere.

16. In my opinion, all the tracks can be enjoyed in clubs with proper sound systems, and the best experience in terms of emotions and sensory quality is in the club.

17. I simulated both options in my mind and selected the one that I predicted would be more enjoyable.
18. I looked at the use of BPM, melody, and drums in the tracks.
19. I decided whether the vibe/energy of the track was suitable for listening in a club or with headphones.
20. I asked myself if the track would sound good in a nightclub while listening to it.
21. As a new producer, I am not very knowledgeable about technical aspects, but I answered the questions based on how they made me feel.
22. I believe that every song deserves to be listened to in venues with good acoustics and technical equipment.
23. Well done, it was a very productive test. Seems like kick drums are important, good luck!
24. As a performance artist who enjoys entertaining people with my own musical culture and selections.
25. I made my decisions based on the impression the tracks created in me. For example, if a track was calmer, I preferred the option of listening with headphones. But if it was more lively, with more elements, I leaned towards listening to it in a nightclub.
26. I made my selection based on the energy level of the song.
27. Only rhythm.
28. I marked the more danceable tracks as nightclub options, and the others as headphone options, as I thought I could listen to them during moments when I need to focus.
29. I thought that some tracks would be better enjoyed up close and in an isolated environment with headphones, while others would be better enjoyed in the enclosed atmosphere of a nightclub while dancing. I answered based on the feeling that the track gave me. It is likely influenced by the habits and aesthetic codes that I have acquired over the years.
30. For me, listening to tracks with high volume in a nightclub, feeling the kicks hitting my body and the bass area, is always more enjoyable than listening with headphones. When listening to something with a lot of stereo movement -panning, etc.- or something that is created with three-dimensional thinking, I might prefer headphones because it is more effective and controlled.
31. I prefer not to choose music with rhythmic characteristics that I cannot dance to or that play at a slower tempo in a nightclub. I kept this in mind.
32. I considered the tracks' complexity and depth. Of course, many sounds that I mentioned can also have special events with headphones, which can be enjoyable as well.

Index

About the Author

Bahadırhan Koçer has a diverse background in music composition, music production, sound design, and cinematography. He gained a foundation in sonic arts through London instructors and studied modular synthesis and mixing. He is a scholar of musicology, focusing on spatiality, noise, and texture, and exploring various sub-genres within electronic music. His academic contributions include published works in reputable journals. He has produced international-recognized projects. His dedication to sound design and music production drives his career, making significant strides in both academic and artistic pursuits.

Contact

E-mail Adress

bahadirhankocer@gmail.com

Social Links

https://linktr.ee/bahadirhankocer

Made in the USA
Las Vegas, NV
21 February 2025

18505384R00162